BLACK ANXIETY, WHITE GUILT, AND THE POLITICS OF STATUS FRUSTRATION

T. Alexander Smith
and
Lenahan O'Connell

PRAEGER

Westport, Connecticut
London

Library of Congress Cataloging-in-Publication Data

Smith, T. Alexander, 1936–
    Black anxiety, white guilt, and the politics of status frustration
/ T. Alexander Smith and Lenahan O'Connell.
        p.   cm.
    Includes bibliographical references and index.
    ISBN 0–275–96054–4 (alk. paper)
        1. United States—Race relations.   2. Racism—United States.
    3. Afro-Americans—Social conditions—1975–   I. O'Connell, Lenahan.
    II. Title.
    E185.615.S5836   1997
    305.8'00973—dc21   97–19232

British Library Cataloguing in Publication Data is available.

Library of Congress Catalog Card Number: 97–19232
ISBN: 0–275–96054–4

First published in 1997

Praeger Publishers, 88 Post Road West, Westport, CT 06881
An imprint of Greenwood Publishing Group, Inc.

Printed in the United States of America

The paper used in this book complies with the
Permanent Paper Standard issued by the National
Information Standards Organization (Z39.48–1984).

10 9 8 7 6 5 4 3 2 1

For J. T. Lenahan O'Connell
and Sandra Ransier Smith

Contents

Preface

For some time now, we have been concerned about, and perplexed by, the apparent inability of our society to improve relations between African Americans and the white majority. The optimism that attended passage of the 1964 Civil Rights Act seems to have been swamped by waves of ugly accusation and counter-accusation. This book is our attempt to come to grips with the often racially charged events of the past 30 years—the successes as well as the failures. It arises from the conviction that so many of our race relations specialists and intellectuals remain prisoners of outdated theories of race relations. As a nation, we are immured, it seems, in the categories and preconceptions of our past—a time when African Americans were accurately depicted as the victims of white racism. Today, however, the companion images of blacks as victims and whites as oppressors serve to obscure and mislead people rather than reveal and illuminate the difficulties experienced by blacks in their contacts with whites.

We are convinced that much of today's racial conflict is caused less by racism and discrimination than by the myriad frustrations occasioned by the very advances that have produced the emergence of the nation's first substantial black middle class. To us, this constitutes a paradox of progress in which material and economic inclusion sets the stage for the specific encounters with whites that so many blacks label offensive. Surely, feelings of status deprivation and threats to identity play a far more crucial role in our current crisis than is commonly acknowledged. Often frustrated claims to status honor can account for the passionate denunciations that accompany accusations of the previously unknown offense of "insensitivity" or the frequent charges of underrepresentation in the more prestigious occupations and workplaces.

Clearly, then, one of our failures as a nation in addressing racial issues is intellectual. But, as worthy as the pursuit of accurate theory is in its own right, a new understanding or theory of race relations is a matter of vital interest to more than the intellectuals and social scientists who specialize in matters of race. As ever, social policies are rooted in our perceptions of reality, and, more than we care to admit, bad theories have contributed to failed policies. As Americans these failures frighten us.

The theory that blacks are held back by chains of racism has given rise to a system of racial preferences from which we all suffer—black and white alike. One consequence is increased distrust and division. Policies based upon group preferences, no matter how well-intentioned, are likely to widen rather than narrow racial cleavages. Why should the losers in the struggle for government-sponsored preferential treatment ever accept the outcomes of such an arbitrary and transparently political regime? Especially troubling, moreover, are the insidious effects of these programs upon our legal and economic practices. Without a doubt they cannot but violate the basic principle that all citizens are equal before the law. And, much like other interventions that violate the rule of law, they are bound to impose heavy costs in the form of regulation and inefficiency, costs which can only impede the proper functioning of the market economy—the fountainhead of the prosperity upon which racial cooperation ultimately will depend.

The study of race relations in contemporary America is, thus, far more than a philosophical parlor game. Those who would use political power to substitute goals, timetables, and quota schemes for private market exchanges rest their case upon the alleged effects of white discrimination and bigotry. If, as we demonstrate, white racism is a minor obstacle with few if any material consequences and racial preferences confer few if any benefits, then all justification for this threat to economic freedom is lost. Affirmative action becomes a cure far worse than the disease.

Lenahan O'Connell

This book arose from a conviction that neither academic specialists in race relations nor the intellectual classes in general were assessing the current state of race relations in a satisfactory manner. We became convinced that much of the conflict between black and white is caused less by racism and resistance to change in American society than by frustrations associated with growing African-American material and social progress. A consequence of this paradoxical situation in which increasing alienation and socioeconomic progress coincide in much of the black community is that interracial disagreements are as likely to arise from what blacks regard as offenses to dignity and self-respect as from overt discrimination. Therefore, feelings of status deprivation and threats to identity play a far more crucial part in daily face-to-face contact than is commonly acknowledged. Consequently, in the struggle for personal and group respect, black claims to status honor typically take place amid accusations of white "insensitivity." Grievances may also be framed in a more ideological, all-encompassing manner, as when the entire nation is called upon to apologize for slavery or renounce racism by establishing special events, days, and other occasions for honoring African-American heroes and black accomplishments.

Black Americans' entry into mainstream life following the eradication of legal separation of the races created an emotional and psychological chasm between two competing, largely contradictory value systems: a modern one based upon ascribed status and group achievement. Success and adaptation in the modern world, however, depend in no small way upon the renunciation of many values and behaviors of the traditional ethnic or racial group in order to meet the demands of an abstract, impersonal, and competitive social and economic order in which social mobility is rapid and failure continually looms as a distinct possibility. Achievement by personal merit is ultimately incompatible with achievement by ascribed status. Nevertheless, the persistent demand for respect and deference to racial group traditions is at heart an effort to escape the effects of modernity and somehow recapture a sense of community through an ideological and emotional retreat into a more or less static social order. Indeed, the proponents of affirmative action attempt to reconcile that which in reality is irreconcilable; namely, the proposition that the principle of individual merit will be adhered to under a legal and administrative system dedicated to group promotion.

It is easy to envisage two possible outcomes if state-imposed racial preferences expand as significant factors in our national life. First, other racial and ethnic groups in growing numbers will insist that they too be singled out for special consideration by the state. On the other hand, those groups presently "covered" will find themselves deprived of their own present positions of privilege by the political leadership—a dangerous option for political incumbents, since groups threatened with potential losses are more likely to respond forcefully than those who are slated for potential rewards. Thus, policies based upon group preferences, no matter how well-intentioned, are likely to stimulate rather than reduce ethnic and racial cleavages, since the losers in the struggle for government-sponsored preferential treatment are unlikely to accept the prevailing status quo on a permanent basis. Especially troubling in the absence of reform of the present system of racial quotas and timetables, however, are the insidious effects of these programs upon our legal and economic practices. Without a doubt they violate the basic principle that all citizens are equal before the law, and the heavy costs they impose in regulation and compliance undermine the proper functioning of the market economy upon which the prosperity of all Americans depends.

Many experts and more casual commentators on race relations have been so doggedly determined to expose every trace of racist behavior in American life that they have shown an inclination to employ illiberal means in the pursuit of liberal ends. In their endeavors they have been supported by civil rights organizations, much of the political leadership, an array of "diversity" professionals, and academic opinion. In their zeal to create a perfect color-blind society, they have been led to support an array of regulations on individuals and organizations, costly both in money and personal freedoms. But by insisting American society is hopelessly racist, they have unintentionally made more of their fellow citizens acutely conscious of race. When they assume, contrary to global evidence, that were it not for racism, the elements of the "rainbow" would fall more or less proportionately into place in the occupational and other hierarchies, these "multiculturalists" do not only retreat from reality but encourage individuals to substitute raw political power for private market exchanges. Whether the politicization of ethnic and racial disputes is eventually reversed by referenda and the courts or whether the balkanization of our political life gathers steam depends upon how we address the issue of affirmative action and the victimist ideology upon which it rests in the next few years. This book considers the personal, social, and political forces surrounding this debate.

T. Alexander Smith

In the course of writing this book we have received support from various friends and colleagues. A special debt is owed to Professor Augustus M. Burns of the University of Florida, who was a continual source of inspiration throughout this project. We owe a debt of gratitude to Professors Thomas D. Ungs of the University of Tennessee and Raymond Tatalovich of Loyola University, Chicago. Sandra Ransier Smith patiently read different versions of several chapters and was especially helpful with organizational problems. Debby McCauley typed the original manuscript. We should also express our appreciation to the staff at Greenwood Publishing Group, especially to Dr. James T. Sabin, Ms. Norine Mudrick, and Ms. Susan Badger. Their patience is much appreciated.

1

Progress and Anxiety: Defining the Racial Problem

In the summer of 1989 a young black intellectual penned a gripping account of his race's current plight in America. In his essay, at once highly personal but coldly intellectual in its thrust, Anthony Walton expressed the bitterness of an upwardly mobile and prosperous middle-class intelligentsia that plays by the rules of the white world and seeks to live by the myth of the American Dream but that nevertheless finds itself increasingly alienated from American life.[1] Although it dutifully fulfills the demands made upon it by a middle-class society, this black intelligentsia is unable to find sufficient satisfaction in its own successes.

For the author, the face of Willie Horton and the issue of crime so cleverly tailored to George Bush's campaign for the presidency in 1988 symbolize only too well those forces arrayed against blacks today. While out of prison on a furlough, Horton, it will be recalled, had raped a young white woman as her fiancé had looked on helplessly in horror. In the opinion of Walton and many other observers, the Horton episode cynically exploited the idea that blacks are typically criminal in intent, prone to violence and robbery. No matter how successful in life or how law-abiding and faithful to middle-class values and responsibilities, if one happens to be a black American it is well-nigh impossible to receive one's just deserts from the dominant white majority in terms of respect, deference, and common understanding. The refusal of a cabbie to pick up the black passenger at night, the suspicious stares when one shops at the local department store, or the mindless racial slurs one overhears at work or along the street are only three examples that occur with sufficient regularity to bring even the most optimistic black back down to earthly reality.

A society based on personal liberty and equality before the law might in theory afford its black citizens the means to achieve a measure of recognition and power, but for those who must surmount any number of subtle and not-so-subtle forms of discrimination along the way, an emptiness in the soul still remains in the midst of nominal success, even when their status is confirmed by elites in government, the arts, the professions, and business. The black who rigidly conforms to the rules of the game as laid down by the white world may be called successful, even privileged, by whites themselves, but his daily encounters with the dominant majority ineluctably evoke an awareness that he is believed to belong to a despised race. Hence, he has that sinking feeling that he is forever forfeiting those very rewards he has so painfully won through intelligence and energy. "[W]e children of the dream," concludes Walton so poignantly, "often feel as if we are holding 30-year bonds that have matured and are suddenly worthless." If Walton is correct, alienation from white society would seem to be a pervasive phenomenon in the black middle-class community.

But why is there so much anger and discontent? Surely economic and social progress for blacks over the past 30 years is undeniable. In fact, in a material sense the "Dream" has already been realized by many black Americans. Even during the 1980s, a time when blacks were said to be neglected by two successive Republican administrations, the number of black Americans earning $50,000 a year or more grew from 810,000 to 1.3 million by the end of the decade. In inflation-adjusted dollars, the proportion of black households with earnings over $50,000 went from 1 in 17 in 1967 to 1 in 7 in 1989. Indeed, since 1950, blacks in white-collar occupations have expanded by 900 percent.[2]

By many measures, race relations are much improved. For instance, there are four times as many black-white marriages today as there were in 1970. Eighty percent of blacks and 66 percent of whites say that they have a close friend of the other race. On college campuses one half of the African Americans study with whites. Increasingly, the black middle class resides in predominantly white suburbs. A *Reader's Digest* poll in 1994 reported that 74 percent of blacks and 82 percent of whites agreed that they would prefer the United States to any other nation.[3]

These statistics suggest that we are entering an age of true integration. Instead, increasing black and white interaction seemingly generates the tensions we somewhat naively hoped would disappear with the decline of discrimination and the rise of integration. Why, then, are things worse when they ought to be much improved? Why do many of the more successful members of the black bourgeoisie feel so hostile toward white America? Why do allegations of racism multiply at a moment in history when discrimination is at its lowest point? And why is the civil rights establishment more committed now than at any previous time to racial preferences and quotas, policies that ostensibly were to be temporary? We propose a paradoxical explanation for these puzzling developments by advancing the argument that the black middle class is primarily responding to status frustrations associated with social and material advancement.

THE RISE OF MIDDLE-CLASS ALIENATION

Walton's assessment of the state of race relations is in all probability shared by most blacks as well as a significant number of whites. Many African Americans have concluded that their race is being systematically oppressed in a historical period when both government action on their behalf as well as their own advancement would seem to imply a much more favorable interpretation about the state of race relations. Indeed, neither government support, better economic prospects, nor growing black political influence appear to reduce the pessimism of many prominent black intellectuals and political leaders. It is hard to conclude otherwise when ordinarily serious leaders, for example, can believe that whites introduced crack cocaine and the AIDS (acquired immunodeficiency syndrome) virus into American cities to eliminate the black population or that whites are forever on the prowl for black victims, as in the well-publicized Tawana Brawley case in 1987 when black leaders in New York City accepted without question a farfetched account by a young teenager of white brutality and rape.

Plainly, the middle- to upper-class segment of the black community has done very well, but having worked so hard for success, it finds itself unfulfilled, deprived of the enjoyment of its labors by what it believes is an absence of goodwill within the white community. In its view, blacks are constantly being denied their complete share of respect from an indifferent, disrespectful, or suspicious white majority.

We intend to demonstrate, however, that this interpretation is misplaced in important respects. It grossly exaggerates the actual degree of white antipathy. But by seeming to make blacks helpless victims of white racism, this interpretation of race relations underestimates the importance of class and cultural factors just as surely as it exaggerates white prejudice and bigotry. In addition, it ignores the very real obstacles to racial understanding. Black crime is especially feared and resented by whites. The violence and anomie of the black ghetto—crimes against person and property, drugs, welfare dependency, disorganized family life, and unemployment—are vivid reminders of an out-of-control black "underclass" whose cultural life is anathema to middle-class norms and values. Should we be surprised at white suspicion of blacks in those impersonal settings where property and person may possibly be endangered, especially when it is widely known that the black murder rate is approximately 8 times as high as that of whites and the rate for robberies is more than 10 times as high? Put another way, if we subtract the violent crimes committed by blacks and leave those committed by whites, the American crime rate compares favorably with that of Great Britain.[4] Such comparisons, however, are seldom raised in public debate, although it is highly unlikely that the typical urban white would be surprised by these statistics.

Sadly, hardworking blue-collar and white-collar black Americans are struck from two sides. Because of their race, they may feel themselves to be variously shunned, ignored, and insulted by whites in ways large and small. On the other hand, white fear or antagonism is itself linked mainly to the persistence of cultural characteristics found in the black lower classes, traits that many blacks believe are all too often generalized to include an entire race of people.[5]

BLACK FEAR AND WHITE CONFUSION

If blacks are angry and alienated, whites are more than a little confused, fearful, and disappointed. Their hope that with the advance of black social and material progress race as a public issue would simply disappear has been dashed. If anything, race looms larger than ever, despite all that reform has presumably done to compensate black Americans for the misdeeds of previous generations of whites. Has not a political leadership peopled mostly by whites offered, at considerable public expense, job training, Head Start, laws forbidding discrimination, affirmative action in employment, minority scholarships for college and professional training, and a host of other programs designed to foster black progress? Whatever America's shortcomings, her apologists say, surely her attempts to eradicate past evils are worthy of praise.

Yet the dreaded accusation of "racist" is thrown about with increasing abandon, indiscriminately applied to all manner of statements and behaviors. Without warning, it may suddenly be attached to any particular statement, position, or policy that may be claimed to injure sensibilities. What is more, this broad approach to what may be said to constitute racism has sometimes led to attempts to suppress ideas properly belonging to the areas of fundamental freedoms. What we have designated as the Sensitivity Imperative has frequently compromised both freedom of expression and social scientific research where racial issues are concerned, not to mention everyday civil discourse.

Walton's account, as are so many similar accounts by members of the black middle classes, is replete with examples of small, hurtful indignities and slights suffered by members of the black working and middle classes seeking only to live as peaceful and upright citizens. It is this reality of daily life, however, that enrages blacks and undermines interracial trust and respect. When the white cabbie, for instance, refuses to give the well-intentioned black male a ride at midnight or when the white clerk carefully scrutinizes the activities of a black teenager, many blacks (and not a few whites) perceive the whites as insensitive bigots. For their part, the cabbie and storeowner would maintain that given the reality of black crime their own behavior ought to be accepted as merely prudent and normal behavior. It is at the point where white fears for their safety and property intersect with black embarrassment and humiliation that we find the prime source of our present racial dilemma.[6]

If this is true, a sharp decline in black social pathologies would in all probability lead to a similar reduction in those white behaviors that blacks—especially the black middle classes—find so distasteful and reprehensible. In cities and on campuses where the races repeatedly interact as social equals, the perceived affronts to black sensibilities, however unintentional, will surely continue for some time, no matter how much political effort is devoted to "consciousness raising" and the enforcement of "politically correct" norms and values on recalcitrant whites. In a word, no amount of moralizing by suburban whites, clergy, reporters, politicians, and intellectuals in the absence of a marked change within the black lower classes is likely to alter white attitudes and behavior.

THE ISSUE OF WHITE STEREOTYPING

Many black elites in the civil rights leadership would probably dismiss the analysis above as simpleminded stereotyping. White intellectuals, politicians, and scholars usually would agree with the former's assessment. The received opinion is that blacks are victims of racist stereotypes. Not only are stereotypes false and degrading, but they severely limit the opportunities for black occupational success. In any event, what well-meaning members of both races devoutly wish for is a decline in racial stereotyping.

Conventional wisdom states that rigidly held generalizations (i.e., stereotypes) when applied to the races are not just morally repugnant but rest upon sheer ignorance or superstition. That they may actually correspond to social reality in important ways is summarily dismissed as too outrageous for serious consideration. Properly understood, however, in many instances such generalizations capture existing behavioral differences between groups with far more accuracy than is usually admitted.[7]

Seen from a certain perspective, stereotyping is in fact a necessary component of human mental processes. As various social scientists have pointed out, all behavior is "typical" behavior. That is to say, in that our daily experiences are of people and events, we anticipate that an event will recur and that the behaviors of others are repeatable over time. In other words, we typify events and the behavior of our fellow humans. Were it otherwise, we would be unable to make sense of the world around us. Experience, whether "on the ground" or derived from the visual and print media, thus provides the foundation for the formation of expectations that are typically derived within the mind. We normally expect dogs to bark, postal workers to pick up mail, drivers in the United States to keep to the right side of the road, and to anticipate our argument, whites (and blacks) to conclude that young black males are more likely than young white males to commit street crimes.[8]

These considerations lead us to proffer an intriguing question: When and to what extent are stereotypes valid? The answer is far from obvious, but as we argue in Chapter 4, many stereotypes are quite valid in the statistical sense (e.g., blacks on average do less well in school than do whites). Thus, any interpretation of race relations that ignores the complex role of stereotypes in typification processes generally is not only an inadequate one; as we observe repeatedly in this study, its assumptions may lead to misguided and pernicious public policies. If inner-city white merchants, for instance, have come to anticipate from their prior experiences that black teenagers are on average more likely than their white counterparts to steal merchandise, they will obviously look on the former with greater suspicion. No amount of television and other media documentation of "white racism" is likely to alter their behavior and opinions. In reality, their behavior may derive from real or potential fears, imagined or otherwise, that threats to their persons, livelihoods, and properties are possible if they place themselves in particular kinds of situations.

AFFIRMATIVE ACTION AND THE QUOTA REVOLUTION

If it is true that racism is as widespread and deep-seated as the civil rights lobby and many white intellectuals claim it is, then nothing short of coercive intervention in the distribution of rewards can work if the war against racism is ever to be won. At the very least, the disproportionate allocation of blacks at present to the less attractive occupations must be reduced in the interest of social justice. To that end, we are now witnessing an attempt to institutionalize the idea that blacks be distributed evenly throughout the institutional structure, from the workplaces and classrooms to the legislatures and corporate boardrooms. Financially strapped cities, already balkanized, are to be balkanized still further to guarantee black political representation, and state and national legislative districts must be carefully gerrymandered so that minorities are guaranteed a strong physical presence in legislative chambers at all levels of government. Private companies and public bureaucracies must set aside positions for minorities to prove in advance, not after the fact, that they do not discriminate in hiring or awarding contracts. Colleges and universities must offer unique inducements and programs in the form of cultural centers, financial aid, student representation on important administration committees, and less stringent standards for admission. And they must devote special resources and considerable time to recruit minorities for their faculties and administrations. Only with government-enforced preferential treatment, it is assumed, can black Americans achieve equality, however defined, with other Americans. Unfortunately, there is neither empirical nor theoretical justification to believe that a policy favoring one race over the other through state-coerced means will produce either material prosperity or racial harmony for the great majority of Americans.

STATUS FRUSTRATION AND ITS BURDENS

Yet alienation persists. Although many commentators would undoubtedly assess the causes of middle-class black alienation differently, it does seem somewhat strange that such a profound disillusionment with "white society" would coincide with a marked growth in black political, economic, and social participation in American life. Still, it is hard to deny that the equality in political and social status so highly acclaimed by whites as a fact of life in interracial relations after 1964 has been viewed by many blacks as little more than an empty promise. Sociologists and other social scientists ought to have anticipated this reaction as much more than an attempt to abolish the remaining traces of racism. They ought to have anticipated that, having come so far so quickly, many black Americans, as upwardly mobile groups before them, would experience frustrations not amenable to the quick fixes of enacted legislation and government programs.

It is this growing economic and social advancement in well-being combined with increasing pessimism among the more upwardly mobile and successful middle classes in the black community that comprise the elements of what we term the *paradox of progress*, a phenomenon whose general outlines are known to social scientists. Socioeconomic change, if rapid and disruptive of traditional social bonds, may stimulate a status panic not only among traditional, downwardly mobile elites but also among those individuals and groups most subject to social and material progress. It is the latter, the upwardly mobile, that concerns us in this study.

In a competitive, market-driven economy in which personal success is determined by the decisions of countless consumers, success may be rather elusive and failure difficult to explain away. After all, following the civil rights revolution, many blacks were ill-equipped, relatively speaking, with the skills and values necessary to adapt to an economic and social order in which status prestige and sense of self are so closely tied to occupational and material position. The traditional fear that legal subjugation to the white man might simply be replaced by a new form of domination that really did bear some resemblance to a racist's conception of the "natural order" of things has undoubtedly enhanced status doubts and fears of failure, delivering along the way countless blows to self-esteem. America is, after all, a society in which achieved success carries more social weight than does inherited status.

If socioeconomic progress often stimulates status frustration among the more socially mobile elements within the minority group, one likely sign of its existence may be observed in attempts to gain special recognition and respect from the majority for the deeds and accomplishments of the minority. That blacks seek the esteem of whites may be seen in the demand that the majority scrupulously observe certain elaborate and prescribed forms of interracial etiquette. Words, gestures, topics, and symbols that have only recently come to be judged "offensive" or "insensitive" in public discourse are now harshly condemned on grounds of insensitivity for the feelings of the aggrieved. The insistence that white society atone for its racist past has formed the backdrop for claims to recognition in the form of material restitution, public apologies for slavery and segregation, special occasions honoring black achievements and heroes, black history courses, sensitivity seminars, special scholarships and grants, and so on. These demands have taken place in a period when interracial relations are in fact becoming more and more equal.

Rather than seeing in many of these demands a symptom of status anxiety arising out of a growing social parity between the races, social scientists have simply assumed that racism is a sufficient explanation in itself. So obsessed is the scholarly community with white racism that we have failed to appreciate the psychosociological burden that freedom itself has recently imposed on the black community, not least on its more upwardly mobile middle class. Many social scientists, of course, have long been well aware that when the barriers to participation are dismantled, ethnic groups may experience powerful emotional and psychological frustrations, including a loss of solidarity with the ethnic group; this theme has played an important role in the work of comparative political scientists for some time in their cross-national studies of developing nations. Similarly, among sociologists, status frustrations, anxieties, and ambiguities between and within various ethnic groups have been periodically topical for quite a few years. Whatever one may say about these ethnic studies, it has been assumed not only that status frustration and ethnic "marginality" are closely joined but that the former often accompanies ethnic advancement and power.

In America, the status anxieties of various ethnic groups have come under intense sociological analysis (as have those of subgroups of white Protestants) in the search for clues as to the effects of marginal social and economic status on social and political attitudes.[9] Although sociologists and political scientists have devoted many hours to studying the role of status frustration in the adjustment of white ethnic groups to American society, it is an interesting sociopsychological datum that recent black experiences that might lend themselves to similar kinds of analyses have largely escaped their critical gaze. That the experiences of black Americans might be similar in fundamental ways to those of other emerging racial, ethnic, or religious peoples in this country and abroad has seldom been raised, perhaps for understandable political and ideological reasons.[10]

WHITE RACISM AND BLACK MIDDLE-CLASS STATUS ANXIETY

There clearly exists among the more affluent and better-educated members of the black community an intense desire for status recognition, which in turn suffuses the racial debate. Certainly questions of relative status rank high on the priority lists of black intellectuals, professionals, civil servants, businessmen, politicians, and thousands of other upwardly mobile individuals. It is these middle- and upper-middle-class groups, not the poorer members of the black community, who usually find themselves in status-provoking encounters with whites. Among those groups are found the black opinion leaders who present "the" black position to the public.

Without a doubt, racial discrimination exists, but its legitimacy among whites in the last several years is often exaggerated. Indeed, the extent to which whites have come to accept the value of equal opportunity for all races implies a shift in the balance of moral forces almost no one would have predicted in 1964. The present ideological antagonism between the races is therefore much less a reflection of disinterested demands for racial justice and equal treatment under the law than a struggle for status esteem in a society increasingly open to diverse groups and individual talents.

It is thus significant that at the moment in American history when blacks are being invited to compete as social and political equals with their fellow Americans that their leaders seek to transform the racial debate into one of *group* claims, material and symbolic, against a social order that they claim to be stuck in racial malevolence. As a consequence, integration with whites is simultaneously demanded and rejected; individual liberty is loudly proclaimed, but so are group rights. In these rather contradictory aims, we encounter an overt manifestation of an identity crisis within the soul of the black bourgeoisie. But group pride, as we shall see, provides a temporary balm for the troubled psyche of the individual as blacks struggle with longing for social recognition and approval while feeling unsure of their own preparation for social and occupational competition in the modern economy.

In sum, an obsession with white malevolence has led many black Americans to view their opportunities in American society as severely limited. Many social scientists agree that it is discrimination which accounts for the persistence of black poverty, the social pathologies of the ghetto, and the failure of aggregate incomes in the black community to approach more closely those of whites. In reality, as we intend to demonstrate, white racism is much less a barrier to black advancement overall than are a weak commitment to middle-class values and a paucity of skills, especially within the black underclass. Even a nation so dedicated as our own to welfare programs, public housing, job training, affirmative action, antidiscrimination laws, and other reforms has found it difficult to "legislate" a belief in the utility of education, diligence, attention to detail, lengthy time horizons, and other "bourgeois" habits so critical to the development of the skills necessary for success in the marketplace.[11]

Since social scientists and journalists give so much of their attention either to the economic plight of poorer blacks or to the ways in which white racism restricts black progress, the more mundane social status needs of the black middle classes are usually neglected. It is the poor who make the headlines, swell welfare rolls, and frighten whites when violence erupts in the cities, but it is the educated, more articulate sectors of the black middle classes who determine which policies are to receive priority and how interracial tensions ought to be managed. In addition, it is predominantly individuals from the middle classes who obtain the jobs, status, and incomes as a result of affirmative action, whereas the working poor and the underclass receive little more than the right to borrow prestige in the knowledge that "one of ours" is a corporate manager, legislator, or government official. This truth is occasionally acknowledged by black intellectuals, if not in quite the way that we address it in this work.[12] That the black middle classes also strongly support the Democratic Party and the "liberal" agenda of massive state intervention on behalf of the poor gives the appearance that blacks speak with a single voice.

In the public mind, at least, the black middle classes are conflated with the black lower classes. Whereas the defense of the poor and the urban underclass may express a genuine concern for the plight of the less fortunate, the persistence of black poverty, crime, welfare, and illegitimacy within the black community at a time when other ethnic groups are prospering poses an ever-present threat to the way the black middle classes see themselves and how they think others look upon them. The underclass, in a word, is an embarrassment to the black middle class. No less a luminary in the civil rights establishment than the Reverend Jesse Jackson admitted as much when he remarked, "There is nothing more painful for me than to walk down the street and hear footsteps and start to think about robbery, and then see it is somebody white and feel relieved."[13]

It is also the status struggle and the demands it makes on other ethnic and racial groups that help to explain the tendency for blacks to speak with a single voice when their interests are perceived as threatened. The desire to circle the wagons is partly a product of historical oppression, a time when racial unity was essential to survival. Today, however, racial unity is a means for the stimulation of group pride and individual self-worth, especially in the middle classes where competition with whites is most intense and therefore strongly affected by status concerns and comparisons. As a consequence, those individuals who deviate from the "official" line of the civil rights establishment may be subjected to sanctions ranging from ridicule to outright ostracism. *Uncle Tomism* and *acting white* are accusations heaped upon those blacks who stake out political positions opposed by the civil rights establishment or who, particularly in the case of the young, are inclined to adopt white standards in dress, speech, manners, or study habits.[14]

THE CHAINS OF MUTUAL DEPENDENCY[15]

The reader will gain a better appreciation of the current state of race relations if he or she keeps certain points in mind. It is our contention that racial harmony may be impeded at present less by a lack of goodwill on the part of the majority of citizens than by a particular relationship that presently characterizes three loosely defined groups: (1) a large majority of nonblack citizens who are relatively uninvolved or indifferent but otherwise consider themselves as personally enlightened in their racial attitudes; (2) a rising, status-conscious black middle class that bitterly resents being subjected daily to what it perceives as racist treatment by white society; and (3) a black underclass whose social pathology is an embarrassment for the black middle classes and a constant source of fear and resentment in much of the American population.

The aims of these groups diverge, and the resources they command are unequal. But each is bound to the other, directly or indirectly, by some form of dependency. Whites, for example, hold by far the most political and economic resources. On the other hand, if the economic and social powers of the underclass are negligible, the potential threat it poses to social peace and the movement of commerce in our major cities compels the authorities, in the interests of social peace, to divert a share of public resources in its direction.

The place of the black middle class in this chain of dependency is rather more complex. Thus, it must take account of the numerous white-dominated institutions upon which its members' life chances depend for economic and social advancement. Its powerful need for respect and esteem from its peers makes it dependent on the attitudes and expectations of predominantly white managers, coworkers, and customers. More generally, its status will be confirmed or disconfirmed by the actions of the numerous whites it encounters in the wider public.

But it must also look below to the underclass and working and non-working poor whose interests its middle-class intellectuals, interest group representatives, and political elites presume to represent. In speaking for "all" African Americans, the middle class lays claim to the trappings and symbols of black unity, not only as a means to alleviate the burden of guilt it shoulders for its own success but for the envy it presumably wishes to deflect.[16]

Aside from the facts of historical oppression in America, the pressure from the lower classes, and the need to alleviate status anxiety in general, there is another factor that encourages strategies of group mobility. Simply put, for the black middle class there is a monetary and occupational advantage to be derived from affirmative action timetables and quotas, race norming, set-asides, and the like. A sense of siege and victimology serve to reinforce group cohesion in the ongoing status struggle between whites and blacks. Much of the remainder of this study will be devoted to sorting out the meaning of these complex relationships.

THE PLAN OF THE BOOK

In Chapter 2, we assess the part played by status struggles and anxieties in intergroup relations and the crises of identity that so often give rise to them. It is our contention that progress, while admittedly uneven, has nonetheless been substantial for many blacks who under new conditions of legal and social equality are compelled to adhere to competitive norms and achievement values. For those blacks in the emerging middle classes, the benefits of social and economic advancement are a mixed blessing from a psychological standpoint. Thus, economic advancement and rising expectations combine with status frustration and anxiety to create a sense of estrangement from whites and what are typically referred to as "white institutions." It is this that we refer to as the paradox of progress.

In Chapter 3, the "victim vision" of race relations is dissected. After we analyze its components—especially its theory of economics as group domination and power politics—we criticize its utility for social science research and record many instances in which social scientists permit sensitivity to minority sensibilities, not objectivity, to dictate their assessments of contemporary racial problems.

Chapter 4 confronts the explosive issue of racial stereotypes. We suggest an approach to them at odds with the conventional wisdom, although it is an explanation quite consistent with the state of our present empirical knowledge of cultural and cognitive processes. Contrary to the mythology that surrounds this complex issue, whites are hardly unthinking slaves to racist stereotypes. In reality, they *typically* construct stereotypes in such a way that they can respond to blacks as concrete individuals rather than as members of an abstract, all-embracing racial category.

Chapter 5 considers the unfortunate consequences of what has been aptly called the "quota revolution." Building on the theory of race relations presented in Chapters 2 through 4, we demonstrate that affirmative action predictably fails in its purpose to raise average black income. Nor does it promote racial respect and cooperation. Not only is affirmative action basically illogical, but the utilization of legal and administrative coercion has actually harmed the economic order and stimulated racial division within the political community. Quite simply, the confused notion of "affirmative action" is inimical to the "rule of law" upon which Western freedoms are historically grounded, although the case against it is seldom, if ever, put in this manner. That it is supported by many sincere individuals and by the major civil rights organizations in no way invalidates this argument.[17]

Finally, if status anxiety plays an increasingly more important role in intergroup struggles as group power relations are more frequently characterized by social and political parity, it would seem to follow that there are rather strict limits to what social reform can conceivably hope to accomplish. *Reform* in this sense would imply that it is possible to legislate states of mind that are themselves a result of social and economic "progress." This conclusion implies that racism per se has less to do with current social conditions in black America than is usually supposed. In general, more indirect forces such as technological innovation, global interdependence, immigration, misguided welfare policies, and certain kinds of cultural values pose far more serious threats to the incomes and employment opportunities of less affluent black Americans than do traces of white racism.

NOTES

1. Anthony Walton, "Willie Horton and Me," *New York Times Magazine*, August 20, 1989, pp. 52, 77.

2. See, for example, the following sources for references to the growth of the black middle classes: Thomas Byrne Edsall with Mary D. Edsall, *Chain Reaction: The Impact of Race, Rights, and Taxes on American Politics* (New York: W. W. Norton, 1992), pp. 117–20; David Frum, "The Prophet of Resentment," *National Review*, April 3, 1995, p. 62; Associated Press, "Study Finds Gains for Black Middle Class," *New York Times*, August 10, 1991, p. 3–A; U.S. Department of Commerce, *Statistical Abstract of the United States* (Washington, D.C.: Government Printing Office, 1992), p. 26; Jared Taylor, *Paved with Good Intentions: The Failure of Race Relations in Contemporary America* (New York: Carroll & Graf, 1992), pp. 23–29.

3. "Up from Separatism," *The Economist*, October 21, 1995, p. 30.

4. See, especially, the remarks of Jared Taylor as well as William F. Buckley, Jr., in a symposium entitled "Blacks, Jews, Liberals, and Crime" as published in the *National Review*, May 16, 1994, pp. 44–45. What is routinely pointed out in the media and elsewhere by black spokesmen, television commentators, and academics, however, is that whites commit more crimes than blacks. True enough, but these same critics usually neglect to add that the black population comprises only about 12 percent of the total population.

5. On these issues, see the enlightening study of William A. Kelso, *Poverty and the Underclass: Changing Perceptions of the Poor in America* (New York: New York University Press, 1994), pp. 21–30. Kelso argues that "all commentators agree that if there is any one trait that seems to characterize the underclass it is their

willingness to flout the traditional norms of what society generally considers acceptable behavior" (p. 25). In addition to crime, the incidence of illegitimacy, divorce, illicit drugs, persistent unemployment, and low educational levels, which characterize the American underclass, is especially high within the black community. Taken by itself the black underclass, while smaller in the aggregate than its white counterpart, is much higher as a percentage of all blacks than is its white opposite. Moreover, unlike the white underclass, which is more scattered about within predominantly white areas, the black one is visibly concentrated in predominantly urban areas. It is this demographic and geographic concentration that tends to make white opinion in general so aware of black social pathologies. It is not crime alone that alienates whites but cultural and class differences as well. It is here that we observe a cultural aspect of the black-white dialogue. Why anyone should be surprised that under these circumstances many whites would convey attitudes that respectable and law-abiding blacks would find insulting and racist is hardly surprising.

6. It is ironic that in our creation of a certain homogeneity of dress and culture in which it has become acceptable, even chic, among the American middle classes of all races to adopt casual everyday clothing such as jeans and sneakers the chances for embarrassment may have actually increased for those younger, middle-class, law-abiding blacks whose own dress and behavior in less egalitarian times would have distinguished them in white eyes from potential underclass criminals. Thus, unlike those traditional, less mobile social orders in which the various classes are easily recognizable, the combination of black crime and the erosion of dress codes more or less specific to rank increases the propensity of whites in settings characterized by anonymity to lump all blacks together, law-abiding and criminal alike.

7. It is rather amusing in this respect to observe many students of comparative political cultures in casual discussions regarding differences in national cultures. Nothing is likely to turn them cold more quickly than when the uninitiated student or layman speaks of "national character." The point here is not that the "culture" concept somehow lacks scientific precision and status; it is that by referring to a particular cultural trait as an expression of national character the offender has breached good taste and therefore warrants social disapproval. "Culture" sanitizes for proper scientific conversation, whereas to describe the same trait as one of national character makes it illegitimate on its face.

8. We shall defend this point in much detail in Chapter 4. Our chief source of inspiration for the study of typical behavior and its potential utility in the study of stereotypes is Alfred Schutz and those who follow in his footsteps. See, for example, Alfred Schutz, *The Phenomenology of the Social World* (Evanston, Ill.: Northwestern University Press, 1967), pp. 176–214.

9. For example, see Seymour Martin Lipset, *Political Man* (Garden City: Doubleday, 1960, pp. 297–98); Daniel Bell, ed., *The New American Right* (New York: Criterion Books, 1955).

10. For a position that seems to agree with ours, compare David Riesman, *Individualism Reconsidered, and Other Essays* (Glencoe, Ill.: Free Press, 1954), p. 60.

11. Despite the exorbitant cost to the taxpayer of programs on behalf of the black underclass, most antipoverty measures have, by most accounts, been failures, even from the standpoint of their intended beneficiaries. It may be possible to make

a case for food stamps or Head Start, but the affirmative action timetables and quotas that help line the pocketbooks of many white-collar blacks are another matter. In general, affirmative action has done little to improve the overall social and occupational standing of black Americans, but it has surely both exacerbated racial tensions and raised the costs of regulations for all Americans. On this point, see Charles Murray, *Losing Ground: American Social Policy 1950–1980* (New York: Basic Books, 1984).

12. See, for example, Cornel West, *Race Matters* (New York: Random House, 1994).

13. Jackson is quoted in Lynne Duke, "Confronting Violence," *Washington Post*, January 8, 1994, p. A10.

14. The effort to maintain black cohesion has come at a high price for those black intellectuals who have defended the values of individualism and free markets. In this regard, such writers as Thomas Sowell, Walter Williams, Shelby Steele, Glenn C. Loury, and others have fought a rather lonely battle.

15. The following is heavily indebted to the formulation of the late Norbert Elias. See, for example, his *What Is Sociology?* (New York: Columbia University Press, 1978), pp. 111–33.

16. See, for example, Clarence Page, *Showing My Color: Impolite Essays on Race and Identity* (New York: HarperCollins, 1996), pp. 46–69.

17. See Peter Brimelow, in *The American Spectator* of November 1992, p. 74; Aaron Wildavsky, *The Rise of Radical Egalitarianism* (Washington, D.C.: American University Press, 1991).

2

Status Anxiety and the Paradox of Progress

In many ways America's blacks appear to be more alienated than ever from whites. Some opinion polls find that the more prosperous and educated among them are, if anything, even more estranged than their lower-status counterparts struggling to make their incomes match their outgo. Yet it is the more privileged middle classes within the black population who have reaped the major benefits of affirmative action but who also seem to be the most dissatisfied. In general, it is they who have received the greater access to the political, social, and economic resources generally controlled by the white majority.

This gulf between material and social advancement, on the one hand, and a growing estrangement from dominant institutions and authorities, on the other hand, constitutes a paradox of progress. A major effect on many individuals is status anxiety or frustration. Black Americans have now won their citizenship rights in the political and constitutional spheres, and increasing numbers from their ranks are entering the broad middle classes. Despite these impressive gains, however, the freedom to compete with whites as individuals on a more or less equal footing for a share of the so-called American Dream has come to have its downside as well, since the warmth and protection of the ethnic group must inevitably give way to values oriented toward individual achievement criteria. The very real possibility of failure in a society in which individual competition and personal merit are highly valued but where some of us would prefer the comfort and support of the traditional group poses not a few problems of social and psychological adjustment.[1]

The upshot is that what we usually call "progress" can itself generate feelings of ambivalence and social isolation. To be both black and middle class, we argue below, may make it difficult for one to feel completely at home in either the white or the black world. This longing for the company of like-minded members of one's group is clear from the response of a middle-class black woman at the summer resort island of Martha's Vineyard:

> Affirmation comes from many places, one of which is seeing yourself reflected in the world around you . . . in the very unspecialness of knowing there are thousands of folks pretty much like you in hollering distance. . . . If the black summer community on Martha's Vineyard forms its own world, it is a world absent the assumptions of inferiority rife elsewhere. It is, I think, the burden of carrying around both the negative assumptions of others, and my own. On the vineyard, as the old spiritual goes, I can lay my burdens down. . . . Here, there is no feeling of unearned, condescending specialness, so often bestowed on African-Americans by others, that "Golly, gosh, you're not like most black people. You're different."[2]

As the statement implies, the burden of history on the black American is not easily lifted by social and financial success, since many of the emotional scars would not exist in the first place but for the wounds long visited on black Americans during slavery and segregation. Personal achievement may therefore be emotionally and psychologically insufficient if one believes that the particular group to which he or she belongs is itself demeaned or pitied by outsiders; and when the achievements and prestige of one's own group are believed to be relatively less esteemed than the accomplishments of other groups, the status identification of the minority member, whose own success would seem to most outsiders as quite sufficient according to accepted standards, may be threatened.

In 1903 W.E.B. Du Bois captured well the experience of black status anxiety in his day in his notion of "double-consciousness": "[T]he sense of always looking at one's self through the eyes of others, of measuring one's soul by the tape of a world that looks on in contempt and pity . . . an American, a negro; two souls, two thoughts; two unreconciled strivings; two warring ideals in one dark body."[3] Mere "progress" cannot entirely erase this double consciousness—in the short run, at any rate.

The phenomenon of status frustration is hardly foreign to the experiences of many whites, as both the modern novel and contemporary sociology attest. Many a book, for instance, depicts the sorrows and frustrations of individuals from humble backgrounds whose good fortune leads them to seek entry into the established upper classes. But there is a qualitative difference between majority and minority status anxiety. Surely the upwardly mobile member of a racial or ethnic caste, only recently liberated from the bonds of subjugation, is typically confronted with far greater inner turmoil than is his or her white counterpart under similar circumstances. One coping device for easing the transition to new or threatening circumstances is to retreat emotionally into the warmth and solidarity of the group from which one has sprung.

In this chapter, we demonstrate that the contemporary dynamics of race relations in the United States are influenced not so much by racism in the traditional meaning of the term as by status frustration and strong feelings of insecurity within significant segments of the black community. Status anxiety, in turn, stimulates a powerful sense of victimization and varieties of group chauvinism that bolster demands for affirmative action and other group entitlements. When social mobility is combined with a gnawing need for status affirmation, the way is potentially cleared for the development of status-inspired movements. The consequence is the transformation of the racial issue from one in which a formal equality before the law is guaranteed into one in which groups compete for signs of status, prestige, and state-enforced preferential treatment.

By a process of collectivizing personal resentments, status politics tends to undermine interracial harmony and generate what we designate as the Sensitivity Imperative. To avoid the charge of racial insensitivity, whites are sometimes put under intense political and social pressures to avoid comments and analyses that assess various conditions in an unfavorable light within the black community, as Dinesh D'Souza has recently learned, apparently to his chagrin.[4] The purpose is to hold "society" responsible for many current social problems in black America. To be seen as "blaming the victim" is often considered unacceptable social behavior. A failure to conform risks the accusation of insensitivity at best, racism at worst. As we shall see, status anxiety and status politics have changed the very meaning of racism to such an extent that almost any statement that fails to treat black Americans as victims of white malice may be deemed hostile to the fundamental interests of the minority.

STATUS IDENTITY IN MODERN SOCIETY

The problems of class and status have long been a major preoccupation of sociology and political science. We shall distinguish status from material interests by keeping the two concepts analytically distinct. From this perspective, *class position* is essentially synonymous with *market position*. It describes the degree to which one can effectively control economic resources in terms of income and capital. *Status position* suggests the degree of honor and prestige attached to one's profession, place, or standing in the community. If class may be said to represent income or economic influence, then status expresses more or less one's cultural power. To this extent status honor, or status prestige, today is not so much tied to specific institutional forms such as guilds or estates (e.g., clergy or aristocrats) as to occupation, formal education, degrees, speech, dress, consumption, and taste. Class implies a market-based condition in which income is the measure of success, whereas status implies that social standing depends upon factors that are extraneous to the market.[5]

We wish to highlight the problem of status as it presently exists among black Americans. Given their historical condition of social, economic, and physical privation, it may seem strange to speak of status frustration or anxiety as the engine of race relations. After all, it is black poverty and isolation that initially strike us with such force. But while poverty and isolation afflict many black Americans in the urban ghettos and in rural areas of the South, many other blacks are not poor. Indeed, they are well educated and prosperous.

Affluence, however, does not guarantee a secure status identification. Status anxiety and the search for an esteemed identity, we argue, explain much of the political and social agitation that arises in the black middle classes today. The civil rights era was an astounding success, but it left blacks in competition with whites as formal equals, a condition for which many were unprepared. The consequence was a loss in self-esteem and confidence, as hopes were soon dashed in the wake of inflated expectations of progress.

Status anxiety or frustration is essentially a modern phenomenon, closely linked with changing lifestyles, social mobility, economic growth, and freedom. The settled life of traditional orders in which status positions were mostly inherited and unquestioned has given way to individualism and status confusion. Uncertain roles, unstable expectations, and fragile personal relationships have led to frantic, never-ending searches for secure personal identities. It is natural, therefore, that the question, Who am I? would be raised with increasing frequency. But the social and psychological conditions under which a secure self and identity can be forged are not easily fixed by the social engineers, in that the psychological and social factors at work impinge on one another in multiple ways.

We humans are eminently social beings, vitally dependent on our fellows for companionship, spiritual sustenance, and physical well-being. Born into a world inhabited by others like us, we employ language and shared meanings for purposes of communication. We learn that some types of conduct are approved and other kinds are disapproved. We internalize the expectations of others, and they do the same in our case. As the social scientists put it, we adopt "roles" or "expected patterns of conduct." By imagining the likely responses of other role takers to us—by assuming their attitudes—we are able to anticipate their expectations and to act accordingly.[6]

How are the self and personal identity related? There is an unfortunate tendency to employ the terms interchangeably. In reality, however, they are conceptually different. As social psychologist Gregory P. Stone pointed out quite some time ago, what is called "identity" establishes *what* and *where* one is *situated* in terms of other individuals, groups, classes, or whatever. One possesses an identity, says Stone, "when others PLACE him as a social object by assigning him the same words of identity that he appropriates for himself or ANNOUNCES. It is in the coincidence of placements and announcements that identity becomes a meaning of the self."[7] For instance, in traditional societies, custom and habit dictate role and status, binding the individual closely to his alloted place within a close-knit community. But think how much more difficult it is for "announcements" and "placements" to coincide when a complex division of labor, social change, and geographical mobility confuse or reduce our knowledge about the roles we and others occupy and when agreement about the degrees of deference and respect that ought to be accorded to us and to others become so problematical.

The facts of historic servitude and subordination to whites can hardly fail to leave many black Americans today with uneasy feelings of insecurity or inferiority vis-à-vis the descendants of those who enslaved their ancestors and then proceeded to reduce subsequent generations to a lowly caste. Suspended simultaneously between an emotional desire for group pride, on the one hand, and a nagging sense of inferiority, on the other hand, blacks in America, whether moderate or militant in outlook, are caught between an idealized and intellectualized solidarity and all the failures and fears of the American present.

The present status identity crisis in black America is associated to a greater extent with processes of modernization now taking place within the black community than with white discrimination and racism. These processes are ones to which all traditional groups are subjected with varying intensities and ones we all attempt to resist to some extent. In general, in the necessity to adjust to the many demands of modern society, the traditional individual confronts a plethora of institutions and values at odds with the older ways. Thus, mobility and status increasingly depend on the talents, interests, or plain luck of the individual rather than on location in a particular caste, race, or class. Due to expanding markets, technology, and higher incomes, we seem to be free as never before to write our own biographies. Simultaneously, modern organizational life locks us into more complicated and demanding forms of social and occupational role-playing. Institutions—not least market institutions—in general seem more remote and abstract at the same time that we seem to have fewer social restraints placed in our way.

Perhaps these differences may be shown more clearly by comparing the American "latecomer" with latecomers elsewhere, most notably in the former European colonies.[8] Difficult as it may be for many of us to accept, given the rigid political and moral interests so easily aroused by issues of race, many of the strains that now exist between white and black are in all probability due less to racism per se than to the kinds of tensions inevitably aroused with the establishment of new sets of relationships between late-comers and those who at present control cultural, social, and economic power. To this extent the *form* of latecomer–early comer disputes is roughly similar in all societies, although the depth and volatility are dependent on local factors, including the pace and impact of modernization on the different social groups.

For the relative latecomers to modernization who find their traditional cultures under siege, the "excruciating pain" of adjustment, in Mary Matossian's words, to modern technology, bureaucracy, capitalism, and the values associated with them have had much to do with the anti-Western sentiment in so much of the developing world.[9] As the structures and the values to which modernization gives expression relentlessly permeate traditional orders, tensions invariably build, not only between the relatively more modernized and the relatively less modernized nations as a whole but also between old and new elites within individual polities. In general, the people from relatively more modernized nations have difficulty comprehending the latter's refusal to appreciate the presumed blessings of "capitalism," "liberalism" (individualism), and laws applied equally irrespective of status, whereas the new elites, seeking their own particular visions of the "good" and resentful of the West's dominance in the material and technological domains, disparage many of the benefits of Western "progress."[10]

This pattern has often been observed in the ex-colonies where the former European rulers and native elites established new relationships, but it has also been seen in the relations between ethnic and racial groups *within* particular nations, including the United States. America has also had its share of latecomers to modernization—Irish, Poles, Italians, Jews, blacks, and so on—although the excruciating pain of adjustment to the dominant white Anglo-Saxon Protestant (WASP) culture on the whole has been a far less painful one than in most of the developing countries of Asia, Africa, and Latin America.[11]

If we can agree that the "colonial" designation is an apt one for those traditional individuals and groups who are latecomers to modernization, we may also suggest that it is applicable to those American latecomers who have differed ethnically and/or racially from the dominant white, Protestant majority. As is true of the peoples in the Third World to whom the terms *colonial* and *ex-colonial* are ordinarily applied, black Americans were likewise originally thrust into a master-servant relationship buttressed by legal and customary rules that relegated them to an inferior status. Moreover, it cannot be emphasized too strongly that, unlike most of our other colonials, they are visibly different in color from the dominant majority. In that legal and political fetters were imposed on a race of conquered people, their position obviously more closely resembles that of colonial peoples ruled by the European nations.

Adjustment to new situations is always difficult, but for the latecomer, once liberated from the bonds of caste and placed on a new footing of formal equality, the emotional pressures may prove especially stressful for those caught between the demands of the traditional group and the need to conform to new ways of behavior. The psychological risks can be enormous. Not only do old friends and acquaintances question one's adherence to the new ways, but the individual, now feeling alone and estranged from the traditional group, has no assurance of acceptance in the new world. Having been liberated from the restrictions of the traditional status group, does one simply stride forth boldly and attempt to seize the opportunities now presumably available, keeping in mind that all manner of slights, insults, and perceived failures may await one at every turn in the struggle for individual advancement? Does one risk the possibility of personal embarrassment in those inevitable social situations that are required in business and professional competition? Can one faithfully comply with the impersonal standards, expectations, behaviors, and values of the workplace yet simultaneously retain one's own dignity? In a word, am I respected for who I am and what I have accomplished as an individual, or am I to be judged by my membership in a racial group whose collective accomplishments are not highly esteemed by the dominant group? Does it make any difference? Yes? No? How much?[12]

By their very nature these questions are difficult to answer, for status depends on claims to honor and high standing from one side and the bestowal of honor and standing from the other side. It is a two-way street of communicated agreement. If agreement is absent or if people are unsure of the grounds for being ranked or for ranking others, a consensus with regard to prestige ranking is difficult to attain. Worse, failures in communication may occur. Bruised egos, misunderstandings, excessive wariness, mistrust, and any number of frustrations can mar social relationships as individuals disagree over the relative weights that ought to be attached to qualities of speech, taste, and behavior associated with social background, education, income, occupation, and ethnicity.[13]

Here we encounter one of the costs to be paid to modernity. Unlike people in more traditional orders, the modern individual has much more scope for social advancement, but he or she likewise has a much greater chance to decline or fail outright. As regional barriers are eroded and national economies become increasingly integrated and interdependent, and as capital flows rapidly within and between nations, the relative positions of individuals and groups are influenced by forces far beyond their immediate environs. Free markets and the establishment of the rule of law enable people to escape many traditional controls based on occupation, class, and status, only to be faced with new kinds of disruptions in their social relations.

A major consequence of these alterations in social structures is the erosion of the more obvious status distinctions, which renders social standing with one's fellows ever more ambiguous.[14] In that it stimulates an increase in status awareness and conflict between groups, economic progress has its own drawbacks. For if class and status divisions are no longer so easily recognized, if people are no longer quite sure where they "stand" in terms of their fellow human beings, if the criteria by which prestige is received and bestowed is often questioned, then they are likely to assert more or less strenuously their own prestige claims, often in idiosyncratic ways, on those with whom they come in contact. But how is status to be determined? By family background? By money? By type of occupation? By education level? By race or ethnicity? In what combinations? The list is endless, but we may be relatively confident that the ones mentioned here are among the more significant signifiers of status. Whether these claims are made aggressively in the political arena in more or less open conflict with others, or whether they involve the quiet processes of individual attainment in the market, the search for status is highly complex and often frustrating.[15]

The quest for status is complicated in still other ways. As work becomes specialized and complex, assessments of the social standing and worth of those who perform tasks also tends to become more difficult.[16] Whereas the prestige ranking of positions in the higher reaches of bureaucracies is relatively unambiguous, it is in the great "middle" that status ambiguity and anxiety are likely to be so keenly felt. Wondering just where they stand, many people are constantly on the lookout for signs of appreciation and recognition from their fellows. Specialization, complexity, and the routinization of tasks necessarily put status systems in some disarray, the effects of which are to reduce knowledge and agreement as to how status ought to be allocated. Social conflict, hurt feelings, anticipated rejection by others, and feelings of inferiority are often coupled with an insistence that one be given his or her due respect from others.[17]

STATUS ANXIETY AND THE BLACK MIDDLE CLASSES

If the dominant white majority finds that coping with the uncertainties of modernization can be a frustrating endeavor, there is ample reason to believe that a black minority, recently freed from state-imposed legal shackles and growing rapidly in political and moral influence, would find the experience still more problematical. Yet the impact of status frustration on these latecomers is not the same for all blacks across the board. Special factors peculiar to the Hobbesian existence of the urban ghetto threaten the self-images of the urban poor in ways rather foreign to the more affluent and educated black middle classes.[18]

Many in the economically successful black working and middle classes, however, are also alienated from white society, but they tend to express their alienation quite differently. Their grievances are characterized by a strong symbolic component. Aside from any concrete desire to secure a particular change in policy or society, the quiet rage of the middle classes, so well articulated in a recent work by Ellis Cose, is expressed by a resentment for the many petty humiliations and embarrassments to which white society is believed to subject black Americans on a daily basis.[19] Polls suggest that the black middle classes "consistently report more encounters with racial prejudice and voice stronger reservations about the country's success at delivering on the American dream." College-educated blacks appear to be particularly disillusioned with their occupational and educational experiences. Contrary to what we might expect, the higher the education and income, the greater the estrangement of the individual.[20]

Much of the mistrust ought to have been anticipated. One is struck in particular by the uneven pace of black progress in comparison with most other groups. About one third of this population remains in poverty. At the same time, black-white contacts on a new and much more equal basis have steadily expanded. The apparent need to explain or justify this relative black "backwardness" has assumed a growing sense of urgency within the black intelligentsia. The realization that despite all the trappings of political and legal equality blacks as a social group have advanced less quickly than expected in terms of their white counterparts and various Asian groups on a number of social and economic fronts has inclined many minority spokesmen to attribute the cause to an abiding, deeply entrenched white racism. Aside from any concrete evidence of racism, however, the combination of historical subjugation, uneven economic advancement, and increased interracial contacts on a basis of relative equality are quite sufficient in themselves to stimulate group tensions.

In the United States, status politics in its various guises has been a principal means for ethnic groups to enhance their own power and status in terms of the dominant Protestant majority. As a consequence of growing interracial political and material parity, we observe in our time a growth in competition between blacks and whites. Since the 1960s, themes articulating black pride and black achievements have assumed much importance in the interracial dialogue. In a period of increasing individualism, a stress on ethnic pride, as well as claims to various group entitlements, functions to reinforce a sense of racial cohesion forged initially during an era of white repression. Now, however, group unity does not so much exist for the physical survival of the individual as for the status protection of the individual in an alien, abstract, and mostly white-dominated world. Accordingly, within the black community, the biracial dialogue has increasingly functioned as a vehicle for the creation and maintenance of personal and status group identification.

As other Americans, blacks devoutly wish to be judged not by their race or ethnic origins but by their individual merits. But they also do not want to be pressured into adopting what they regard as white cultural norms and values calculated to call their own group identity into question.[21] As such, they have supported the ideal of formal equality before the law irrespective of race, but they have by no means rejected affirmative action rent-seeking activities based on ascriptive criteria of race when it has suited their purposes. Needless to say, it is not an equilibrium likely to endure.

Status politics always entails issues of identity and group entitlement. Affirmative action, in particular, depends for its legitimacy on the idea that racial identity is prior to individual self-identity. Government-imposed racial preferences have thus been considered as perfectly appropriate and defensible in the drive for social and economic advancement. Given the overriding support that affirmative action holds among the black middle and upper classes, it is easily understandable why status disputes would come to play such a significant part in political struggles. Affirmative action can last only so long as the ascriptive status of its beneficiaries is accepted as morally and legally superior to individual achievement.

It has often been remarked that the black lower class is highly dependent on public welfare. What has received less comment is that in its growing reliance on public service employment and jobs in the huge private bureaucracies where affirmative action programs are most easily monitored and enforced the black middle class has developed a strong stake in the growth and permanence of major programs in the modern welfare state. For example, with 16 percent of the civilian workforce employed by government, 24 percent of blacks hold government jobs at some level; and according to one estimate, among black professionals, about one half of the males and two thirds of the females work for the state.[22]

Not surprisingly, the black minority, as compared with most other ethnic groups, has as yet to develop a strong entrepreneurial class. In 1987, blacks owned around 420,000 small businesses with receipts of $19 billion, whereas Asians, with only 3 percent of the population, owned some 350,000 small enterprises having receipts of $33 billion. With roughly 12 percent of the population, they own less than 3 percent of the business establishments. In Dinesh D'Souza's words, "[B]lack enterprise is so fragile that 60 percent of its receipts come from the government; many black enterprises would collapse instantly if they were taken off government contracting preferences and set-asides."[23]

The growth of a middle class mainly dependent on public sector employment and affirmative action policies has left the black community largely bereft of a class possessed of those virtues traditionally attributable to a bourgeoisie, such as thrift, self-reliance, independence, and a healthy suspicion of large government.[24] Moreover, the relatively large gains associated with successful entrepreneurship have come under suspicion in much of the black community. It would seem that success in business activities in the marketplace somehow threatens the "imperatives of black solidarity."[25] This attitude is not uncommon among members of traditional groups who value custom and group solidarity over individualism. The marketplace and its rewards liberate the individual from custom and habit by placing him or her in opposition to the demands of the group. In these circumstances envy can become a powerful weapon for imposing conformity. "Getting above one's raisings," "acting white," and other such phrases are a means to sanction the individual who would resist conformity with the norms of the group. In its opposition to uncontrolled mobility, it also appeals to egalitarianism over and against individualism.[26]

As it is, the development of a black middle class highly dependent on government jobs and funding and a weak entrepreneurial sector within that class has probably reinforced black *intra*class unity. As a result, a certain coincidence of interest between the middle class and the underclass and poor has emerged. In championing the interests of the black lower classes in general, the black middle class, highly dependent on government employment and funding for the welfare state, is able to present a more or less united racial front to the white world.

Affirmative action plays a highly significant role in this regard. As we shall see in Chapter 5, its existence benefits only a relatively small number of black Americans in any material sense. Due to its powerful symbolic value, however, affirmative action not only opens up positions that might otherwise have been unavailable for many middle class blacks, but it enlists the support of less fortunate black Americans, irrespective of social and material circumstances. Defended on the grounds that it serves the entire black community, it is thought by many to be a boon for *all* blacks.

If a disproportionate black middle-class dependence on government jobs and affirmative action facilitates a certain harmony of interests between the black upper and lower classes, and if this common interest enhances black political power, it potentially exposes the individual who is surrounded by whites to a slew of interracial social strains. If white attitudes appear more enlightened than elsewhere, but if competition is also strong and status not clearly defined, affronts to status are easily aroused. The promise of equal treatment in these cases does not eliminate fears of failure by any means. This is more or less true for government agencies, the large corporations, and other white-collar bureaucracies in which conformity with group norms and values is highly prized—and rewarded for reasons that may sometimes have more to do with manipulative and interpersonal skills than with raw talent. In any event, values specific to the racial group may prove a hindrance. "Race, ethnicity, or occupational networks," reports Clarence Page, "are powerful identities around which to organize your life, but they are not life, although for many African Americans, blackness comes remarkably and, I would submit, hazardously close."[27]

It is understandable why these competitive, white-collar environments would be a source of status insecurity within the black middle classes. First, given the place occupied by affirmative action in American economic life, the individual cannot be at all confident that his (or her) own status position and success are due entirely to his own effort and talents. He may be haunted, rightly or wrongly, with a nagging fear that were it not for the imposition of racial preferences, he might never have attained his present position. Second, the individual may feel himself overwhelmed and alienated in terms of the sheer numbers of whites that surround him, especially if his background and customary attitudes diverge somewhat from those of his white peers. Because there are so many whites with whom he must contend and who, besides, exercise authority at so many levels, he is inevitably dependent on their goodwill for recognition, moral support, or professional advancement. A perceived slight, communication snag, or failure to gain the proper recognition that is his due may therefore be magnified and chalked up to racism of white superiors and peers, leading him to conclude that "all" whites are determined to thwart his ambitions.

"The quest for black identity," Cornel West informs us, "involves self-respect and self-regard, realms inseparable from, yet not identical to, political power and economic status. The flagrant self-loathing among black middle-class professionals bears witness to this painful process."[28] Indeed, various surveys suggest that it is this "privileged class" of black Americans that is *most* alienated from important American institutions.[29] It is also this middle class that is more likely to come into frequent and intimate contact with whites in professional and business settings where competition can be fierce, if subdued in tone, and where discourse and behavior are subject to ritualized restraints. In that these individuals are likely to have traveled the greatest psychological distance from their ethnic roots, they may feel more keenly than blacks exposed to less integrated settings the doubts and contradictions inherent in situations in which both ethnic integration and ethnic competition with the dominant majority occur more or less simultaneously.

Modern life is saturated with social and cultural ambiguity. Despite the efforts of liberal politicians and respected elites, the rapid acknowledgment by whites after 1964 that the new state of race relations implied greater social equality among individuals in both races was slowed partly by events within the black community itself. First, the relatively high rate of crime and other social pathologies within the black community came to the attention of the public, leading many whites to adopt avoidance behaviors, which in turn were perceived by law-abiding, respectable black citizens as brutally indiscriminate in their effects. A consequence, we have seen, was a staggering blow to the respect and pride of many black Americans who would now find themselves being lumped together with criminals and welfare mothers.

To carry the weight of white suspicion, fear, and avoidance is bad enough. Perhaps even more distasteful and humiliating, especially for upwardly mobile middle-class black Americans, are the perceived affronts to status, that is, the denial entirely or at least insufficiently of the kinds of recognition and respect that define who one is and would like to be. In these instances, the individual who wishes to "announce" one kind of social or occupational status may find himself (or herself) ranked more lowly by others. In other words, a status ranking may be attributed to him that he would just as soon like to forget.

The affronts can certainly be intentional, but more likely, they are the result of ignorance or insensitivity. As it is, they are usually open to diverse interpretations. Take the wealthy black owner of an apartment in an upscale area of a metropolitan city who is dropped at the employees' entrance by a cabdriver; the lawyer who comes to work in casual dress on a Sunday afternoon only to find himself under close interrogation by a security guard; or the couple checking out a home in a white suburb who observe two individuals looking in their direction from the house next door. For the individual who has struggled so hard and has met and overcome the many challenges thrown at him (or her) but who now believes his status is being implicitly questioned, the blow to the self and identity can be staggering.

The search for acceptance is made more difficult when status is open to challenge from so many directions. It is instructive that many black intellectuals and politicians routinely attribute racist motives and behaviors to whites whose actions with equal plausibility might be described in terms of insensitivity, indifference, or inadequate information. Motives are not always correctly interpreted. No two individuals process information in exactly the same way, since none of us calls on exactly the same kinds of past experiences. Individual expectations and hence interpretations of events may vary widely. To interpret the meaning that lies behind the act is essential. That task, however, can be a daunting one. For example, should the cabdriver have assumed, given the dress and demeanor of his black passenger, that the latter was the owner of an expensive high-rise apartment rather than an employee? Was the cabbie trying to insult his passenger deliberately? It is difficult to know for sure. Such personal recollections and anecdotes play an important role in black alienation at the present time, especially within the ranks of the middle class. The issue seems to come down to the following: White Americans fail to acknowledge in an appropriate manner the legitimate status demands of black Americans.

As a result, many misunderstandings arise in those gray areas where interracial contacts are prevalent, where social equality obtains, and where some combination of white ignorance, poor manners, or indifference to blacks is perceived to have taken place. Similarly, if information is scarce and cues must be taken from dress, speech, and adherence to certain forms of etiquette, whites may attribute behaviors and attitudes to well-intentioned, upstanding black citizens that in reality characterize lower-status individuals or underclass life. That is, the white may rely on superficial generalizations that by no means accurately assess the true qualities of the specific black individual with whom he or she interacts. In a myriad of ways the typical white may demonstrate insufficient respect or consideration for the particular role the black individual occupies. The latter in turn may interpret the white behavior as racist.

As blacks advance in various areas of American life, the occasions on which misunderstandings can arise will inevitably occur. From the standpoint of whites, what appears as the most innocent statement or act can take on a racist meaning for the black. For instance, as a college student the black may have perceived racist intent when a professor called on white students to answer the more difficult questions or, in his (or her) opinion, appeared "deliberately" to refuse to recognize his outstretched hand. Perhaps he received a lower grade than he thought he deserved because, as he saw it, his instructor probably assumed that, being black, he would perform inadequately. If following graduation he subsequently enters a prestigious, white-controlled law firm or company, he may come to feel that, due to race, his older and more experienced colleagues do not wish to help him surmount any number of daily hurdles, although he notes that without any apparent hesitation they offer support to whites. Or he may not be invited into their homes or asked to join their clubs. But even if he finds ready acceptance among his white-collar peers, he may find himself being mistaken for a blue-collar worker if he arrives at his office casually dressed on a Sunday. Indeed, he may find that if he does not satisfy the security guard, he may be refused entry altogether. Naturally, he suspects that his color may have been behind the guard's action.

In short, whenever the black enters the public world of strangers, his or her status as independent professional, higher civil servant, or other esteemed position may come under threat in any number of ways, depending on the particular circumstances, the level of information available to the participants on both black and white sides, and the tact and sensitivity of the whites.

It cannot be doubted that black "announcements" and white "acceptances" are easily thrown into disarray where race is concerned, occasionally coming into correspondence only to unravel at the next moment. The fear of a loss in status respect can be so overwhelming on occasion as to make not a few outsiders wonder why all the fuss in the first place, as when, for example, a former New York City Schools chancellor reportedly had so much difficulty in deciding which predominantly white country club he would agree to join. What delayed his decision was a fear of being mistaken at some future date for a caddy.[30]

On the other hand, the threats to status may be much more direct. For example, a sociology professor is refused entry into a dress shop until his white wife arrives; a prosperous newspaperman is shown a slum apartment by an insensitive real estate broker; a well-known journalist, working in the yard at his suburban home, is mistaken by a passerby for the gardner; or a young female lawyer finds the suspicious stares of clerks in expensive dress shops highly disturbing.

Why do we find a discrepancy between white respect for African Americans in some settings and an apparent lack of respect in other, more impersonal situations? Why do black college professors, for example, who garner the attentive respect of their colleagues at professional gatherings and in the faculty coffee rooms find themselves suspected as potential shoplifters in upscale stores? *The extent to which whites harbor negative stereotypes of blacks and the extent to which blacks in turn perceive that the white majority carries such images in its collective mind are mainly the result of a large underclass within the heart of the black community itself.*

Most blacks are keenly aware that a large black underclass grows within the inner cities, one dependent on welfare, often subject to criminal behavior, hostile to educational institutions, and in general, an affront to middle-class and working-class values alike. Because blacks make up only about 12 percent of the total population but are associated with a disproportionate amount of the violent crime, illegitimacy, and school failure in America, the effect on many whites is to taint all blacks to some extent. No doubt the characterization is grossly unfair to the great majority of black Americans. But when whites cannot clearly distinguish between middle-class, lawful blacks and possible criminals from the lower-class, they are likely to think first and foremost about their own persons and property. It is this dilemma that may explain Ellis Cose's remark to talk show host Dennis Prager (May 31, 1995) that in the minority community it is widely held that whites think of "all" blacks as being "on welfare, lazy, and ignorant."

Blacks react strongly to the implication that they are relatively more prone than other ethnic groups to seek welfare checks and unemployment relief, to have babies out of wedlock, and to engage in criminal activities. They rightly regard it as a gross and unfair stereotype placed on respectable black Americans. Why should they be called on to pay the price for white fear and ignorance? Are the white middle classes blamed for the social pathologies of disadvantaged and poorer whites? Is this not "blaming the victim"?

These black Americans ask only that the white world judge members of their race as individuals to be accorded the same respect and compassion that whites in the collective themselves receive. They, their families, and their friends can recall humiliating experiences in which they themselves were singled out as potential shoplifters or muggers by clerks, policemen, or whomever. Whenever they or their friends are subjected to mistaken identity, the effect is to raise all the old unresolved historical questions of black servitude in the past as well as their own current status problems vis-à-vis whites. One may be sure that the last thing with which they wish to be confused and identified is the underclass, since it is from that source that most of the negative stereotypes of blacks now prevalent among whites are derived. Indeed, the disorganization of ghetto life, which figures so prominently in white conversation, is in all probability clearly understood by most blacks. It is a source for "group disgrace."[31]

Black confidence, therefore, is severely shaken because of a strong conviction that much of the majority population behaves as if it thinks most blacks are low achievers, destined to occupy the lower rungs of the social ladder. The mere presence of the underclass is marked down as a serious racial deficit.

On the other hand, whites, fearful for their own safety and keenly aware of the disproportionate level of black crime, either avoid contact with black strangers as much as possible or take special precautions on the streets and in their business establishments. For black Americans, the implication is that every black stranger is lumped by the majority into a single "potential criminal" category. Thus, how blacks tend to see themselves often fails to correspond with how whites actually perceive them. And to the extent that by their words and gestures whites fail to confirm positive black self-images, racial tensions will persist and status struggles will flourish.

In his autobiography, Henry Louis Gates, Jr., would seem to agree with the point we have been making; namely, that middle-class blacks want to be judged as unique individuals in their own right. The preface to his book, written in the form of a letter to his children, may be seen in this light. Gates, a black and chairman of the Afro-American Studies program at Harvard University, expresses the profound black "resentment at being lumped together with thirty million African Americans . . . with whom we may or may not have something in common, just because we are 'black'. . . . What do the misdeeds of Mike Tyson have to do with me? So why do I feel implicated?"[32]

Tyson, we suggest, is a metaphor for the black underclass. In this regard, West maintains that the black middle classes conflate their own identity problems with the "siege raging" in poor communities. "The uncritical acceptance of self-degrading ideals that call into question black intelligence, possibility, and beauty," he argues, "not only compounds black social misery but also paralyzes black middle-class efforts to defend broad redistributive measures."[33] Strangely, he concludes that an antidote to the black middle-class identity crisis and its estrangement lies in a massive redistribution of wealth by government from the taxpayer to the poor and the underclass. The implication is that the black underclass is merely the result of low incomes and "society's" refusal to tax itself at a sufficient level.

Indeed, we must read somewhat between the lines. If the manifest purpose of this proposal is to raise the material and educational standards of less fortunate blacks, the latent one, it seems, is to facilitate racial cohesion by overcoming the centrifugal forces of intraclass division and egoistic in-dividualism within the black community. Public-spirited middle-class blacks would join hands with similarly motivated whites in a heroic strug-gle to eliminate poverty and its effects. Once the scourge of poverty is eliminated, the social pathologies so long indiscriminately associated in white minds with the underclass and the middle classes will tend to dis-appear. At that time, it will be possible to speak to whites as true equals.

But Gates and West recognize that the alienation of the black middle class from white society is by no means due to white prejudice alone. If white insensitivity and prejudice were to undergo a marked decline tomor-row, the problem of self-esteem and identity would remain, and many blacks would continue to attribute their dissatisfaction to majority malev-olence. One cannnot exclude, therefore, the unintended effects of "intrar-acial class embarrassment" as an important contributor to interracial tensions.

Embarrassment, however, extends well beyond the underclass to include in general those less educated, lower-status blacks who in the opinion of other, higher-status African Americans are, as Page puts it, guilty of "show-ing their color" or, in Gates's words, of "speaking too loudly, dressing too loudly, and just *being* too loudly" in public.[34] The embarrassment probably derives less from "loudness" in dress and behavior per se than that it is observed by whites, depriving blacks of white respect. In one sense, we encounter the attitude of the upwardly mobile arriviste in search of respect and embarrassed for himself (or herself), his class, and/or his ethnic group. More broadly, it reflects the perpetual social struggle between the estab-lished and outsider groups in which the former attempt to define standards of behavior, speech, dress, and culture either to regulate access to their ranks or to insulate entirely from the influence of the latter. Emotional self-restraint and understatement are more typical of cultural and social elites than of members of traditional groups.[35]

Gates, as many other middle-class blacks, would prefer to keep a foot in the traditional group while enjoying the fruits of individualism. Typical of elite latecomers to modernity, he apparently longs for the "warmth and nuturance of the womblike colored world" of the traditional ethnic group. "I want to be black, to know black, to luxuriate in whatever I might be calling blackness at any particular time," he says, taking "special pride" in the accomplishments of a Nelson Mandela, Jessye Norman, Toni Morrison, or Spike Lee, among others. As many middle-class blacks, he is, as he puts it, "divided."[36]

Whereas "divided" expresses this attitude in a concrete way, it is also somewhat inadequate. Standing in the shadows, ever critical of the middle class, are both whites and the black masses: "[T]oday's black middle class is frustrated over being subject to contempt, not only from whites, but also from . . . other blacks."[37] Suspended between the demands of the traditional ethnic group and a modernity in which individualism, formal rules, abstract institutions, and impersonal relations govern his or her conduct, the black middle classes navigate emotionally and psychologically between each sphere of social existence, never entirely at home in either realm.

Once this divided position is staked out by black opinion leaders, however, it becomes necessary for psychological and strategic reasons to attribute underclass social pathologies to racism. To admit that the prevalence of black crime, illegitimacy, and endemic welfare, for instance, is at heart a *black* problem would lend credence to many negative white stereotypes. It would be a betrayal of the group. Moreover, intraracial cohesion would be threatened. As a keen observer of black America has pointed out, "There is no significant faction in Afro America that *confidently* pursues total assimilation. To do so invites instant ridicule for abandoning the poorest among us."[38]

Indeed, the erosion of group cohesion would impose specific costs on many members of the black middle classes specifically. Unity of purpose is essential if affirmative action and other public policies are to remain viable. Because it serves to legitimate racial preferences in public policy, victimism plays an indispensable part in the allocation of resources, material and psychic, to those who are able to take advantage of affirmative action. Hence, the occupational opportunities and incomes of many members of the black middle classes who are at present dependent on affirmative action policies would be greatly threatened by a middle-class individualism whose major goals lay outside the group. They would also be pressured to admit that social pathology in the underclass, not white discrimination, may be a major obstacle to the status affirmation they so earnestly desire.

UNDERACHIEVEMENT AND THE PROBLEM OF STATUS

In modern social orders, we have suggested, occupation provides a major source of status identity. Yet modernity itself creates conditions under which a secure self and identity are not easily established and maintained. Whereas the more preferred occupations may offer some support of status security through pecuniary gain and social recognition, the reality of fierce market competition looms as a constant threat to professional standing and social status in today's world. These aspects of modern life render reduction of income, loss of employment, and consequently status more difficult to bear than in traditional societies where occupational roles were determined by accident of birth and where status positions were relatively secure.[39]

Be that as it may, it behooves us not to exaggerate unduly the importance of occupation alone. Other factors may also affect social status and therefore status identification. The influences on self and identity are undoubtedly *cumulative* over the life span of the individual. The impact of family, education, peers, occupational life, and so on, play a most important role in this regard. Thus, when the individual "announces" who he (or she) is—that is, his identity—not only is his sense of self at issue, but the kinds of "acceptances" that his "announcements" receive from others will likely be determinative. The nature of the acceptance of announcements by others may turn on any number of factors, sometimes unpredictable and idiosyncratic but normally predictable from both sides. If anticipated "success," however defined, does not go according to plan, efforts may be made to justify, deflect, or rationalize perceived personal failures.

It is for this reason that one of the most important means necessary for ensuring success—specifically, education—is so avidly sought. If educational attainment is increasingly recognized as the chief means for social mobility and material and symbolic resources, we ought to expect upwardly mobile working- and middle-class blacks to place a relatively high value on its worth and the cognitive abilities associated with it. No doubt they do, but regrettably, black Americans as a group have not advanced through educational attainments as rapidly as many had anticipated following the end of legal discrimination. Much academic and political controversy has revolved in particular around black performance on cognitive ability tests. Contemporary opinion has attributed the relatively low level of black performance to a history of slavery, poverty, family breakups, and especially, racial discrimination.

The issue of testing has implications for the nature and consequences of status anxiety among black Americans. It is bound up with a potential loss of respect if the African-American test taker does poorly, thus confirming what he (or she) believes is the white assumption and what he secretly fears may be true, that blacks are generally not as intelligent as whites. A test of mental abilities does indeed leave many blacks vulnerable to a feeling of inadequacy in areas where group standards have generally lagged behind those of other groups.[40] It stimulates fear of failure.

How can blacks not experience anxiety about where they stand? In recent years publicity about test scores has increased. As a result, the conventional wisdom about black pathology and the role of white racism has been questioned. It was therefore inevitable that data would be supplied that had the effect of making unfavorable comparisons between blacks and whites on several fronts, implying that whites were no longer primarily responsible for the major ills of the black community. These data would exacerbate black insecurities at the same moment that African Americans were joining the major corporate, educational, and political worlds in unprecedented numbers.

In short, notwithstanding the effects of negative white attitudes, a significant threat to group self-esteem is the general awareness by blacks themselves that they fare poorly on several esteemed attributes as compared with other groups. This phenomenon has been observed at elite universities in which authorities have found it particularly difficult to explain to critics why their black students would score significantly lower on standard aptitude and achievement tests than would whites or Asians. These test results are bound to affect the self-esteem of educated blacks, precisely the ones who are most likely to possess knowledge of these tests and who are most likely to vent their status frustrations in the public arena.

That these tests not only are a subject of controversy but are utilized by governments, corporations, and universities raises fears that the relative black underachievement in schools and colleges signifies something more than historical discrimination alone. Thus, when distinguished social scientists vehemently deny that these test score differences between the races have anything to do with innate intelligence, their protests are not quite convincing to much of the black intelligentsia. The same may be said for the charge of "cultural bias."[41]

Can one doubt not only that many younger and accomplished blacks are quite aware of these comparative scores but that the attack on the legitimacy of cognitive ability tests is itself linked to the threat they pose to collective status?[42] Indeed, the present tensions between the races are motivated in part by a need to allay status anxiety. Much of the recent writng on race is obviously driven by these concerns. "The basic aim of much multicultural scholarship," argues William A. Henry III, "is to explain away the lack of success of groups designated (in the case of blacks, with undeniable validity) as victims. However artful and diverting the phrasing, the purpose is to blame their failure on the people who have succeeded, turning that success from a legitimate source of pride into proof positive of blame."[43] Even the most questionable criticisms of the West are routinely accepted in many scholarly circles. For example, despite devastating attacks from academic experts in his own field, Martin Bernal's thesis that ancient Egypt was strongly influenced by sub-Saharan sources and that Egypt, not Greece, is the true birthplace of the West has been eagerly adopted by many blacks as evidence of black cultural achievement.[44]

In fact, the insistence that "Eurocentric" curricula be eliminated or deemphasized and that black studies play a larger role in American education implies a sense of insecurity and a need to justify oneself before whites. "If we lose our black cultural perspective," a black Harvard student revealed to policy analyst Dinesh D'Souza, "we have nothing left—only our murder rate, infant mortality, the bad stuff. Without our culture, all we are is a bunch of pathologies."[45] Or in the opinion of another student, "We feel that Africans did great things in the past. It's a contrast with what this society says about blacks. History teaches us we can be great again. We are not just ignorant savages in the jungle, which is the idea you get. We have culture too."[46] When D'Souza asked still another opponent of Eurocentrism how he would feel about substituting such non-Occidental subjects as Japanese capitalism and Islamic fundamentalism in current academic curricula, he replied: "Who gives a damn about those things; I want to study myself."[47] Perhaps in his insistence on self-examination, this student heeds the call of the wounded self and the frantic search for a stable identity.

"WHITE INSTITUTIONS" AND BLACK MISTRUST

Although we have so far concentrated on the estrangement of the middle classes, it must not be supposed that feelings of estrangement from whites are confined to higher socioeconomic income groups alone. Indeed, outright mistrust of whites and "their" institutions characterize much of black opinion. The extent of fear and apprehension may be seen in a 1992 WCBS-TV poll of blacks in New York that found that 60 percent "thought it true or possibly true" that the government was making drugs available in black neighborhoods in order to harm black people, and 29 percent "thought it true or possibly true" that the AIDS virus was invented by racist conspirators to kill blacks.[48]

Still, as we have seen, the belief that whites will eventually undermine their positions is strongest among the middle classes. It is an interesting, if sad, datum that many young blacks who attend elite educational institutions are themselves highly mistrustful of the colleges that prepare them for future entry into the professions.[49] Feelings of estrangement, it apppears, have no class boundaries within the black community.

Mistrust, it goes without saying, enormously increases the extent to which whites are believed to hold negative stereotypes of blacks. This exaggeration of white malevolence is found in opinion polls. For example, a *Time/*CNN opinion poll found that 65 percent of the blacks who were questioned thought that whites believe blacks to have no self-discipline, whereas only 17 percent of whites in fact took that position. With regard to committing violent crimes, white beliefs were even more moderate than blacks might have expected. Thus, 75 percent of the blacks sampled said that whites believe blacks are more likely to commit violent crime, whereas only 34 percent of the whites actually held that belief.[50] Since professional criminologists conclude that blacks on average are in truth more likely to commit violent crimes than are whites, the degree of white moderation is rather remarkable.

Under conditions of mistrust, the temptation grows to seek moral and spiritual sustenance in the cultural milieu of the black community itself. The withdrawal from sustained contact with whites and a marked hostility toward white institutions take many forms, from multicultural ideals to physical separation in universities and professional societies. It is not going too far to say that emotions inspired by status insecurity, pessimism about the future, and a general distrust of whites inform virtually all public issues bearing on race, such as affirmative action, multicultural education, race-normed testing, black nationalism, separate black campus organizations, and set-aside programs.

Many blacks believe that it is necessary to divide the world mentally into a black in-group and a white out-group. In defense of group solidarity, they then enter the public arena in pursuit of collective objectives. In all probability, material gain is secondary to a need for pride in the achievements of black people and for white acknowledgment of these accomplishments. By asserting pride in all things black, their activism often provides an anchor for status identity. For growing numbers of black Americans, their own special historical tradition and their triumph over discrimination are a source of pride and dignity. And as we have previously argued, by easing the pain of adjustment to an "abstract" society dominated by remote institutions and large bureaucracies in which powerful whites seem to be everywhere, especially in positions of authority, group pride encourages a sense of power and meaning for a people caught between tradition and change.

A heightened sense of racial pride has both positive and negative implications. On the positive side, one finds a justifiable pride in the heroic struggles to endure in an alien and hostile environment. Yet group pride in itself cannot erase all self-doubts with regard to the relative position of blacks in American society today. By inviting comparison with other groups, the individual may rejoice in the accomplishments of his or her own race or ethnic group. But unless care is taken, the strategy may backfire, raising questions about the relative qualities and accomplishments of one's own group vis-à-vis other groups. When these racial and ethnic claims to special status rights become part of the public discourse, the probability that invidious comparisons between the contenders will become more frequent is also likely. This poisonous debate can arise when the group that claims first bragging rights arouses other groups to demand bragging rights for themselves. Assertions of racial or ethnic pride (in the form of multiculturalism or nationalism) have a way of producing their own countervailing forces.

Status politics has another fundamental weakness: The primordial pull of the ethnic or racial group, however compelling, is inimical to adaptation to life in a modern society based on the individual, an extended division of labor, and market competition. Social and geographical mobility, economic innovation, expanding international trade, and constant consumer change do not cater to those forces in the service of ascription. Participation in the "great society" requires a degree of trust and support from others of different color, religion, or culture. Minority group members must labor with majority group members in various social-institutional contexts (banks, stores, offices, factories, schools, and so on). The cultural and emotional retreat into the group, if seriously pursued, only intensifies mistrust and thereby reduces the likelihood of successful mobility.

THE SENSITIVITY IMPERATIVE

The Sensitivity Imperative arises in interpersonal relations when a designated victim, either self-defined or defined by others, insists that the nonvictim demonstrate sufficient sympathy and respect for the plight of the victim, usually by demonstrations of emotional support and goodwill but sometimes by public largesse as well. More than courtesy and fair treatment are at stake—two norms of behavior endorsed by all Americans. It is particularly important that nonvictims be sensitive to the emotional needs of the victim. As Charles J. Sykes puts it: "[I]t is not enough to behave correctly—one must be *attuned* to the feelings of others and adapt oneself to the kaleidoscopic shades of grievance, injury, and ego that make up the subjective sensibilities of the 'victim.' " " 'Sensitivity,' " he concludes, "transforms the self—especially the aggrieved self—into the inspired arbiter of behavior."[51] As we shall see, the extent to which nonvictims defer to the status needs of the victim determines in no small way his or her social and moral authority over them.

Before proceeding with the Sensitivity Imperative and its role in contemporary race relations, we wish to make it clear that we wholeheartedly embrace the moral precept that the feelings and self-esteem of others are important considerations in our daily conduct. Our criticism is aimed at that extreme form of sensitivity that undermines the legitimate discussion of ideas. The Sensitivity Imperative indeed goes so far as to censure any statement, no matter how accurate and valid, if it is believed to inflict harm on the self-image of black Americans.

Today, racism has less to do with *overt* behaviors and the denial of legal right for black Americans than with entrenched moral failure on the part of whites to express sufficient sensitivity in the form of compassion and understanding. It is no longer sufficient that whites merely consent to obey the civil rights laws and adhere to ordinary rules of civility. Over and above these considerations, they must prove their good intentions by displaying appropriate deference to certain social conventions and by giving their support to the political and economic agendas of the leading civil rights organizations. It was apparently this mode of thought that led Congressman Charles Rangel in the course of a speech prior to the 1995 congressional elections to equate the proponents of supply-side tax cuts with members of the Ku Klux Klan.

This shift in emphasis ought not to be underestimated. The concept of racism is now so general, spongy, and far removed from the particular behaviors and customs easily comprehensible to ordinary citizens in their daily lives that the term risks being reduced to banality. In particular, the concept of racism erodes the basis for the formation of those stable mutual expectations so necessary for interpersonal communication and trust between individuals whose backgrounds and primary social needs vary greatly.

Since racism is so omnipresent, ubiquitous, and elusive, the specific targets at which it is aimed are likely to be abstruse, abstract, and remote.[52] Thus, we encounter more and more criticism directed, depending on circumstances, at the "white power structure," the "system," "institutional racism," "systemic oppression," or "covert" racism rather than at specific acts of overt racism in which laws are willfully ignored or clear standards of conduct are violated. This symbolic component may be observed in the way racism has come to be seen by each race on college campuses. Whereas whites generally adopt the conventional definition of racism as hostility toward blacks based on race and/or discrimination based on race, blacks perceive its presence in their relationship to white institutions. The latter maintain that manifestations of white dominance of important institutions are necessarily racist. Hence, when faculty positions, campus organizations, grading systems, and curricula content are dominated by whites or when the majority controls the overwhelming proportion of managerial positions in corporations or governments, it is often charged that racism exists.[53]

These attacks on remote structures and general features of the environment suggest that specific acts of racism may be far less frequent or damaging to black people in any specific way than many civil rights advocates like to admit. For if the institutional environment is perceived as threatening to one's long-run interests, if the barriers it creates in the name of merit appear forbidding, and if the individual generally anticipates that he or she may well not live up to expectations with regard to established criteria for success, racism provides an excuse for any potential failure. As such, the "new" racism may serve political and psychological functions that ought not to be taken at face value.[54]

How are whites of goodwill to demonstrate conclusively that they have purged racism from their thoughts? It seems that a new race etiquette has emerged to help them navigate the treacherous rapids of "political correctness." As we have already pointed out, in biracial situations the racially attuned white must develop keen intellectual, moral, and linguistic skills for sending appropriate signals of sensitivity. The failure to address "people of color" by the title that the latter deem most appropriate for civil discourse, for example, can produce embarrassment all around, not least for the white who happens to be unacquainted with recent changes in the etiquette of racial or ethnic designations. Agreement about how blacks wish to be addressed or distinguished from other racial and ethnic groups has undergone four changes in the course of a single generation, the consequence of which is to confuse those whites who wish to avoid embarrassment to themselves or to others. "Negro," "black," "Afro American," and "African American" have all moved quickly across the historical stage since the passage of civil rights legislation in the 1960s. At present, either "black" or "African-American" is said to be the appropriate form of designation, although the latter seems somewhat more preferred by black elites and the former by the black majority.

From the otherwise well-meaning white's perspective, a slip of the tongue, an unintended breach of the new etiquette, may be interpreted as a deliberate insult. Similarly, a reference to historical situations and events may be construed as demonstrating an inadequate understanding, awareness, and concern for black suffering in the past or a lack of appreciation for black contributions to American and world history. In other words, current fashion and what the designated victim consider as insensitive behavior and a lack of compassion can make an instant racist of the unthinking, indifferent, or unwary white.

Once racism is redefined as a *state of mind*, the status struggle may be viewed in all its purity. No longer is a racist merely the individual who denies another individual his or her fundamental or contractual rights in the social, economic, and legal realms of daily existence. Rather, he (or she) is one who harbors certain thoughts that express themselves in unintentional assumptions, gestures, attitudes, or behaviors that are felt to threaten the self-respect of a member of another race. In this regard, one may be a covert no less than an overt racist. The underlying attitude of the white may be readily discovered in his or her "insensitivity," "lack of compassion," or "understanding" for the feelings of the minority individual or group. And since *insensitivity* is an ambiguous term at best, depending as it does on what the other thinks it to mean at the moment, it provides a powerful moral and political tool for the putative victim's use.

"Power," a distinguished French sociologist has argued, has much to do with control over areas of uncertainty. Thus, the "power of A over B depends on A's ability to predict B's behavior and on the uncertainty of B about A's behavior. As long as the requirements of action create situations of uncertainty, the individuals who have to face them have power over those who are affected by the results of their choice."[55]

Surely uncertainty will govern much of the social interaction between the races when almost any particular gesture, facial expression, statement, or attitude may be interpreted as hostile to the interests of the victim. Indeed, since the majority has allowed the minority to define the situation of blacks as one of more or less helpless victims of white malevolence, and since black elites and their allies have broadened the meaning of racism to include covert discrimination, it is to be expected that much uncertainty would characterize the relationship between the races. In a word, so long as the white majority implicitly or explicitly accepts the notion that covert racism is a problem, the uncertainty that results will function to increase the social and moral authority of the victim in various areas of special interest to the black minority.

Obviously, becoming attuned to the emotional needs of others can present problems to those nonvictims who must continually seek to discern what the victim may consider as insensitive and racist behavior. "Taking the role of the other" becomes difficult when victimized black and nonvictimized white fail to read one another's actions reliably. Mutual expectations and the performance of roles are consequently undermined once racism is routinely made identical to acts of insensitivity. If victimism can encourage pessimissm, prickliness, and paranoia, under the right conditions it may also enable the victim to claim social and political influence out of all proportion to his or her numbers or material resources, especially if the victim can persuade the majority that it is responsible for his or her plight.

Buttressed by the imperative that others be sensitive to his or her feelings, the victim is well positioned to define which particular actions may be legitimately regarded as proper or improper. A demand for sympathy and respect, after all, is at bottom an insistence that others sacrifice their own interests to the feelings, self-esteem, and other needs of the victim.

Racism is therefore whatever the victim declares it to be. For example, it has been argued that because black students may become uncomfortable during college classroom discussions in which, let us say, the problems of the ghetto are discussed, it is incumbent on the instructor that he (or she) not add to the students' discomfort by looking in their direction either too often or too seldom. As they say, the instructor is "damned if he does and damned if he doesn't." In either case, he or she is guilty of a subtle form of racial insensitivity and therefore vulnerable to charges of racism—or so it has been suggested with all seriousness in some scholarly circles.[56]

If what in our time is labeled racism in the course of public discourse is in reality a state of mind that is manifested in any particular utterance, gesture, or behavior that may or may not be recognizable as such to black and white in everyday situations, then how are we to find agreement as to which statement, opinion, or individual ought to be appropriately condemned as truly racist? Can one not be a racist without even realizing it, as some whites and blacks have seriously argued? Of course, we now go far beyond the conventional realms of public policy debate into those hazy areas in which any statement, omission, or gesture said to be offensive, insensitive, lacking in compassion, unfair, or unjust may be interpreted as an outward sign of inner racism.

Who determines when standards of decency and decorum are violated? The most appropriate answer apparently is the designated victim who happens to be offended by the particular remark, gesture, or statement in question. The black middle classes and their white allies therefore appropriate for themselves the power to determine what is proper in public or even private discourse. But he or she who can decide just which particular statement, reference, or gesture is racist can also decide the question of who, when, and under what conditions any individual may be appropriately condemned as racist. This control over the terms of public discourse is a powerful social and cultural weapon for the victim, particularly if the targeted racist accepts the terms of the debate. Abject capitulation has often occurred, not least in universities and in political debate.

Make no mistake: A major consequence of the Sensitivity Imperative is a transfer of significant social and moral power no less than economic resources to a relatively small number of political and cultural arbitrators. When and if the targeted racist acts to protest his or her own innocence or treatment, the minority members or their allies making the original charges can still accuse him or her of lacking in sensitivity and compassion. It is obvious that in such a charged atmosphere communication between the races will tend to be characterized by tenseness and a lack of forthrightness, if not dishonesty.

A second consequence is that black Americans can more easily discover clear evidence of racism once the term is defined as a lack of sensitivity or compassion. Racism may then be discovered in a variety of areas of social, political, and economic life no one would have imagined only a decade ago. This can only lead to witch hunts in which the most unlikely behaviors and attitudes are read as signs of underlying racist intent. The results are predictable. When racism is redefined to include covert norms, values, and insensitive behaviors, then charges, countercharges, and allegations of racism can only increase. Much as the communist leaders who ceaselessly sought for evidence of bourgeois and reactionary thought and behavior, our guardians against racial immorality will look for evidence of racism in even the most benign statements and gestures.

Thus, redefining racism as insensitivity opens a Pandora's box of racial ill will and conflict. It no doubt exacerbates an already difficult American dilemma. Why, then, did black activists and their supporters become obsessed with subtle forms of white behavior and expression, and why do they insist that whites adopt the new etiquette of race relations?

The source of this contemporary obsession is not difficult to find. If we look beneath the surface for the meaning behind so many of the charges of insensitivity or lack of compassion, we find an underlying plea for respect and esteem by many members of a group historically relegated to the lower ranks of the American social order. Such charges are in actuality usually an open manifestation of an inner need to repair the self through the struggle for status identification.

Nothing said so far ought to be taken to imply that the Sensitivity Imperative is found only among black Americans. Indeed, it has strong support among ideological liberals in the media, universities, the political class, and the upper reaches of many corporate structures. While the majority of whites resent being pressured to conform to its dictates, others accord it legitimacy. In particular, it appeals to liberals on emotional and intellectual grounds alike. Holding white society mainly responsible for current problems in the black community appeals to their historical mission on behalf of the group or class they deem as *most* oppressed at this specific historical juncture.[57] Consequently, policies and programs enacted on behalf of black Americans as a group are in harmony with modern liberalism's egalitarian thrust. For example, the strong commitment to affirmative action is justified not only because blacks have suffered oppression historically but also because present-day America is dominated by entrenched inequality. Liberals thus see blacks as "shackled runners," doomed to failure unless special treatment is meted out in law and policy.[58]

American liberalism's message has produced an ambivalent reaction in the black community. On the one hand, the hand of friendship is extended by white intellectuals, politicians, and administrators to a group historically excluded from power and consideration. On the other hand, there is the implied message that in the hurly-burly of political and economic competition blacks are somehow not up to the struggle. Indeed, this was the unstated assumption that underlay much of the early justification for school busing and affirmative action. Already undergoing the pangs of modernization, however, middle-class blacks could hardly express their gratitude for what seemed to be rank evidence of patronizing by their white "allies."[59]

CONCLUSIONS: THE PARADOX OF PROGRESS

Black Americans, as latecomers to modernization, have remained unsure of their status in an environment in which the traditional group can no longer offer the emotional and spiritual sustenance that it provided in the more settled and rural settings. The security of status and the emotional bonds of the traditional group are being severely tested by competing values and institutions. This point has been put no better than by the syndicated columnist Clarence Page:

> Group identity—the *tribe*—provides a soothing, healing balm for the pain of being black in a white world, but it also shoots a chastening jolt of guilt into the flanks of those who would dare bolt out of the pack or challenge the party-line "groupthink." Any dissension from "unity in the community" or any "airing of dirty laundry" in public threatens the group, which is held together by its mutually felt sense of vulnerability.[60]

The gales of modernity threaten the tenuous status identification of members of a race suspended precariously between the warmth of the traditional status group and the pull of an achievement-oriented, individualist society. The traditional group, however, will not give up without a fight for the loyalty of those who belong to it. They demand conformity to its norms and values. Once blacks achieved formal freedom and the individual was declared a full citizen along with the white majority, the possibility of failure, embarrassment, and rejection loomed larger than ever as the individual was now thrust back on his (or her) own inner resources, somewhat unsure of his place, and told in multiple ways that he alone is responsible for his destiny. Failure cannnot so easily be dismissed or rationalized as racism once one is legally free and repeatedly informed that he can rise as high as talent and effort allow. But since many black Americans have entered this competition unequipped to compete with whites in the marketplace and elsewhere, a justification for the lack of progress that had been so eagerly anticipated following their liberation from segregation had to be found.

Burdened by painful historical memories that they believe are linked to their present relatively low group status in the American racial and ethnic pecking order, many blacks, as individuals, have encountered what we have called the paradox of progress. Many individuals have prospered according to standards by which status and rank are earned, but they cannot truly enjoy the fruits of their labors, either because they do not believe that white society fully recognizes their worth as individuals or because they feel that whites do not sufficiently respect the virtues and accomplishments of their race. After all, whites cannot help but matter; they are everywhere; and they occupy most of the important positions of prestige, power, and authority. They cannot help but play a powerful part in the way blacks see themselves.

In this chapter, we have painted a picture of status identity and frustration that at first glance may give an impression that we are not sufficiently aware that discrimination continues to exist in American society. Racial hatred has certainly caused much harm to black Americans. On the other hand, when compared with other nations, the progress in racial tolerance and acceptance of full citizenship rights for black Americans in the course of the past generation has been astounding. Although other nations have created racial preferences in law for their own *majority* ethnic or racial group, what other important nation has created laws and regulations that under the umbrella of affirmative action actually award preferential treatment to an economically and politically weak racial *minority*? Indeed, in our fervent attempts to right old wrongs, we have occasionally violated the rights of our nonminority citizens. Formal rights are today guaranteed to black Americans, and public opinion is united in its effort to eliminate any remaining traces of discrimination, as any casual observer of American events would admit.

The fact is that there are limits to what can be done and what we would even wish to do to end all group disparities in the ways preferred by many black intellectuals and politicians. As we shall see in Chapter 5, the social and political costs of affirmative action are rapidly becoming unacceptable to many Americans. Moreover, our ability to address by political means and government coercion the status frustrations of black America is quite limited, short of the creation of a police state. Besides, how do we prevent those numerous incidents to which blacks so often refer, especially in cases where whites believe their persons or property may be at risk? Undoubtedly, whites would have to display a far greater sensitivity to the black American's need for respect and deference than they have thus far been willing to demonstrate. It is rather clear that only a sharp reduction in black crime would sufficiently reduce white fear so as to encourage more trusting behavior in the presence of blacks. As for the creation of secure personal identities within the black community and the sought-after white empathy, we may suggest that solutions to these kinds of problems require the enlistment of religious authorities and moral philosophers rather than the tools of the policy analysts!

To be sure, what one is tempted to call the victim revolution of the past couple of decades has utterly failed in its mission to reform whites. Many whites, who feel strongly that they have never discriminated against anyone and consequently deserve no criticism, continue to remain either openly or secretly defiant when faced with accusations of racial malevolence. We anticipate no changes in majority attitudes. After all, in the final analysis, status frustration and anxiety are problems of the psyche, useful to political elites in their quest for votes swayed by collective resentments. But precisely because the qualities of frustration and anxiety are at once unique to each individual, they are resistant to treatment by the physicians of social science. So unless we intend to adopt the communist tactic of reeducating entire populations, we must rest content that positive change will be slower in coming than many would wish.

NOTES

1. For a consideration of the problem of individual versus group, see the remarks of Arthur M. Schlesinger, Jr., *The Disuniting of America: Reflections on a Multicultural Society* (New York: Norton, 1992), pp. 117–20.

2. Jill Nelson, "An Island on an Island: Cherishing a Special Part of Martha's Vineyard," *New York Times*, August 23, 1993, p. B4.

3. W. E. B. Du Bois, *The Souls of Black Folks* (New York: Penguin Books, 1969), p. 4.

4. Dinesh D'Souza, *The End of Racism: Principles for a Multiracial Society* (New York: Free Press, 1995).

5. See Pierre Bourdieu, *Distinction: A Social Critique of the Judgement of Taste* (Cambridge, Mass.: Harvard University Press, 1984); especially C. Wright Mills, "The Sociology of Stratification," in Irving Louis Horowitz, ed., *Power, Politics and People: The Collected Essays of C. Wright Mills* (New York: Ballantine, 1963), pp. 305–23, also the useful survey by Bryan S. Turner, *Status* (Milton Keynes, England: Open University Press, 1988), p. 66. For the classic discussion of Max Weber, see H. H. Gerth and C. Wright Mills, eds., *From Max Weber: Essays in Sociology* (New York: Oxford University Press, 1958), pp. 180–95.

6. See, for example, Hans Gerth and C. Wright Mills, *Character and Social Structure* (New York: Harcourt, Brace & World, 1953), pp. 80–111. This general theme owes its inspiration in the first instance to the classic work of George Herbert Mead, who is generally considered the father of social psychology. See, for example, his *Mind, Self and Society: From the Standpoint of a Social Behaviorist* (Chicago: University of Chicago Press, 1934).

7. See Gregory P. Stone, "Appearance and the Self," in Arnold M. Rose, ed., *Human Behavior and Social Processes* (Boston: Houghton Mifflin, 1962), pp. 93–94. For an excellent overall account of the nature of identity, see Orrin E. Klapp, *The Collective Search for Identity* (New York: Holt, Rinehart and Winston, 1969).

8. The notion of the "latecomer" is discussed extensively in Marion J. Levy, *Modernization: Latecomers and Survivors* (New York: Basic Books, 1972).

9. Mary Matossian, "Ideologies of Delayed Industrialization: Some Tensions and Ambiguities," in John H. Kautsky, ed., *Political Change in Underdeveloped Countries: Nationalism and Communism* (New York: Wiley, 1962), pp. 252–64.

10. Different aspects of the pains of modernization may be found in Peter Berger, Brigitte Berger, and Hansfried Kellner, *The Homeless Mind: Modernization and Consciousness* (New York: Vintage Books, 1973); David Riesman, *Individualism Reconsidered and other essays* (Glencoe, Ill.: Free Press, 1954); Levy, *Modernization: Latecomers and Survivors*; Norbert Elias, *The Civilizing Process: The History of Manners*, vol. 1 (New York: Pantheon, 1978); John Murray Cuddihy, *The Ordeal of Civility: Freud, Marx, Lévi-Strauss, and the Jewish Search for Modernity* (New York: Basic Books, 1974).

11. Matossian, "Ideologies of Delayed Industrialization."

12. For an excellent discussion of this problem, see William A. Henry III, *In Defense of Elitism* (New York: Doubleday, 1994), pp. 64–99.

13. See, for instance, David R. Schweitzer, *Status Frustration and Conservatism in Comparative Perspective: The Swiss Case* (Beverly Hills, Calif.: Sage Publications, 1974), pp. 11–12; and C. Wright Mills, *White Collar: The American Middle Classes* (New York: Oxford University Press, 1956).

14. An excellent study is Peter Berger and Thomas Luckmann, "Social Mobility and Personal Identity," in Thomas Luckmann, *Life-World and Social Realities* (London: Heinemann Educational Books, 1983), pp. 110–23.

15. For example see Daniel Bell, *The Cultural Contradictions of Capitalism* (New York: Basic Books, 1976); and Seymour M. Lipset, *Political Man* (Garden City: Doubleday, 1960).

16. Peter Berger, *The Human Shape of Work* (New York: Macmillan, 1964). The altered nature of the workplace and the meaning attached to work take place in a general environment that is increasingly pluralized. We moderns migrate between divergent, often discordant realms of social life. The division of labor and specialization require people of diverse educational and occupational experiences to interact, however awkwardly; the same pressures arise in cases of religion, ethnicity, and race. Again, diverse lifestyles and ideologies put severe strains on communication, it goes without saying. Coping with any number of potential threats to identity requires that we become accomplished role-players, performers, as it were, on the social stage of life. It is especially in large bureaucratic settings that, given their intricate division of labor and specialization, the tendency toward elaborate role-playing is of such importance for individuals.

17. Berger and Luckmann, "Social Mobility and Personal Identity."

18. In the urban areas, crime, illegitimacy, absent fathers, and welfare mothers perpetually undermine that essential growth of trust in the infant and adolescent stages that are so necessary for self-esteem. Despite incomes far superior, say, to more recent arrivals in this country such as Mexicans and Indochinese, black infant mortality is nonetheless far higher. The cause is primarily behavioral in nature in that drug addiction and sexual disease are much more prevalent among poor black women. Moreover, risky and unpredictable early years tend to foster anxious and mistrustful individuals, hostile to all kinds of authority, including schoolteachers and administrators, cultural symbols, standard English, and acceptable manners. See, for example, Edward Banfield, "Present-Orientedness and Crime," in Randy E. Barnett and John Hagel, eds., *Assessing the Criminal: Restitution, Retribution, and the Legal Process* (Cambridge: Ballinger, 1977), pp. 133–42; idem, *The Unheavenly City Revisited* (Boston: Little, Brown, 1974); also see Signithia Fordham and John U. Ogbu, "Black Students' School Success: Coping with the 'Burden of Acting White,' " The *Urban Review* 18 (3) (1986): 176–205.

19. See, in particular, Ellis Cose, *The Rage of a Privileged Class* (New York: HarperCollins, 1993), pp. 38–39; also see John Bunzel, *Race Relations on Campus: Stanford Students Speak* (Stanford, Calif.: Stanford Alumni Association, 1992); Schlesinger, *The Disuniting of America*; and Clarence Page, *Showing My Color: Impolite Essays on Race and Identity* (New York: HarperCollins, 1996).

20. Cose, *The Rage of a Privileged Class*, pp. 15–16.

21. Ibid., pp. 55–56.

22. D'Souza, *End of Racism*, p. 496.

23. Ibid., p. 495.

24. For example, for a keen analysis of the need for a healthy bourgeoisie, see Wilhelm Roepke, *A Humane Economy: The Social Framework of the Free Market* (Chicago: Henry Regnery, 1960).

25. Page, *Showing My Color*, p. 46.

26. On the role played by envy and the social pressures arrayed against rapid upward mobility, see, in general, Helmut Schoeck, *Envy: A Theory of Social Behavior* (New York: Harcourt, Brace & World, 1969).

27. Page, *Showing My Color*, pp. 38–39.

28. Cornel West, *Race Matters* (New York: Vintage Books, 1994), p. 97.

29. Cose, *The Rage of a Privileged Class*, pp. 36–39.

30. Interestingly, the reporter who gives us the case of the avid golfer sees mistaken identity as an example of racism, although one might think that an individual so avidly sought by various country clubs would have relatively little about which to complain. In any event, to treat this case as one of racism does seem to stretch the concept somewhat. See the article of Sam Roberts, "Once Again, Racism Proves to Be Fatal in New York City," *New York Times*, September 3, 1989. Cose, however, provides the best source for various examples of affronts to status identity, and we have drawn extensively from his work in preparing this chapter. See also the autobiography of Henry Louis Gates, Jr., *Colored People: A Memoir* (New York: Alfred A. Knopf, 1994).

31. See Cose, *The Rage of a Privileged Class*, pp. 2, 38. Many critics believe the cause for black alienation not only in the past but in present-day America is due to the persistent strength of negative stereotypes held by whites for the black mi-

nority. We argue in Chapter 4 that not only are such stereotypes much more subject to erosion than is generally believed, but the ways in which individual whites assess the qualities of black individuals are much more dependent on class and culture than on race-related phenomena. The notion of "group disgrace" is drawn from Norbert Elias. For an interesting discussion, see Stephen Mennell, *Norbert Elias: Civilization and the Human Self-Image* (London: Basil Blackwell, 1989), p. 120.

32. See Gates, *Colored People*, xii–xiii.

33. West, *Race Matters*, p. 98. West's insistence on what can only be called a radical redistribution of resources toward the black poor through the government would in all probability lead to decumulation and wastage of capital and falling productivity.

34. See Page, *Showing My Color*, pp. 4–5. For a detailed analysis of Page's book, see David Horowitz, "Clarence Page's Race Problem, and Mine," *Heterodoxy* (May/June 1996): 4; the Gates quote is in *Colored People*, pp. xiii–xiv.

35. The notion of "established" and "outsider" groups is found in Norbert Elias and J. L. Scotson, *The Established and the Outsiders: A Sociological Inquiry into Community Problems* (London: Frank Cass, 1965). Also see the fascinating study of John Murray Cuddihy, *Ordeal of Civility*.

36. Elias and Scotson, *The Established* pp. xiii–xiv, 184.

37. See Page, *Showing My Color*, p. 57.

38. Author's italics. See Hugh Pearson, "Blacks and Jews View the Holocaust," *Wall Street Journal*, April 19, 1966, p. A12.

39. The amorphous, abstract, and conditional qualities of modern life mean that the relative paucity of settled customs and traditions in the "external" worlds of individuals tend to undermine as well the stability of their "internal" ones. Fewer social and institutional supports are available. "Objective" standards are found wanting in an environment in which a multiplicity of roles must be played amid a diversity of lifestyles and ideologies. The resulting insecurity makes us highly sensitive to slights or affronts, real or imagined. And since a basic attribute of modernity is its tendency to erode established and well-understood systems of social ranking, it is obvious that threats to self-worth become a pervasive aspect of modern life. The absence of secure systems of social ranking enhances efforts to validate one's own worth, while simultaneously the numbers of people said to be characterized as having an "inferiority complex" are multiplied. If this is true for entire populations in modern democracies, is it not likely to be even more evident among groups subject to rapid mobility and change? For a fascinating account of these problems, see Arnold Gehlen, *Man in the Age of Technology* (New York: Columbia University Press, 1980), pp. 73–91.

40. On the notion of "stereotype vulnerability" or "stereotype threat," see the work of social psychologists Claude M. Steele and Joshua Aronson, "Stereotype Threat and the Intellectual Test Performance of African Americans," *Journal of Personality and Social Psychology* 69 (November 1995): 797–811. A discussion of Steele in particular may be found in Ethan Watters, "Claude Steele Has Scores to Settle," *New York Times Magazine*, September 17, 1995, pp. 45–47. On the notion of "anticipatory socialization," see Berger and Luckmann, "Social Mobility and Personal Identity."

41. Examples may be found throughout Bunzel, *Race Relations on Campus*.

42. In all probability the *Bell Curve* has reinforced black insecurities. In fact,

there were some very thoughtful assessments of this work, but on the whole, these kinds of contributions were lost in a swell of moralistic hand-wringing and charges of racism. See Richard Herrnstein and Churles Murray, *The Bell Curve: Intelligence and Class Structure in American Life* (New York: Frees Press, 1994). For two good critiques of Herrnstein and Murray, see Stephen Jay Gould, "Curveball," *The New Yorker*, November 28, 1994, pp. 139–49; and Thomas Sowell, "Measuring Ethnic Intelligence," *The American Spectator* 28 (February 1995): 30–37. We shall consider the nature and durability of stereotypes in Chapter 4. Suffice it to say at this point that one cannot wish them away, although contradictory data over time can erode their hold on opinion.

43. See, for example, Henry, *In Defense of Elitism*, pp. 69–70; also see Hugh Pearson's thoughtful piece, "Blacks and Jews View the Holocaust."

44. Martin Bernal, *Black Athena: The Afroasiatic Roots of Classical Civilization*, vol 1, *The Fabrication of Ancient Greece, 1785–1985* (New Brunswick, N.J.: Rutgers University Press, 1989).

45. See Dinesh D'Souza, *Illiberal Education: The Politics of Race and Sex on Campus* (New York: Free Press, 1991), p. 221.

46. Ibid., p. 114.

47. Ibid., p. 75.

48. Schlesinger, *The Disuniting of America*, p. 110.

49. Bunzel, *Race Relations on Campus*; Fordham and Ogbu, "Black Students' School Success"; and the perceptive account of Shelby Steele, *The Content of Our Character: A New Vision of Race in America* (New York: St. Martin's Press, 1990).

50. See the analysis of George Church, "The Fire this Time" in *Time Magazine*, May 11, 1992, p. 24.

51. Charles J. Sykes, *A Nation of Victims: The Decay of the American Character* (New York: St. Martin's Press, 1992), p. 168. Sykes quite rightly calls our attention to a culture dominated by an obsession with psychological explanation. As in most areas of human behavior, however, complexity rules here as well. Hence, as we shall see, in their demand for victim status, the black middle classes are motivated by more than just a need to care for the self, as Sykes suggests. In addition, the specific material benefits that victim status can bestow on the recipient of affirmative action preferences ought not to be underestimated. If and when the black American no longer enjoys the status of premier designated victim, the moral authority of affirmative action will likewise decline. For the black intelligentsia and middle classes, what the economists call "rent seeking" and victim status reinforce one another. See Joseph Epstein, "The Joys of Victimhood," *New York Times Magazine*, July 2, 1989; for a good analysis of America's obsession with the psychological, see Philip Rieff, *The Feeling Intellect: Selected Writings* (Chicago: Chicago University Press, 1990).

52. On the abstract aspects of modernity, see the stimulating analysis of Anton C. Zijderveld, *The Abstract Society: A Cultural Analysis of Our Time* (Garden City, N.Y.: Doubleday, 1970); and Gehlen, *Man in the Age of Technology*.

53. For example, see the analysis of Bunzel, *Race Relations on Campus*, pp. 72–74.

54. Ibid.

55. See Michel Crozier, *The Bureaucratic Phenomenon* (Chicago: University of Chicago Press, 1964), p. 158.

56. For an example of this kind of advocacy, see Dhyana Ziegler and Camille Hazeur, "Challenging Racism on Campus," *NEA Higher Education Journal* 5 (Fall 1989): 31–36.

57. This aspect of American culture in general is discussed in T. Alexander Smith, *Time and Public Policy* (Knoxville: University of Tennessee Press, 1988), pp. 211–15; and Andrew Hacker, *The End of the American Era* (New York: Atheneum, 1971), pp. 150–51.

58. The logical inconsistencies in the notion of the "shackled runner" are deftly explored in Nicholas Capaldi, *Out of Order: Affirmative Action and the Crisis of Doctrinaire Liberalism* (New York: Prometheus, 1985).

59. We would do well to ponder the words of a wise South African, a champion for racial tolerance and freedom in his own country, who was writing with the American case in mind in the midst of racial change in the United States:

The non-white peoples of my country are smoldering at the continued slur which, they think, attaches to their color. It is useless for the whites to deny that there is any stigma when their actions suggest the opposite. And sheer white arrogance sometimes aggravates the position, an arrogance which tends (in South Africa at any rate) to be greater the lower the intelligence or economic status of the whites, while resentment at the slur tends to be greatest in those non-whites who have risen most above the rest in income and education. The mere wish to segregate may, not unnaturally, strike the cultured non-whites as inherently insulting.

See Svetozar Pejovich and David Klingaman, eds., *Individual Freedom: Selected Works of William H. Hutt* (Westport, Conn.: Greenwood, 1975), p. 9.

60. Page, *Showing My Color*, p. 39. His italics.

APPENDIX 2.1
SOURCES OF STATUS INSECURITY: SELF AND SHAME

According to psychologists, the self-image of the individual begins to develop early in life as the child becomes aware that certain forms of conduct are found to be acceptable or unacceptable. If he (or she) finds that his actions do not earn the approval of others, and if he is subjected to negative appraisals from those who are significant to him, he may develop a weak sense of self. By the time he is an adult, he will have learned what models of conduct are expected of him, but he may nevertheless be left with emotional scars because of early experiences.

But what if his self tells him that he is less than he might be or that he is not "as good as" others? Such self-appraisals, often formed in early life and immediately aroused under certain conditions, may bear heavily on subsequent interpersonal relationships. Whereas threats to the self may also arise in circumstances where role expectations diverge, a mere divergence in our mutual appraisals of one another is by no means the only source of insecurity. Indeed, as is well known, institutions based on discrimination were well understood and marked by little role confusion in the eras of slavery and segregation, but incalculable damage to the self-esteem of black Americans has nevertheless occurred down to the present time.

In general, however, the more institutionalized the habits and customs, the easier it is for the individual to anticipate correctly the attitudes of others and for the latter in turn to anticipate the actions of the individual. A predictable external environment, as it were, readily imposes itself on our "subjective" inner worlds, making our environments more plausible than otherwise. The opinions of some people matter much more than others, particularly those individuals with whom we regularly come into contact. In the case of parents and peers, especially, their impact may be downright destructive to the individual's self. Thus, the less subjected one is to slights, humiliations, and general abuse by parents, family members, peers, and others of significance to him during the course of childhood, the less the probability that a wounded self will emerge.

As a rule, a secure self is most likely to arise when a basic trust in others, usually parents, has been established, when the many potential risks that may occur daily are not unduly exaggerated, and when the individual self over the course of time is able to interact with the social environment in a positive manner. In a word, the secure individual gains a sense of where he has been and where he is going once he trusts those around him, shows confidence in his own actions, and can exclude from his concerns those potential minefields that might otherwise inhibit positive action in the world. To the extent that the individual fails to follow the role expectations of others of significance to him, his sense of self may be threatened when they disappoint his own hopes or expectations.[1]

Research on black self-esteem has found that young blacks have as much self-esteem as do young whites in that they do not appear to devalue those attributes that characterize their race such as facial features and skin color. On the other hand, they do seem to possess lower self-esteem in many integrated settings in which they are compelled to compete with whites. A number of studies that have looked at black self-esteem before and after school integration have found that blacks in predominantly white schools have relatively lower levels of self-esteem. Quite possibly, black students in predominantly majority settings tend to make invidious comparisons about their own academic abilities. To the extent that identity and self-esteem are social products, they will likely change if the environment sends a different message about the particular individual's capacities relative to others.

It must not be supposed that low self-esteem is limited to the less privileged blacks; indeed, on college campuses, it seems to be prevalent among many of those blacks whose futures would appear to be most secure. As former university president and political scientist John Bunzel has demonstrated in detail, black students at Stanford University and other elite schools tend to search feverishly for ways to avoid unfavorable comparisons with their white peers. In arguing for separate campus organizations, one Stanford black student claimed that "in black-controlled arenas, blacks are freed from the pressure to evaluate themselves in comparison with whites. This, I can assure you, is a serious matter in the black community."[2] As Bunzel poignantly summarizes this problem, "In the personal interviews a number of blacks spoke of 'feeling the burden of comparison with whites,' a burden that sometimes gets so heavy that they try to escape the pressure by withdrawing into their own social circles."[3]

Affirmative action policies, in particular, have the perverse effect of setting black students up for invidious comparisons that can shake their academic self-confidence, since minority admission requirements are so often lowered in order to accommodate minority applicants. At Stanford, for example, 20 percent of the white students felt that black freshmen were less academically qualified, whereas 30 percent of the black freshmen felt the same way.[4]

We ought not be too surprised that blacks would express even more negative comments about their qualifications than did their white peers. "When circumstances," says psychologist Morris Rosenberg, "stimulate minority children to compare themselves with the majority, their self esteem does suffer." "Our self esteem," he goes on to say, "may be damaged if we find ourselves immersed in contexts in which others . . . outstrip us . . . because self esteem is related to the performance level of others. It is not only how good the individual is but how good others around him are that affects his self-attitudes."[5] This may be especially true for academic settings where grading, if anything, stimlates competitive impulses.

Adult identity and self-esteem are related to the achievement and respect we derive from the various roles we perform. Moreover, role performance is evaluated with reference to the performances of others who share the same or similar roles. Consequently, when the Reverend Jesse Jackson and other activists engage in ritualistic chants calculated to invoke a sense of self-worth, the effects are likely to be minimal at best. Proclaiming that "I am somebody" is unlikely to have any lasting effects on self-esteem, since at its root self-esteem occurs when individuals have a sense of personal efficacy and believe that they can master the challenges of everyday living in our complex social order.

At the extreme, if people lack confidence in their abilities, they may well experience a sense of shame. Psychologists are now beginning to argue that shame informs virtually all mental illness and that in all likelihood it contributes to such maladaptive behaviors as drug use, passivity, and alcoholism. This so-called master emotion must not be confused with "guilt," although admittedly the two emotions are somewhat similar in nature. Guilt refers more to what ought or ought not to be done in particular circumstances. It involves harm to others and is directed at specific actions taken by an individual. Shame, however, arises not so much from any wrongdoing as from what others may think of us. It derives from a diffuse sense of inadequacy and insufficiency, from a general feeling that we just cannot be what we would wish to be. It is an emotion turned inward on the self, one in which the individual is continually judging himself to be flawed or scarred. Since it is so closely associated with feelings of anxiety, mistrust, and inadequacy—usually developed in childhood—shame poses a constant threat to the self. As such, it is a barrier to a sense of pride.[6]

Shame seems especially adaptable to conditions of modernity, which may explain the increasing attention it has received from psychologists and psychiatrists in recent years. Whereas guilt is most likely aroused when customs, standards, and institutional behaviors are transgressed, shame makes us obsessively concerned that others are forever judging us and finding us wanting in intellect, money, dress, manners, taste, and so on. Therefore, in the more traditional social orders where class and rank are clearly delineated, where roles are relatively well defined, where demands for social equality are relatively weak, and where competition is played down, feelings of shame are less likely to be aroused. Conversely, when these conditions are absent, the individual is more easily thrown back on his own mental and moral resources, his own subjective world of unguided feelings and obsessions. True, once freed from the tyranny of custom and clear standards of expected behavior, the individual may hopefully choose his work and fashion his identity. But this freedom may also stimulate fears of failure, inadequacy, and shame.[7]

The role of shame has received far too little systematic attention in assessments of black-white disputes, although by referring constantly to "self-esteem" and "pride," black social commentators and propagandists surely attest to its salience within their ranks. The blanket charge of insensitivity, so often leveled at whites and "white" institutions, would seem to lend support to the shame hypothesis. Recall that insecure personalities, lacking a basic sense of self and deficient in trust, tend to turn inward, in the process becoming anxious about their environments. According to this notion, weak identities focus more readily on general aspects of their environments, on what others *may* think, than do those more trustful selves who find it much easier to filter out so many potential dangers "out there."

NOTES TO APPENDIX

1. See Anthony Giddens, *Modernity and Self-Identity: Self and Society in the Late Modern Age* (Cambridge, England: Polity Press, 1991), pp. 64–68; also, in general, see Heinz Kohut, *The Analysis of the Self* (New York: International Universities Press, 1971).
2. John Bunzel, *Race Relations on Campus: Stanford Students Speak* (Stanford, Calif.: Stanford Alumni Association, 1992), p. 66.
3. Ibid.
4. Ibid.

5. Morris Rosenberg, "The Self-Concept: Social Product and Social Force," in Morris Rosenberg and Ralph H. Turner, eds., *Social Psychology* (New York: Basic Books, 1981), pp. 605–53.

6. Robert Karen, "Shame," *The Atlantic Monthly*, February 1992, pp. 40–70.

7. See Arnold Gehlen, *Man in the Age of Technology* (New York: Columbia University Press, 1980), pp. 73–92; Giddens, *Modernity and Self-Identity*, pp. 64–68, 153; and Karen, "Shame."

3

Visions of Victims

A racial crisis undermines a rather uneasy consensus in American public life. Contrary to what one might expect, however, the academic study of race relations seems more steadfastly attuned to received opinion than to asking new questions. What may be called the "orthodox" account, which is subscribed to by the majority of social scientists and race relations authors, typically depicts blacks in the latter part of our century as hapless victims of white discrimination and racism, unjustly and more or less consciously relegated to marginal occupations, undesirable dwellings, and ineffective schools and perpetually victimized by a hostile white majority. We label the theory that the problems of black America are due mainly to white hostility and discrimination the "Victim Vision" of race relations. As the more or less official version of the current plight of blacks, its ideology suffuses the vast majority of race relations reports, essays, and textbooks, discussions of curriculum reform on college campuses, and the recommendations of race relations experts. In addition, it is a vivid expression of various exploitation theories of socioeconomic life, that type of social science indebted primarily to Marxism and socialism in which capitalists, industrial barons, and the politicians in their service are said to employ their vast controls over economic resources in order to exclude ordinary citizens from the good life. Blacks, as other powerless groups, invariably lose out, since the economy, after all, can be little more than a zero-sum game in which the gains of some groups must inevitably entail losses for other groups.

The purpose of this chapter is roughly threefold in nature. We wish to describe this regnant theory of race relations expounded with such intensity by many academics and black activists alike. Second, we shall expose its weaknesses and errors. Finally, in order to illustrate its intellectual power to reduce social science to ideology, we shall demonstrate the way in which it is linked to the Sensitivity Imperative. As we conclude in this and subsequent chapters, the Victim Vision has little empirical or theoretical justification. It survives as orthodoxy because it meets many ideological, emotional, and even material needs of ordinary whites, liberal elites, and the majority of black Americans. To the extent that it attributes the current plight of black Americans to white discrimination and malevolence, it remains faithful to the logic of the Sensitivity Imperative.

In our efforts to comprehend the intellectual and ideological hegemony of the Victim Vision in social science, we shall quote generously from four leading textbooks on race relations as well as from the works of such important scholars as Stanley Lieberson, Milton Gordan, Andrew Hacker, Edna Bonacich, Thomas Pettigrew, Joel Steinberg, Joe Feagin, and Charles Willie.[1] These writers are in agreement with a fundamental notion of contemporary race relations theory—namely, that powerful whites control the life chances of victimized and passive blacks. We deliberately employ the term *passive*, for passivity is surely implicit in the idea that whites control the life chances of blacks and, moreover, that white Americans are primarily responsible for the current conditions in black America. Let us therefore turn to six major components that may be said to constitute the Victim Vision.

WHITES CONTROL THE ECONOMY

According to the Victim Vision, whites monopolize access to desired economic resources—well-paying occupations, housing, property, business opportunities, and even marketable skills. This dominance is due less to any superior white knowledge, industry, or skill than to a control over the levers of economic and political power. In this view wealth is not so much created as expropriated. As Feagin and Feagin write, "[P]rivileges or resources gained at the expense of another group remain massed in the hands of the dominant group unless acted on by that other group."[2] Since it is implicitly assumed that minority groups are unable to generate their own resources through hard work, entrepreneurship, and the development of the special skills demanded in the marketplace, this vision of social reality resembles the old-fashioned socialist and academic Marxist belief that the economic pie is somehow fixed in size over time, subject to little alteration so far as the poorer classes in the community are concerned.

The notion that whites unfairly amass and control economic resources may be likened to the so-called cargo cult theory of production and distribution. The cargo cult arose in the aftermath of World War II in the South Pacific among certain indigenous peoples (notably in New Guinea and Melanesia). The indigenous population envied the material wealth of Europeans, whose wealth and power were a marvel demanding explanation. Seemingly, the Europeans possessed goods that they in no way worked to produce. The understandable amazement and confusion of the natives were intensified in that goods were so often airdropped to European outposts and plantations.

The cargo cults were therefore created by native prophets offering a plausible explanation for European wealth. The white man, said the prophets, had stolen ancestral goods intended for the natives themselves. However, the white man's wealth was believed to be a temporary phenomenon, for in time the ancestors would send more goods to the intended beneficiaries. At that point an era of great prosperity would be ushered in for the indigenous people.

Our modern race relations specialists also tend to assume that, like manna from heaven, wealth falls in the direction of some people—or, to be more precise, on the way to the ground, it is diverted from some people to other people. Blacks are poor, and whites are wealthy, not so much because whites are on average more productive but because the latter are somehow able to expropriate for themselves the more lucrative and preferred positions. Material life is thus reduced to group conflict in which the powerful players hold all the cards. White dominance is the centerpiece of the Dworkins' assessment of race relations. "When the powerful majority controls resources," they write, "it also controls the life chances of the minority: their access to resources, jobs, education, wealth, even food and health care. So doing guarantees that the minority will remain dependent upon the majority in a colonial type relationship."[3]

Once political and social controls over economic resources are posited as the underlying determinants of the relative financial and occupational positions of minorities and majorities in the United States, and once it is assumed that what matters is not so much how wealth is produced but how it is to be redistributed after it has been produced, one can easily find all manner of exploitation at work. Many authors actually call on the colonialist metaphor to characterize current black-white relationships. "[T]he two models that most closely describe the black position in the society are," says the sociologist Harry Kitano, "domestic colonialism and neo-colonialism. Like colonized natives, blacks are there to serve the larger community with a supply of cheap labor."[4] Neocolonialism, according to this argument, aptly portrays the current situation of blacks inasmuch as the latter are said to be superexploited in the workplace and culturally stigmatized as inferior beings.[5]

At first glance the description of blacks as a source of cheap labor seems reasonable enough. After all, relatively few blacks are employers, and many work at low-wage jobs. But this begs some obvious questions: How do whites maintain their control over the best jobs? How do they keep blacks from acquiring adequate marketable skills?

We shall address these questions by assessing the most common explanation for white domination—namely, the so-called split-labor market theory. This analysis of white control, however, is basically similar to all exploitation theories in that labor is invariably depicted as hostage to labor markets consciously designed by white elites to ensure the latter's dominance. In the concept of split-labor markets, white workers are said to join hands with employers against the interests of black workers.[6] In this version of exploitation black employees are split off from the white working class and assigned to the most poorly remunerated occupations. As a result, white employees constitute a "labor aristocracy with the ability to exclude low-priced labor, or minority labor, or to create labor castes in which better jobs are allocated to high-priced labor and poorer jobs to low-priced labor."[7]

Split-labor market theorists are hardly alone in contending that due to discrimination the white working class derives some advantage over blacks. In one way or another, the majority of commentators on racial issues are addicted to an image of economic life in which class and group conflict are the essence of socioeconomic existence. To their lights, white exploitation is so pervasive that even the white working class can depend on some material and/or psychological scraps from the white capitalist's table.

In truth, those who depict capitalist economies as exploitive fail to appreciate the dynamic qualities of market-driven phenomena, and they ignore the historical connection between free markets and working-class prosperity. Worse, they attribute to markets what are in reality the ill effects of government intervention. Thus, they cannot see that economic oppression of minorities requires government intervention, because in order to exclude minorities from particular occupations, it is necessary to make laws that limit the powers of employers and employees to contract freely with one another in the marketplace. Such laws may exclude minorities from particular occupations altogether or impose special requirements for preferred positions that are so stringent, time-consuming, or expensive (e.g., licenses, seniority systems, special training, or educational demands) as to discourage minority individuals.

It is especially when discrimination against minorities is codified into law by legislative majorities that something bearing a resemblance to the "segmentation" of labor markets into racial and ethnic enclaves can thrive. Not surprisingly, South Africa in its apartheid period provides a very good example for proponents of split-labor market theory. When the power of the state and social prejudice were legally joined, it was possible for workers from the white majority to receive much higher wages than would otherwise have been possible. Similarly, it is significant that in the American South prior to the 1960s the black-white gap in wages was greater than that in any other region of the country. Following the elimination of legal segregation, however, the wage difference has narrowed more rapidly in the South than in any other section.

Split-labor markets, wherever they appear, are mainly a product of political power, especially the state-sanctioned capacity to form unions and deny employers the right to hire nonunion labor. Whereas the deleterious consequences of state-sponsored segregation are well known, the damage to minorities wrought by government-conferred union power is not well understood.

William H. Hutt, himself a distinguished economic theorist and trenchant critic of the racial policy of his own country of South Africa, has argued that what is variously termed in collective bargaining as "equal pay for equal work," "the rate for the job," or the "standard rate" is more harmful to minority interests than even those more obnoxious and blatant forms of racial discrimination with which we are so familiar. Unlike government-sponsored segregation in places of residence, work, and the use of public facilities, the effects of the union-negotiated standard rates are less easy to trace by the untrained eye. Hence, those of us who support it on the grounds that it is beneficial to the working class are shocked to hear that we unwittingly support a labor policy harmful to the people we most sincerely wish to help.[8]

Nevertheless, a very strong case may be made that the standard rate effectively excludes from consideration for employment those "nonpreferred" categories of workers whose skills, education, language, ethnicity, or race tend to render them objectionable to privileged and employed workers who resist working beside minorities or to employers who fear morale problems among their employees or social stigmatization by their peers or prefer hiring "their own kind." Its scope may be relatively narrow or broad, including contractual agreements within particular industries, special occupations, or even the nation as a whole. Nor need the standard rate be limited to private sector arrangements alone. Minimum wage laws may also be considered a standard rate, although they are a creation of public policy.

No doubt the reader must wonder why and how a standard rate that raises wages can do harm to minorities. The explanation is that such rates increase minority unemployment with all the long-run social consequences that perpetual unemployment encourages. The standard rate prevents those who suffer from discrimination and prejudice from discounting the value of their own services on the market *below* those of "preferred" employees. As a result, nonpreferred workers, whether they are minority blacks in America or majority blacks in South Africa, either tend to remain unemployed altogether or are the first to be laid off when demand for labor falls for their particular kind of labor. Their inability, therefore, to undercut the wage demands of preferred workers creates artificial floors below which wages are not allowed to fall. One consequence is the elimination of a vital source for on-the-job training and the subsequent development of habits, skills, and confidence so necessary for success at work and in the community.[9]

There are two other general consequences flowing from government grants of legal power to unions in labor markets that harm minorities in particular and average wages as a whole. First, other things being equal, since wages may be forced to higher levels in union-organized industries than in unorganized ones, the vast majority of unorganized workers and the public as a whole pay higher prices for goods produced by organized labor. Second, and this point is especially pertinent with regard to the split-labor market theory, the trade union power to exclude nonunionized workers legally through the strike threat and the picket line may well favor higher wages for unionized labor relative to unorganized workers. However, by forcing the unorganized on to markets where labor is relatively more plentiful than it would be in the absence of union monopoly powers, unions tend to encourage both an increase in unemployment and a fall in the real wages of nonunionized labor. If the trade unions have discriminated against black labor on grounds of race, which they undoubtedly have, they have likewise discriminated against white *and* black labor as a whole on economic grounds. Whatever the grounds, minorities suffer the consequences of union efforts to set a standard rate.

Without question, trade unions have discriminated against black labor in other ways, not least through the apprenticeship system. But since they are necessarily organized to defend the interests of specific workers, their interests are detrimental to unorganized whites as well as to unorganized blacks. Logic would suggest that any so-called split would presumably occur between a privileged and relatively senior labor union membership of mostly whites, on the one hand, and a mass of workers, black and white, on the other hand, who are compelled to compete with one another for lower-paying nonunion positions where the supply of labor is higher than otherwise and who also pay higher prices for goods produced by organized labor. This is just another way of saying that minorities do best in markets where state coercion is minimal, as both theory and the historical record indicate.

But split-labor markets harm the interests of employers as well as those of minorities. Because the former will prosper to the extent that they can select the most able and competent workforce possible, restrictions with regard to employment decisions may be detrimental to output. Why employers would cooperate with white employees in order to confine black workers to low-level employment, or just how the white collaborators would enforce their will in any industrial democracy where freedom of contract and the rule of law are observed with some regularity, is a mystery. Common sense and over 200 years of economic theory would teach us that under these circumstances employers would be severely tempted in the absence of physical or the most extreme social coercion to break their "wage agreements" with white workers in order to hire cheaper, from their point of view, black labor. And since our split-labor theorists, not to mention many other social scientists and intellectuals, tend to assume that white and black laborers in the aggregate are more or less easily exchangeable entities—that is, roughly equal so far as their abilities, work habits, and contributions to the final product are concerned—one might suppose that white employers in split-labor markets would have strong incentives to recruit black workers. Thus, in seeking their own interests, they would cause demand for black laborers to grow more than previously, thereby driving up the aggregate wage of black labor relative to that of white labor—which is the last thing that is supposed to happen in the world of split-market theorizing!

In general, exploitation theorists refuse to acknowledge the decisive role played by free markets in the relative distribution of individual incomes. Implicitly, they conceptualize labor as divided into two or more homogeneous wholes or "blobs" of workers, not as individuals possessed of diverse talents who happen to be offering their services in markets at given times. They fail to comprehend that market demand for heretofore oppressed minorities will tend to rise once freedom to contract between employers and employees is honored rather than breached by legalized union monopolies, state-imposed segregation, or physical threats to employers. Indeed, they exaggerate the period of time required before immigrants or previously oppressed groups can be integrated successfully into a workforce, once legal discrimination has been formally outlawed. In any event, other than as unique, nonrecurring historical phenomena, the notion of splits between different kinds of labor—even minority and majority labor—has little theoretical or explanatory value for modern industrial democracies in general and for the United States in particular. Whatever its historical relevance, it would be extremely costly in these times for employers to assign races to separate occupational categories, since they would both violate the law and risk public condemnation.

In general, exploitation models of the economy are seriously flawed in their grasp of the nature of the overall economic order. At most, such models would be applicable to traditional castelike systems or to political orders in which government coercion and legal discrimination are employed in order to create or enforce racial or other forms of blatant discrimination. They are surely inapplicable to modern democratic polities based on the rule of law and more or less open market processes. People, after all, offer their services in the market, and those services are dependent on the desirability to employers of the particular skills that are being offered. Labor's share of the national wealth will depend on its marginal productivity. If the output of capital per worker grows more rapidly than the supply of labor, then labor's share of the social product will increase relative to that of capital. Put another way, the higher the growth of capital relative to that of the population, the greater the demand for labor. In societies where the output per worker is low, the supply of labor will be higher and wages as a result will be lower. This is true for all societies.

Exploitation theories, including the split-labor market one, are therefore inherently political in nature. Politics and power, not economic fundamentals, are what truly matter in the distribution of the national income. In most extant social science accounts, whites continue to exploit blacks in much the same manner as they exploited the ancestors of the latter during slavery and de jure segregation. That blacks are now free from legalized constraints and state-imposed segregation is dismissed as irrelevant, since whites remain as the monopolizers of institutional power. In fact, the failure to comprehend correctly the nature of a social order characterized by a division of labor and private property in which people are free to sell their labor to the highest bidders leads most race relations experts to underestimate the salutary effects of free markets and, perhaps, the benefits of antidiscrimination laws that guarantee access to markets.

It also leads them to exaggerate the importance of political conflicts. For instance, Joel Steinberg, a sociologist, attributes black progress during the late 1960s to the race riots of that turbulent decade. Presumably, the rising black middle class ultimately owes its level of progress to the ghetto revolts of that era. "[A] benefit emerging from the riots," he argues, "is that the nation's corporate elite, fearful of the mounting level of violence in the nation's cities, launched ambitious programs for recruiting and training black workers."[10] He thus rejects the possibility that the 1964 Civil Rights Act may have provided some impetus for black progress in the 1960s. That act gave blacks access to jobs by making employer discrimination against minorities illegal, giving aggrieved victims the right to enter federal court and sue for redress. As is true of many race relations writers, he apparently believes that blacks can advance their interests only through political activities calculated to wrest resources from whites. In this sense, riots are not so much destructive criminal acts as political protests that produce lasting benefits for the downtrodden masses.

In fact, it is highly probable that rather than face the destruction of their property and loss of profits occasioned by rioting many employers simply vacated the central cities. As for the 1964 Civil Rights Act, much evidence suggests that many firms reacted to the fear of lawsuits by increasing their minority payrolls and by creating specific positions for equal employment opportunity (EEO) managers in their personnel departments. An effect, at least in the short run, was to stimulate to some degree a demand for minority labor at the expense of majority labor.

In general, politicized accounts of race relations exaggerate the extent to which any racial group or groups can control markets in which the freedom to buy, sell, and offer one's labor in more or less open markets is protected. Market forces, not ethnicity and race, in the main determine relative shares of incomes in capitalist societies. The explanation for this is easily discerned. When we purchase products or labor services, we have no interest in all probability in the ethnic background of the individual who sells the good or service in question. Rather, price and/or quality are the determinants of our decisions. The "cash nexus," whatever its cultural deficiencies in terms of the "quality of life," is a great leveler. For this reason, traditional elites are usually quite hostile to capitalism. By making way for the parvenu, its spread unsettles older class and status relationships. Values to which ruling groups are attached are undermined, and cultural norms that have previously enhanced their social distance and power are weakened by the lure of money.[11]

The relative openness of markets to minorities helps to explain why many nonwhite or non-Protestant ethnic groups have found escape routes from poverty in the first and second generations through education, self-employment, manual skills, and so on. This list of prosperous groups is a long one: Jews, Greeks, Armenians, Chinese, Japanese, Koreans, Vietnamese, Arabs, Cubans, Catholic ethnics, subcontinent Indians, and second-generation West Indian blacks. Most today have incomes at or above the national average. Especially pertinent in this regard are subcontinent Indians and West Indian blacks whose dark skins and accents make them easily identifiable to the white majority. Obviously, whites do not favor either of these groups, yet each has incomes near or above the national average. And more instructive still, despite their phenotypical similarity to American blacks, the earnings of West Indians are substantially above those of American blacks. As is true of other successful immigrants, the former tend to acquire skills that are in demand. Interestingly, when compared with black Americans, they usually do better at school and are much more likely to create their own enterprises.[12]

In truth, depictions of economic life as one of group and class conflict more closely resemble racial and ethnic relationships in horticultural and agrarian societies than existence in modern, market-driven societies in which prosperous but ethnically separate and identifiable groups interact with one another.[13] Segregated dwellings and distinct ethnic communities do not mean that groups exploit one another. To prosper, however, each group must employ its skills at the behest of consumers.

As is the case with politicized versions of economic reality in which majorities are depicted as an overwhelming force arrayed against an inert and powerless racial or ethnic minority, so workers are basically considered as passive instruments of employer interests. The image of labor markets is one in which workers wait hat in hand for employers to select them for a task. In reality, workers do not stand idle; they actively participate in labor markets by developing those attributes likely to augment their bargaining position with employers. It is a truism that employers seek the best possible workers at the cheapest possible wage. Since potential employees are aware of this desire and wish to put themselves in the best bargaining positions possible under given circumstances, they tend to acquire those particular skills and work records likely to impress prospective employers. According to pessimists, however, workers are likely to be pawns of monopolistic managers, a faceless mass of helpless humanity mostly indistinguishable by talent, motivation, and power. That they may have previously acquired the requisite skills, habits, and attitudes calculated to give them an advantage on the labor market counts for little. We are thus invited to envision a kind of lottery in which workers are assigned more or less arbitrarily to positions within the labor hierarchy.

Basically, the vision of race relations we have been analyzing does not reckon with a fundamental fact of human existence—that is, that the ability to perform different kinds of labor and the availability of nature-given resources are unequally distributed. Talents, interests, and motivations peculiar to individuals no less than a geographical "maldistribution" in land and natural resources lead the individual in the direction of specialization. The outcome is not only growing specialization but, in complex social orders, an enhanced tendency toward social cooperation in an expanding division of labor. It is perhaps more accurate to say that we do not participate in the division of labor in order to specialize, but, to the contrary, we specialize in order to participate in the division of labor.[14] Exchanges by individuals, whether they be products or labor services, are in some sense rooted in human diversity. To conceptualize labor services as of more or less equal value, sealed hermetically in concise categories, is to assume that individual abilities matter little, that mobility between classes of workers is mostly nonexistent, and that the demand for and hence the real income of labor has less to do with worker productivity than with political force. However applicable such notions were to the life of blacks in the southern United States of a half-century ago, they are a gross caricature of the lives of black workers in the America of our day.

If labor markets are forever subject to supply and demand forces, it is obvious that those workers who remain unemployed or who fail to obtain the positions they might have preferred have in general been unable or unwilling to acquire the attributes most conducive to their employment. One implication is that black workers are on average less likely than their white counterparts to acquire the necessary skills sought by prospective employers. For example, the relative absence of skills found among blacks is suggested by their poorer performance, relatively speaking, on aptitude and achievement tests.[15] Another liability for blacks in their search for employment is the manner in which many younger ones, especially, tend to pass their spare time. Studies suggest that they usually spend few of their nonworking hours in constructive and employment-related activities (e.g., car repair, reading, vocational courses, sewing, home improvement projects, etc.).[16] Thus, there is less likelihood that many among them will ultimately acquire marketable skills or build work records that will set them apart from other applicants in the eyes of employers. Indeed, when they fail to accumulate desirable work histories, blacks may find their prospects for employment reduced since older job applicants, in the absence of prior "objective" signs of constructive activity, are simply judged to be less trainable. As a consequence, employers reasonably conclude that those prospects who have failed to acquire skills in the past are less likely to acquire them in the present.

Employers in reality do not arbitrarily assign individuals to positions in labor markets, even to positions that provide extensive on-the-job training. Rather, they base employment decisions on those factors that they believe are likely to contribute most successfully to future output. Experience tells them that the most important indicators of future achievement are previous accomplishments as well as current skills, whatever their particular provenance (i.e., work, school, the military, or leisure-time activities). Certainly the labor market is no random lottery where, barring discrimination, all untrained workers are deemed by employers to be equally qualified for the more coveted positions. In short, blacks are not victims of arbitrary and discriminatory labor practices. They tend to fare more poorly than whites because insufficient numbers of them have as yet acquired the habits and skills demanded in today's marketplace.

WHITE DISCRIMINATION AND RACISM ARE WIDESPREAD

Textbooks on race relations overwhelmingly assume that most whites stereotype blacks in unflattering ways. Whites are presumably so blinded by prejudice that they cannot see blacks as individuals, as possessors of unique attributes and abilities in their own right. Furthermore, they are said to dislike blacks on sight and, because of their skin color, to discriminate against them. According to these authors, the intentions of most white Americans who have the temerity to oppose affirmative action or school busing or call themselves "conservative" are forever suspect.

"Prejudice" and "stereotype" are closely related concepts. The most famous definition of prejudice, that of social psychologist Gordon Allport, defines it as an antipathy based on a faulty and inflexible generalization.[17] His definition has two components: (1) a negative emotion or feeling, antipathy, or dislike; and (2) an inaccurate belief or stereotype (i.e, a generalization). Most subsequent discussions of prejudice are consistent with this definition, depicting the stereotype component of prejudice as an inaccurate, inflexible "overgeneralization" that goes so far beyond existing evidence as to have no basis in fact. Stereotypes are allegedly applied by prejudiced whites not so much to any small percentage or subset of a minority as to most members of the minority group itself. To take an example provided by Feagin: "I hate black and Mexican people because black and Mexican people always smell worse than whites."[18] No doubt this example, cited approvingly in the Kitano text on race relations, gives an inaccurate and irrational generalization that has no factual basis. Because this particular stereotype is so patently false, it provides a straw man with which one may easily dispense. In truth, many stereotypes are not patently false.

Whites, of course, have historically possessed many negative images or stereotypes about black Americans. For instance, the latter have been considered at various times as being more impulsive, less intelligent, less industrious, less responsible, more prone to criminality, and so on. Such stereotypes are routinely dismissed as false, inflexible, and inaccurate generalizations. Yet available data do tell us that black Americans, relatively speaking, do less well on average than whites and Asians in school, do less well than most other groups on tests of ability and achievement, and are far more likely to be involved in street crime. Perhaps, then, some stereotypes of blacks are commensurate with certain facts. But, if this is true, is it scientifically permissible to dismiss all stereotypes as inaccurate, empty generalizations? Oddly enough, their relative accuracy (i.e., their degree of empirical validity) has been little explored. Indeed, many stereotypes may actually represent the known facts at the majority's disposal. These "facts" may be less irrational than we have been led to believe.

For most of us, the word *stereotype* suggests something that is not only incorrect and wrong but, worse, exceedingly dangerous. Most social scientists, not surprisingly, accept as true a necessary causal sequence that leads ineluctably from negative belief (stereotype) to negative affect or feeling (prejudice) to negative behavior (discrimination). So it follows that the white who holds a stereotype must translate it into discrimination against blacks in everyday life. In a word, there is presumed to exist a strong causal linkage between attitudes and concrete behaviors. Yet contrary to conventional opinion, a strong linkage between stereotypes and discrimination cannot be demonstrated, nor can it be shown that discrimination itself is widespread.

Moreover, although both many whites and many blacks hold negative stereotypes with regard to black Americans, we ought not to conclude that they then proceed to apply the stereotypes to all or even to most blacks. As we demonstrate in Chapter 4, stereotypical traits are applied to relatively small numbers of blacks, and when asked, whites base their conclusions about specific blacks on the particular traits of the individual in question. That is to say, any presumed connections between stereotypes and prejudice or prejudice and discrimination are at best quite weak.

Whatever the contribution stereotypes may make to discrimination, we may certainly conclude that there is less racism in the United States today than a generation ago. We observe this decline in a perusal of available statistical data on educational levels and occupations. The gap between black and white Americans in average years of education has declined from 2.5 years in 1950 to just 0.3 years in 1990.[19] Blacks today increasingly enter white-collar occupations that were traditionally closed to them. As a result, black male occupational prestige has grown dramatically.[20]

The reality of declining racial discrimination also appears in data relating to politics and poverty. For example, the number of black elected officials, which had already increased from 100 to 4,900 between 1964 and 1980, expanded further during the Reagan years.[21] The most recent estimate is 7,445. Surely, they often received a share of the white vote.[22] Black politicians have indeed been elected as mayors of large cities, to the U.S. Senate, and to the Virginia governorship. In 1983, 81 percent of whites in a national survey said they would vote for a black president, an increase from 37 percent in 1958.[23] As for poverty, the percentage of black families below the poverty line had declined from 55 percent in 1959 to 32 percent in 1990.[24] If one takes into account the upsurge of single-parent families by comparing intact black families in 1960 with intact black families today, the decline is even more impressive.

Opinion polls conducted by the Gallup organization and the National Opinion Research Center at the University of Chicago suggest that white support for discrimination and segregation has declined markedly. In 1942, only 32 percent of white Americans said blacks and whites should attend the same schools, but by 1982, fully 90 percent agreed that the races ought to attend the same schools. In 1942, 46 percent of whites were opposed to employment discrimination, whereas 88 percent were opposed in 1970. Whites are now quite tolerant of integrated neighborhoods, once social class factors are taken into consideration. In 1942, 36 percent answered no to the following question: "If a negro with the same income and education as you moved into your block, would it make any difference to you?" By 1972, 85 percent said "no."[25]

Perhaps most damaging of all for champions of the discrimination thesis is their difficulty in identifying concrete victims of discrimination. Although thousands of social science researchers and lawyers diligently search the social and political landscape for evidence of racism, only 3 percent of all cases alleging discrimination filed with federal and state discrimination law enforcement agencies result in cause for discrimination findings.[26] In one of the longest and most expensive cases ever prosecuted by the Equal Employment Opportunity Commission (EEOC) to take a prominent example, the U.S. government lost its case. Although it spent millions of dollars against Sears Roebuck and Company, the government failed to identify a single victim.

One possible explanation for the reduction of discrimination may be that most American corporations now have black personnel officials who actively participate in the corporate hiring process.[27] In that they may possess knowledge of the relevant qualifications of prospective employees and can more easily detect unfair treatment than their white counterparts, perhaps blacks in personnel are strategically located to function as brakes on any discriminatory inclinations on the part of management.

We should also take into account some other changes in the system since 1960. Today an infrastructure of fairness exists that makes discrimination a less likely occurrence, for in addition to black personnel managers, most organizations have black employees who can observe and report suspicious racist behavior. There are now objective procedures written into company policy; indeed, employers find it difficult to reserve positions for whites inasmuch as they are required to post and advertise openings. Furthermore, the government refers potential employees in a nondiscriminatory manner through the Employment Service, a clearing house for jobs used by many workers in their search for employment. Of course, victims of discrimination have the EEOC and the courts as well at their disposal. Finally, the 1964 Civil Rights Act required companies with 100 or more employees to file annual reports detailing by occupational category (e.g., manager, skilled worker, laborer, etc.) the number of minorities they hired. Once this regulation went into effect, the recruitment of blacks also increased. Moreover, those companies that receive federal contracts are required to have affirmative action plans with the result that now such firms tend to employ proportionately more blacks than previously.[28]

Many critics respond to the relative dearth of victims with the claim that discrimination is as pervasive and damaging as ever; it is only more subtle in these times. To prove their point, they usually marshal six kinds of arguments: (1) The average black income is low compared with white income; (2) there is black "underrepresentation" in specific occupations (e.g., blacks make up only 3 percent of the doctors but compose 12 percent of the population); (3) high levels of black unemployment persist; (4) there is much white violence against blacks; (5) there is the legacy of past discrimination and its alleged current effects; and (6) there are anecdotal accounts by blacks claiming to have been discriminated against or otherwise victimized by whites. For the present, we set aside the first argument and consider the remaining five.

In a recent best-seller on race relations, Andrew Hacker, a distinguished political scientist, argues that black occupational underrepresentation is proof that whites discriminate.[29] Whites are said to practice intentional discrimination and, as such, are held primarily responsible for the current plight of blacks. Although his discussion of the black-white Scholastic Aptitude Test (SAT) score differences acknowledges that blacks on average possess relatively fewer skills than do whites, he largely ignores the crucial role that skills play in black material advancement. Instead, he lays stress on workplace underrepresentation in three occupations—bartender, waiter/ waitress, and dental hygienist—in which whites and blacks come into close contact with one another. Many more blacks, he believes, would enter such occupations if whites were not so wary of close contact. Anticipating exceptions to his observation, he notes, "While white patients seem willing to be cared for by black nurses, they apparently draw the line at having black fingers in their mouths."[30]

On the other hand, Hacker's implicit assumption that many blacks seek these relatively low-paying positions is questionable. There is no evidence that blacks are currently either applying for or being denied employment in these types of occupations. Most of these jobs, after all, are relatively low-paying positions, so perhaps many blacks do not find them attractive. Moreover, he assumes that whites reject black applicants because they are uncomfortable in dealing with minorities in intimate situations, but he ignores the alternative possibility that blacks themselves may be similarly predisposed. Indeed, given a choice between two jobs paying roughly the same wage, is it not probable that blacks might also prefer the position that exposed them to fewer interracial contacts? One who can perform well as a dental hygienist can presumably also do well as a licensed practical nurse. Yet blacks are much better represented in nursing. The same may be said for bartenders and cooks, the latter being an occupation where blacks are presumably overrepresented. The average pay of cooks in 1987 was $200 per week, whereas bartenders commanded $223. The average pay of licensed practical nurses that year was $316 per week; that of dental hygienists, $247.[31] Even if we agree with Hacker and others that some discrimination in hiring practices persists in these kinds of lower-paying positions, it would hardly account for the overall black poverty rate and for the black-white income gap.

A tendency to hold white society responsible for economic hardship within the black community appears with regularity in studies of black unemployment. In explaining why black unemployment is twice that of white unemployment, Hacker's assessment, for instance, echoes the conventional pessimism: "For as long as records have been kept, in good times and bad, white America has ensured that the unemployment imposed on blacks will be approximately double those [sic] experienced by whites. Stated very simply, if you are black in America, you will find it twice as hard to find or keep a job."[32]

Let us examine this argument. The unemployment rate in 1940, to quibble a bit, was approximately the same for both races,[33] but Hacker tells his reader that in these times "[I]t is twice as hard for blacks to find and keep a job." Actually, as a general rule, about 95 percent of the whites and 90 percent of the blacks are found to be working. A more basic criticism, however, is that unemployment is something that is somehow imposed on blacks by white malevolence or neglect. That high levels of black unemployment might have less to do with race per se than with impersonal market forces in which demand is weak for people with few skills rates little consideration.

One explanation for the popularity of Hacker's book is its antiwhite rhetoric and its interpretation of American society as hopelessly racist. "Given all the misgivings [about blacks as employees] of white executives and supervisors," Hacker worries, "it would seem self-evident that blacks must put in more effort simply to satisfy the standards employers set. It is not as if they can simply walk in and start doing a job. All eyes are on them, as if a Great Experiment is under-way."[34] Although this notion seems to have credence among many blacks, there is no evidence from *any* social science study that the average black employee is compelled to outperform the average white employee. What little evidence we do have suggests another conclusion. According to industrial psychologists Frank Schmidt and John Hunter, black employees tend on average to perform less well than do whites on employment aptitude tests.[35] Since blacks may also have lower test scores in the typical workplace for a variety of reasons, one might infer that, relatively speaking, they tend to perform less well on the job than do whites. At a minimum the relative work performance of the races is an area that needs research.

Another way to prove that entrenched racism blankets the social landscape is to dwell upon incidents of white violence against blacks. In a questionable passage, Feagin makes the following argument:

> The decrease in lynching since World War II is somewhat misleading since legal and secret lynchings had by then replaced public lynchings. Unnecessary killings by police officers have taken many black lives. Secret attacks resulted in the deaths of hundreds of black or black and white civil rights workers in the South between the 1940s and 1960s. Moreover, numerous white supremacy groups such as the ever-present Ku Klux Klan have periodically played an important role in violence directed against blacks in the 1970s and 1980s.[36]

With the sole exception of a pamphlet that was written for U.S. senators and congressmen in 1940, Feagin provides neither studies, statistics, nor scholarly citations in support of this extreme position. At any rate, this 1940 report is hardly pertinent to events in post–World War II America! Nor does he see fit to remark on either the small size of the present-day Klan, the government's effective prosecution of Klan violence, or opinion polls showing that the vast majority of white Americans are unfavorably disposed toward the Klan.[37]

Unfortunately, too many social science tracts ceaselessly accuse whites of aggressing physically against their black neighbors. Of course, nothing better serves to perpetuate the myth of rampant white violence and the social policies built on it than this brand of scholarship. Violence, after all, is the most extreme form of victimization as well as the most blatant expression of discriminatory behavior. By dwelling on such atypical incidents as the Bensonhurst murder (a group of whites killed a black man in New York City) or the pervasive power of the Klan, the scholar in quest of victims has no trouble discovering white bigotry. Yet the scale of white-on-black violence is never addressed, probably because it is so rare. In fact, black-on-white violence is far more prevalent. Of those murder cases occurring in 1988 in which the race of the victim and perpetrator were known, blacks murdered 579 whites, and whites murdered 237 blacks. These data (and the Uniform Crime Report statistics showing that 63 percent of those arrested for armed robbery are black) seldom, if ever, find their way into the race relations textbooks.[38] Since blacks make up only 12 percent of the American population, these omissions are little short of scandalous. They distort the true nature of American race relations and hence our ability to provide helpful solutions to our present crisis.

The tactic most commonly employed in these studies, and one sure to gain the maximum effect, entails the juxtaposition of white discrimination in the past with black social conditions in the present.[39] It is, of course, justifiable to claim that prior conditions of oppression—for example, slavery, Jim Crow segregation, northern discrimination prior to 1950—affected black cultural life in complex ways, including black material development and family organization. It is decidedly impermissible, however, to conclude that past discrimination, rather than contemporary conditions in the black community, is the *primary* cause of present problems. Surely it is a safe rule of thumb that the more remote in time a causal factor, the less useful it is in explaining a current condition. Recent conditions, not remote ones, are the proximate causes of current ills.

Let us briefly provide a few examples. Feagin, for instance, finds no difficulty in linking white attitudes in New York in 1799 to black problems in 1990. "Not until 1799 was a statute of emancipation passed there. Moreover, understanding that slavery was entrenched in the North's legal system is important for understanding the internal colonialism that blacks still face today in the North."[40] No causal connections are offered, much less discussed in this effort at historical sociology. In a similar vein, Farley attributes black family disorganization to a "deliberate disruption of black families under slavery, discrimination, and violence against black males (which certainly has weakened their ability to act as leaders of traditional families)."[41]

It is not unusual to lay the blame for the chaos in so much of black family life on the heritage of slavery and white malevolence. Nonetheless, modern historiography has demonstrated rather conclusively that black families in the nineteenth century were essentially stable.[42] Family disintegration is itself a rather recent phenomenon; indeed, the number of intact families did not drastically decline until after passage of the 1964 Civil Rights Act (which, we hasten to add, is not the cause of illegitimacy and family breakdown). Public policy analyst Charles Murray argues convincingly that alterations in the welfare system during the 1960s made it economically rational for many young and poor women to avoid marriage. The tragic result has been for many black babies born to unwed mothers to grow up in families and communities where absent fathers help very little in the socialization of their children, in the financial support of the family, or in providing stability for their communities.[43]

It is frequently said that black family life, as presently constructed, possesses valuable cultural elements lacking in white family life and that the black family, moreover, is a successful adaptation to white oppression.[44] These cultural and adaptive mechanisms, however, remain unidentified, much less confirmed. How early pregnancy, illegitimacy, and single-parent and female-headed households are well adapted to the building of viable, self-supporting communities is puzzling. What sustains such families and their communities is in reality government money.

Many arguments to the effect that an unremitting discrimination against black Americans continues unabated often rely on anecdotal evidence. One study, frequently cited as proof that discrimination is widespread, combines survey research with anecdotes in order to demonstrate that black managers in large corporations are subject to discrimination. This particular survey, conducted by Edward W. Jones, found that many black managers believed that their lack of success in winning promotions was due to race. Yet Jones offered no proof that these managers were victimized; rather, he demonstrated that a substantial proportion *believed* themselves to be victims of discrimination.[45] Although highly questionable, such flawed data are taken at face value. "This extensive research on upper middle income blacks who have moved into non-traditional managerial positions," says Feagin, who utilizes this research in support of his own discrimination thesis, "clearly documents the firm entrenchment of racial discrimination in the private sector in the 1980s."[46]

As is true of other scholars and journalists who collect similar sorts of anecdotes, Jones (and Feagin) accept without question the statements of blacks alleging discrimination. On the other hand, a willingness to believe the accounts of putative victims is rarely extended to whites who say that they also suffer from discrimination. As the late William Beer informed us, social scientists show little interest in this kind of discrimination.[47]

Interestingly, whites today are as willing as blacks to allege victimization. In a survey of white Federal Bureau of Investigation (FBI) agents, it was found that 68 percent felt that they had suffered discrimination.[48] This is highly unlikely, since affirmative action–inspired programs could conceivably harm no more than 1 in every 10 FBI agents. As it is, blacks and women make up only about one tenth of the FBI workforce.

Needless to say, few students of the race problem take arguments of reverse discrimination seriously. Nevertheless, these allegations are instructive. That such a large number of white males report themselves on the receiving end of discrimination casts much doubt on the validity of survey data for measuring its extent. Perhaps the ubiquitous press and television accounts of discrimination and the persistent demands by black leaders, feminists, politicians, and other opinion elites for affirmative action programs contribute to a climate of fear and suspicion that is in turn highly conducive to false accusations and the growth of a victim industry. In any event, we do know that growing numbers of Americans define themselves as victims.[49]

WHITES ARE TO BLAME FOR MOST UNDESIRABLE QUALITIES ATTRIBUTED TO BLACKS

It is said that whites are primarily responsible, either directly or indirectly, for various undesirable aspects of black life, including broken homes, criminal violence, functional illiteracy, and unemployment. In particular, white discrimination and white institutions are seen as undermining black motivation in the school and in the workplace. The following passage, taken from a 1985 textbook in which the authors offer the thesis that white prejudice and discrimination are related to low wages and functional illiteracy, is instructive:

> By limiting the opportunities of a minority group, by segregating it, by putting it at every competitive disadvantage, white prejudice helps to create the very inferiority by which it seems justified in the minds of the dominant group. Start out by saying the black man is inferior; use this as the reason for giving him poor schools, poor jobs, poor opportunities for advancement, and one soon proves himself correct by creating and enforcing the very inferiority.[50]

We are also informed that "a person deprived of opportunity may be lazy, deprived of schools may be ignorant, deprived of hope may be careless—and the depriving majority may then accuse that person of the very characteristics they have brought about."[51] Nevertheless, there is little evidence to support such statements.

Two observations are pertinent in this regard. In the first place, these arguments more accurately describe the effects of white attitudes and behavior on black Americans prior to 1950. As a consequence, they address few of the fundamental difficulties with which blacks are daily confronted today. Second, the idea that minority status and discrimination in themselves induce negative outcomes—for example, resignation, resentment, an unwillingness to study, inadequate skills, laziness, dependency, violent crime, alcohol and drug abuse, sexual promiscuity—is a dubious proposition at best. Various minorities in America (e.g., Jews, Asians, the Catholic ethnics, Greeks, Armenians) have responded to their own minority status and to majority discrimination by developing appropriate skills useful to employers and consumers in the marketplace. It is significant that these successful minorities have experienced very low levels of family breakdown and other forms of social pathology, even in periods when their incomes were quite low and when discrimination by the dominant majority was a strong barrier to advancement. In other words, there is no simple and direct connection between discrimination and undesirable social behaviors and attitudes.

According to conventional wisdom, a reduction in discrimination against blacks and the increase in relative black wages ought to have been followed by a decline in broken homes, illegitimacy, divorce, desertion, school failure, alcoholism, drug abuse, and violent crime. For if social pathologies are caused by white racism, then a reduction in discrimination (i.e., the overt expression of white racism) ought to have induced a reduction in its effects as well. Nevertheless, family breakdown and illegitimacy have grown apace. The percentage of black children living with a single parent or a single grandparent was 20 percent in 1960, but by 1980, it had grown to 51 percent. Illegitimate births to black women were 22 percent in 1960, whereas 20 years later, the figure had risen to 56 percent. The percentage increases among whites were far smaller.[52] Paradoxically, black income rose while various types of social pathology grew or remained constant. Although the difference in years of education narrowed, the difference in learning and skills, as measured by standardized tests, remained wide. Statistically speaking, blacks steadfastly remain one standard deviation behind whites on virtually all such tests, which means that only 16 percent of the black population performs at the level reached by 50 percent of the white population.[53]

Given the political climate of these times, reaction to these data is what we might have expected. It is insisted that discrimination remains entrenched (only now it is more subtle and covert), relentlessly undermining the life chances of black Americans. Strangely, the more dogmatic proponents of this thesis, such as sociologist Joe Feagin and psychologist Thomas Pettigrew, offer little, if any, evidence for the relative magnitude of the effects of the covert and subtle kind of discrimination on blacks as opposed to the more overt and blatant forms of racism. We are naturally led to wonder just how the "new" discrimination can be as damaging as was the old-fashioned, door-slamming variety.[54] It is highly improbable that the subtle, covert forms of racism can have as deleterious an effect on the black population as did the more traditional discrimination. To put the matter gently, it is less than scientifically rigorous to assume that weaker causes precipitate equally strong, or stronger, effects.

The inclination to seek out white scapegoats is especially evident in the analyses of school performance by poorer blacks. The relatively low levels of minority attainment are generally attributed to inferior and run-down facilities, underpaid or inexperienced teachers, overcrowded classes, and low teacher expectations and to classrooms in which anti-working-class and antiblack sentiments pervade the environment. Conversely, low achievement is seldom said to be caused by family disintegration, by a lack of discipline and instruction in the home, or by the attitudes, literacy levels, and values of black parents. Indeed, the charge of white culpability with regard to black performance in the schools must be considered in some detail if we are to understand why black educational fortunes have continued to lag.

To begin with, little evidence supports the hypothesis that inadequate spending is the cause for the relatively low performance levels of lower-class blacks in school. True, expenditures on average are slightly lower in the central cities than in suburbia, although spending in rural school districts appears to be lower than that in central cities. Turnover of city teachers is higher, but their salaries compare favorably with their suburban peers. Perhaps most fatal to the notion that we can spend ourselves out of this problem is that research in the main shows little or no correlation between expenditures per student and student performance.[55]

Nor does the contention that low teacher expectations cause lower black performance withstand scrutiny. In support of their claim that black achievement levels are inadequate because white teachers enter their profession with low opinions about the potential of their black students, critics cite a well-known study by Rosenthal and Jacobson indicating a strong relationship between teacher expectations of student ability and increases in average student intelligence quotient (IQ) test scores.[56] Race relations texts repeatedly call attention to this study, but they neglect to inform us that follow-up studies have been unable to replicate the earlier findings.[57]

More recent studies fail to discover any evidence that teachers are biased against black students. For instance, in a study of 100 teachers and their 2,600 students, social psychologists Lee Jussim and Jacquelynne Eccles found that the particular race of the student—black or white—had no visible effect on the teachers' perceptions of his or her performance. To the contrary, instructors based their perceptions and expectations on performance and motivation. The authors concluded that teachers did not apply stereotypes in their evaluations. "Abundant research in the laboratory and field," they report, "show that perceivers generally evaluate targets far more on the basis of the target's personal characteristics than on the target's membership in social groups." In other words, they do not assess students according to their racial characteristics.[58]

If numerous works have consistently failed to confirm a significant relationship between teacher expectations and IQ test performance, it nevertheless seems likely that expectations do have an influence on learning.

In fact, a so-called pygmalion effect of teacher expectations is supported by some research,[59] although no evidence supports the proposition that race per se lies at the heart of low expectations. In other words, there is no evidence that arbitrary and racist teacher beliefs contribute to the persistent learning gap between black and white students. The connection between expectations and learning is more complex than most of the orthodox accounts are willing to admit. Indeed, a certain naïveté about the role of stereotypes in human behavior influences the debate about teacher behavior. As it is, we have no justification to conclude that racial stereotyping of lower-class black pupils by their teachers leads instructors to construct inflexible expectations about the future performance of their black students.

It is certainly undeniable that teachers may have low expectations. But pessimistic beliefs about students may be more of an effect than a cause. Perhaps teachers alter their views in concrete cases so that their expectations arise from their observations. Thus, when they observe satisfactory work on the part of a student, they proceed to adjust their expectations upward. If problems are noted, however, they presumably lower them. In either case, actual learning, not racist stereotypes, may be a primary source for the formation of teacher expectations. It is true that their expectations may have the consequence of reducing the levels of achievement slightly, but to draw any inference that stereotyping and racism are the cause is quite unwarranted in any empirical sense. Indeed, a recent Louis Harris poll of new teachers supports our contention that classroom experiences, not racist stereotypes, are the prime source for lowered expectations. It was found that 93 percent of new teachers believe that all children are capable of learning, but after a mere two years on the job, only 86 percent believe that all children are able to learn.[60] Racist beliefs, moreover, do not explain why *both* black and white teachers have equally low expectations for their black students. To the best of our knowledge, reputable studies so far have found no positive correlation between negative stereotypes and low expectations on the part of teachers. To the contrary, experimental evidence that we consider below suggests that in the course of interracial encounters most of us generally respond to objective information about other individuals. Furthermore, few of us base our anticipations about future performance on such sociological categories as race, ethnicity, or religion alone.

The influence of classroom experiences on their expectations notwithstanding, there are other, more concrete explanations for the pessimism of teachers. In all probability, the structure of public education lends itself to the fostering of low expectations. Sociologist James Coleman's comparison of student achievements in public and Catholic schools is instructive in this respect. Once parental socioeconomic status is taken into account, both black and white students learn more in Catholic schools than do their counterparts in public schools.[61] Coleman and his collaborators also observed that the educational gulf between the races was much smaller in the Catholic schools. Why? Higher teacher expectations were a factor, but of more importance were the greater demands made on the private school students. By increasing effort, one increased performance. Catholic schools insisted on more homework and difficult courses as well as greater discipline, parental involvement, and higher attendance in class. Strict sanctions for misbehavior were enforced, and inadequate work was criticized.

These findings strongly imply that teacher expectations influence learning in schools where work and devotion to task are encouraged. Therefore, apart from supportive educational settings, teacher expectations in themselves have little positive effect. After all, it is difficult to believe that Catholic schools make greater demands on students because they employ teachers with higher expectations. In the language of social science, teacher expectations are a "dependent" rather than an "independent" variable (i.e., they are an "effect" as opposed to a "cause"). Teachers, black or white, who insist on good work in an inner-city classroom in which disorder, absenteeism, and little or no student effort are the norm not only will have little influence on the intellectual development of their students; in time, they will lower their expectations in response to the realities of classroom life. But where effective discipline, low absenteeism, parental support for homework, and a sound academic environment exist, the same teachers will probably maintain high expectations for their pupils. Ultimately, it is the effectiveness of the setting that determines the height and rigor of teacher demands of students.

Many social scientists simply refuse to acknowledge that teacher expectations are essentially rooted in actual classroom experiences. In their opinion, white prejudice, not lower-class class culture, ultimately explains black underachievement in school. Thus, when black teachers, much as their white counterparts, are found to call on their black pupils less frequently than on their white ones, these same critics tell us that, yes, it is the whites who are responsible for the misbehavior of black teachers! That both minority and majority teachers, according to the Dworkins, "define minority children as less competent, praise them less often, assign them lower grades and seldom encourage minority students to be full active participants in the classroom" suggests that minority group teachers merely adopt majority interpretations of minority children's abilities and motives, the effect of which is to demean their own race.[62] A more parsimonious and plausible hypothesis is that, contrary to the Dworkins and the Civil Rights Commission report upon which they rely, black and white teachers react in similar ways to similar classroom experiences. It is quite unnecessary and insulting to argue that they somehow absorb the invidious and false attitudes and behaviors of a white culture. There is simply no evidence that many blacks internalize such attitudes. Public opinion polls reveal unequivocally that majorities of each race reject the notion that blacks are intellectually inferior to whites.[63]

Another major criticism is that our schools are suffused with a middle-class bias that fails to take the needs of children from nonwhite and deprived backgrounds into account. Educational institutions are castigated by these experts for stressing middle-class values by insisting on the teaching of standard English rather than Black English (a dialect of English spoken by many poor blacks) and by assigning textbooks that are said to give insufficient attention to black history. Surely black Americans would profit more from being taught the language spoken by the overwhelming majority of the population; and although textbooks devoted to black heroes and events may be of greater interest to some students than the more conventional accounts, there is no evidence that such a change in curricula would have any discernible effect on learning in general. Nor should we suppose, furthermore, that a middle-class bias that insists on punctuality and order suppresses a potential for education. Without a doubt, punctuality, diligence to task, and discipline foster a favorable climate for learning.[64]

It is unreasonable to believe that schools teach values to which the parents of disadvantaged lower-class and working-class children are opposed and ignore those values that they support. Anyway, it would be exceedingly difficult to teach these values in that no one has as yet identified them. Do working-class parents, unlike their middle-class counterparts, wish their children to be disorderly, disrespectful, and nonpunctual in their daily conduct? Such an absurd question answers itself.

Although it is seldom mentioned, in one respect middle-class schools may indeed be detrimental to the interests of children from disadvantaged backgrounds. By requiring students from educationally impoverished home environments to proceed too rapidly in their studies, reformers may unintentionally do incalculable harm to the self-esteem of pupils whose earlier training has not prepared them for competition with their more advanced peers. This conclusion, of course, implies that a different compensatory program of instruction would be advisable for many disadvantaged children of both races.

To summarize, more black than white children do poorly in school for various reasons, most of which are tied to cultural disadvantages associated with broken homes and semiliterate mothers and fathers. These disadvantages, not teacher stereotypes and expectations, are the primary obstacles to school success.

THE LOWER CLASS AND THE MIDDLE CLASS ARE EQUALLY COMMITTED TO THE SAME VALUES

Most books on race relations reject as inconsequential the argument that many lower-class blacks are trapped in a subculture that limits their ability to overcome poverty. They correctly point out that surveys of the values of the poor show that disadvantaged blacks and whites alike endorse such traditional values as hard work, education, marriage, sobriety, and honesty. Hence, many of them conclude that the lower class does not differ cultur- ally from the middle class. Consequently, it is impermissible to speak of a "culture of poverty."

Yet the poor often *behave* as if they are committed to different values. The lifestyles of many in the underclass display a familiar cluster of behav- iors clearly incompatible with the traditional values attributed to the middle class. Indeed, the poor frequently engage in those behaviors said to consti- tute the culture of poverty—drug and alcohol abuse, fatalism, illegitimacy, early and casual sex, violent crime, divorce and desertion, and the impul- siveness associated with short time horizons.[65] These characteristics in turn are closely linked with disorganized family life, poverty, and an inability to adapt successfully to the demands of the marketplace.

Nevertheless, critics of this notion either minimize or reject the role played by culture in the current plight of lower-class black America. In- stead, they reverse the causal sequence, arguing that discrimination causes poverty and that poverty in turn produces the culture of poverty. Most important, they fail to establish a connection between the lifestyle and cul- tural values of the poor and the skills and attitudes that are imparted to their children. They stress the "situational constraints" of exploitation and discrimination. Hence, economic deprivation and prejudice are allegedly responsible for the manifold pathologies and problems associated with the contemporary lower-class experience in America. In other words, values are mostly irrelevant. Poverty causes pathology.

In taking this position, the critics neglect some uncomfortable facts. For instance, between 1960 and 1980, the wages of black males grew, while the unemployment rate for black adults increased only slightly. For ex- ample, among those individuals in the 35–44 age group, the unemployment rate was 7.9 percent in 1960 and 8.1 percent in 1980.[66] Meanwhile, black families disintegrated, and the number of out-of-wedlock births skyrock- eted from 25 to 60 percent of all births. Improved wages and relatively stable unemployment levels in their prime earning years can hardly account for an illegitimacy rate of 60 percent in 1989. One can only conclude that something very much resembling a culture of poverty lifestyle indeed exists when approximately 40 percent of black Americans receive some kind of government assistance in the form of food stamps, housing assistance, and Medicaid and when so many recipients of public largesse are characterized by disorganized families, impulsive behavior, frequent drug and alcohol use, and violent crime.[67]

Despite widespread awareness of such data, most social scientists con- tinue to subscribe to the idea that if only government would give the poor more money and somehow raise their incomes above the poverty line, say, to around 30 or 40 percent above it, then substance abuse, crime, school failure, illegitimacy, and family breakdown would decline. This argument is sometimes couched in propositional form. To quote Harvard sociologist Charles Willie: "As family income decreases, the proportion of families headed by one parent increases."[68] In other words, poverty creates most illegitimacy, desertion, and divorce.

How a correlation establishes a necessary cause-and-effect relationship is left unexplained. Willie apparently thinks it unimportant that while the average black income has been increasing for at least 50 years, the percentage of black families with a father in the house has declined. All social pathology simply cannot be explained by the relative social class positions occupied by blacks and whites. "Among one-time offenders," Harris reports, "holding class effects constant, black youths have a 72 percent higher rate of serious incidence (rape, robbery, assault) than do white youths. Among recidivists, however, this difference increases dramatically to 274 percent."[69] Proportionate to their share of the population, blacks are three times as likely to be poor and black males are six times as likely to serve a prison sentence. The net result, according to a report by *The Sentencing Project*, is that about 25 percent of black men ages 20 to 29 are in prison, on probation, or on parole on any given day. The figure for whites is 6 percent.[70]

Nor can discrimination by the police and the courts explain this substantial difference. According to the National Crime Survey, which is conducted by the Bureau of Justice Statistics, victims of crime report that blacks, once their proportion of the population is taken into account, are 5 times more likely than whites to be the perpetrators of a crime. If anything, the former are even more overrepresented as the perpetrators of violent crimes such as rape (7.5 times) and robbery (13.6 times). Contrary to opinion in many elite circles, black incarceration rates are in all likelihood due less to racial discrimination than to the reality of higher involvement in the commission of serious crimes.[71] Poverty in itself can hardly explain this phenomenon, but perhaps it ought to be admitted that cultural factors do play a crucial role.[72]

But if cultural differences exist, how can lower-class blacks and the middle classes share the same values? The answer, we suspect, has much to do with the respective degrees of commitment to the values that the classes tend to hold. As William Kelso, the author of an important work on poverty writes, "The main problem with the poor is that they are loosely committed to their values rather than being partisan advocates of a pathological or deviant set of cultural beliefs."[73] That is, the poor do not dwell in a culture of poverty with a separate set of values and ideals. But for various reasons they are less attached to middle-class standards, perhaps because they are inadequately socialized and/or poorly regulated such that they can engage in impulsive and pathological behavior without fear of punishment and loss. As it is, our society gives them far less reason to abide by traditional norms. They may have casual sex and children without marrying, obtain the basic necessities without having to work, drink excessively, and take drugs without fearing a loss of livelihood.

SKILL DIFFERENCES DO NOT EXPLAIN INCOME AND OCCUPATIONAL DIFFERENCES

The important role that skill differences play in the creation of income inequalities among groups is also underestimated by many students of race relations. In arguing that literacy and numerical skills have little impact on income, they advance at least three main arguments in support of their position. First, differences in the quality of education received by blacks and whites are difficult to document. Second, most skills are learned on the job. And third, there is scant evidence that the income gap between the races would be narrowed simply by equalizing the kind of education the races receive, since statistical studies that compare whites and blacks with the same number of years in school find that whites earn significantly higher incomes than do blacks.[74] None of these arguments, we contend, withstands scrutiny.

Since income differences are so frequently researched, we shall initially address the third argument. Most income studies are significantly flawed in that they employ a highly questionable measure of "skill level," which leads them to conclude that black-white income differences are due primarily to discrimination. They control for skills by equating years of education attained with the skills acquired. By utilizing years of education as a technique to measure skills, researchers assume that the average black high school graduate has acquired as much preparation for the world of work as has the average white high school graduate. Years of education is thus treated as a proxy, or substitute, for actual knowledge or skills acquired. Consequently, they readily conclude that one third to one half of the income difference between the races is due to discrimination. Discrimination, as they measure it, is the years of schooling that remain. They do not measure discrimination directly; rather, they *infer* its existence from the fact that the income gap between blacks and whites is not eliminated once years of education (and other variables) are taken into consideration.

In that significant differences in basic skills between blacks and whites with the same years of education are clearly evident, this particular technique can be highly misleading. Thus, a study in 1986 by the National Assessment of Educational Progress (NAEP) found that blacks between ages 21 and 25 were more than three years (0.91 standard deviations) behind whites at each level of education attained (high school dropout, high school graduate, some college, and college graduate). That is to say, the average black high school graduate reads at the same level as the average white ninth-grade dropout, while the average black college graduate reads at the same level as the average white high school graduate who does not attend college.[75]

We have known for some time that the achievement gap is greater than the corresponding gap in years of education. For the first time, NAEP research accurately measured this differential with a nationally representative sample of the population that includes, among others, both black and white high school dropouts and high school graduates. Because we are now aware that the black-white gap is wide for those individuals who have attained the same number of years of education, it is no longer permissible to assume that "years of schooling" accurately measures the actual level of skills attained. Put somewhat differently, skills amassed by an individual are not necessarily a product of the total number of years he or she attended school. Occupying a classroom seat probably does little in itself to foster the diverse skills useful for success in the modern workplace, especially if the teaching environment is one in which students fail to respond to the demands of teachers, school administrators, parents, and others. Still, researchers often doggedly persist in the use of years in school as a measure of skills.[76]

The difference between blacks and whites with respect to their skill levels is wide. But do these differences contribute to lower performance levels on the job and to lower income? It appears that they do. Since most of us are compelled to cope with printed materials at work, students of American labor markets generally agree, a degree of literacy and numeracy are essential to success in the workplace. In a 1981 review of manuals utilized by skilled blue-collar workers, it was found that the manuals and printed directions were written at an average grade level of 10.5 and that the average grade level of high school textbooks was a 10.6 grade level.[77]

It is noteworthy that the blue-collar workers in this study spent 97 minutes at work each day reading printed material. They also had achieved higher average reading competency scores than a comparison sample of high school students. It is a safe assumption that most skilled workers (i.e., the more highly remunerated as well as most foremen and supervisors of laborers and service workers) read at least at a 10.5 grade level. Presumably, the less literate workers would therefore be placed at a disadvantage. After all, employers understandably desire to recruit, train, and promote those individuals who are likely to "get the job done."

The linkage between skills and literacy, on the one hand, and job performance, on the other hand, is clearly demonstrated in studies relating performance on standardized tests to occupations in which literacy is a requirement. For example, organizational psychologists Frank Schmidt and John Hunter, who specialize in employment testing, find repeatedly that cognitive ability tests validly predict performance both on the job and in training for the job.[78] Whether performance is measured by supervisor evaluations or by objective samples of employee work, those individuals with higher test scores tend to outperform those with lower test scores. These researchers discovered that a given cognitive ability test is valid for entire families of occupations in all organizational settings and that such tests, moreover, predict job performance equally well for black and white employees. In other words, the average black whose test score is at the 50th percentile performs as well at work as does the average white whose test score is at the 50th percentile.

Schmidt and Hunter conclude that employers would save tens of billions of dollars in low productivity and training costs by recruiting from among those prospects who achieve satisfactory scores on standardized tests. These findings obviously have important implications for students of income differences within populations. If test scores predict occupational performance, and if blacks perform less well on average on these tests than do whites, it would seem to follow that the average black will be less likely to succeed on the job as frequently as does the average white. Furthermore, since pay and promotions tend to go to those employees who perform better, one can understand why many blacks, comparatively speaking, are at a disadvantage once they are placed in competition with more adequately prepared whites.

Research on cognitive skills and job performance suggests that many social scientists have failed to grasp the relationship of skills to work. Whether or not a particular worker learns specific skills on the job, it is difficult to deny that his (or her) actual performance is shaped by the cognitive abilities he brings into the workplace. Since so many occupations require on-the-job training, the argument runs, education is not a crucial factor in success at work. Nevertheless, this claim is hardly pertinent to the skills versus discrimination debate over the sources of race differentials in income. Indeed, cognitive skills contribute directly to performance in the workplace and probably as well to one's ability to learn on the job. Relatively speaking, lower cognitive abilities seemingly help to explain the lower incomes blacks tend to command in two respects. First, blacks are more often less well qualified than whites for the more preferred positions; and second, if they are already employed but possess fewer skills than do their white counterparts, they are also less likely to win pay increases and promotions in the future.

Contrary to the opinions of many contemporary race relations specialists, inadequate skills, not employer discrimination, is the main cause of black-white income disparities. It is possible, moreover, to test the proposition that skills explain black-white income differences. As we have seen, studies comparing blacks and whites with the same number of years of education close the income gap somewhat, but they never eliminate it entirely. A large income difference between the races remains. What must be remembered is that blacks and whites with the same years of schooling have different skills. We know from the NAEP study on literacy that black scores on average are consistently more than three years behind those of whites who have been in school for the same number of years. Accordingly, we base our estimate of the relative quality of education received by blacks and whites on the 1986 NAEP study of literacy. These findings suggest that the relative skill levels of each race may be estimated by taking into account the more than three-year difference between blacks and whites, even as years of education remain the same.[79]

If we are to make a useful comparison between blacks and whites, it is necessary that we estimate the relative quality of black education. After all, it is well known that blacks have for the most part received less adequate schooling. We have developed a statistical procedure with the assistance of Michael Bobic by which the years of education attained by blacks are adjusted downward in order to facilitate a meaningful comparison with whites (See Appendix 3.1). By making this adjustment, we find that the white annual income "advantage" is eliminated. Indeed, as Table A.2 makes clear, blacks now earn slightly more than do whites. Skill differences, it appears, account for the entire income gap between the races. As startling as this finding may appear to some readers, it is consistent with studies that use the *National Longitudinal Survey of Youth* and find only a small income difference, once skills are taken into account. Those studies, however, use a sample that is limited to those who are 32 years of age or younger.[80] Here we look at income across the entire working-age population.

Our data imply that the annual incomes of blacks between the ages of 25 and 64 are reduced very little by discrimination. This conclusion will no doubt astound many readers in that it clearly conflicts with current research claiming that blacks suffer discrimination during the hiring process.[81]

We accept the possibility that blacks may have more difficulty than whites in finding employment. How, then, one may ask, can comparable blacks earn as much as comparable whites? The answer seems to be rather straightforward. While some employers discriminate against blacks, others do not; and since blacks are only 10 percent of the workforce, it is unnecessary for all employers to abstain from discrimination in order for blacks to have opportunities in locating jobs that provide appropriate compensation for their skills and marginal contribution.[82] Thus, whereas they may have to spend more effort in locating employment, they do not suffer income discrimination. In other words, if discrimination increases the black unemployment rate, it certainly does not seem to lower the incomes of those already employed.

This point is cleverly made by Christopher Jencks in a discussion of why discrimination does not necessarily produce economic loss in the form of lower wages.[83] Jencks likens today's marketplace to a hypothetical situation in which major league baseball integrates the National League but not the American League. He notes that black income need not suffer so long as blacks are a minority of all qualified players. If, for example, one third of the talented players are black and the American League excludes blacks, then the American League will be entirely white and the National one-third white and two-thirds black. All the most talented baseball players will land a job. Moreover, wages will be the same in both leagues, since there is no reason to pay whites more than blacks and since the owners of teams in both leagues are assumed to seek the best athletes available. That discrimination need not result in lower income is well illustrated by the history of American ethnic groups, many of which have incomes at or above the national average. These successful groups apparently suffer few economic consequences, despite their minority status and the antipathy of some majority group members.[84]

At the very least, our findings suggest that more research about how and when discrimination occurs is essential. For instance, we might speculate that discrimination is more likely to occur during the recruitment process and within the smaller companies in general that frequently pay low wages. In that case, black income would be less adversely affected, although discrimination might increase black unemployment levels.

It is necessary to make a more global observation in this respect. In recent years, an explosion of technology has taken place, particularly in the areas of telecommunications. Innovations have proliferated, influencing the way we do business and shrinking time and space. Not only has this led to massive corporate restructuring and labor redundancy, but a demand for skilled workers has been encouraged. More generally, the demand for educated labor has risen relative to that of uneducated labor, so there has been a tendency for the incomes of the former to increase relative to the latter throughout the industrial democracies, especially in the United States. The implications are obvious, not least for the unskilled black Americans, who in the aggregate make up a disproportionate share of unskilled workers in this country.[85]

Similarly, as international trade has steadily expanded, much of it with the newly industrializing countries (NICs), both Europe and America have been forced to adjust to a pronounced increase in the importation of relatively cheap goods made with low-wage labor. In that much of this imported merchandise competes with similar kinds of goods produced by our own unskilled, less productive domestic labor, the tendency arises for employment and incomes of the latter to fall or grow more slowly than otherwise. Although the effects of cheaper foreign-produced goods on domestic unskilled workers may sometimes be exaggerated—many less-skilled Americans are in the services sector not directly in competition with tradeable foreign goods—the fact remains that in the more mature economies there has occurred a rise in the incomes of workers with relatively higher skills and a fall in the incomes and demand for less-skilled workers.[86]

Since black Americans as a group are more likely to be unskilled relative to their white counterparts, it was to be expected that these international trends would adversely affect their income and employment opportunities relative to better educated whites. It is not so much racism as the supply of and demand for a certain kind(s) of labor that explains the relative stagnation in black incomes and employment at the lower end of the pay scale.[87]

There is an additional, more specifically American factor that, so far as the case of unskilled labor is concerned, ought not to be underestimated— namely, the surge of immigrants from Latin America and elsewhere over the past two decades. One consequence has been an increase in the supply of unskilled workers relative to the demand for their services, therefore contributing to the growing income gap between skilled and unskilled labor. And since blacks in America are found disproportionately among unskilled and less educated workers, it is not surprising that these altered patterns in labor supply would often produce adverse effects on their own income and employment prospects.

It thus seems apparent that technology, economic change, globalization, and immigration all play a role in the declining fortunes of unskilled labor. In other words, if not only the black poor of America but the less well-educated and unskilled in other industrial democracies are being similarly affected by these momentous structural changes, and if these European nations, whose own welfare states are reputedly more "advanced," are also finding themselves faced with a growing underclass, does it not seem plausible that the obstacles encountered by the uneducated and unskilled poor in general, including the black poor, may have less to do with racism than many of us assume? After all, the great majority of the poor in the major European democracies are not black nor were their ancestors subjected to slavery and segregation.

BLACK PROGRESS DEPENDS UPON AFFIRMATIVE ACTION

As we have seen, race relations experts often claim that white control over the levers of economic and political power prevent blacks from acquiring "their fair share" of the national income, to use a phrase much in vogue. Economic activities are seen primarily as political and social struggles over a more or less fixed number of resources between individuals or organized groups. From this static perspective, decisions to employ are based more on the aspirant's ability to fit into the work group (i.e., according to race or some other group characteristic) than on the particular skills, talents, or abilities the individual may possess. Politics is primary; market supply and demand are secondary. So in order to advance materially and socially, it is necessary that blacks utilize political means to wrest group advantages from whites. The major political weapon in this struggle with whites is affirmative action.

The advocates of affirmative action never define it as preferential hiring of the less qualified at the expense of the more qualified, although in practice the insistence that more minorities be hired according to government-determined goals and timetables has led courts and administrators in this direction. Specifically, they demand that blacks and other designated minorities who score lower on aptitude tests or who have less experience than the white applicants with whom they compete for specific positions nevertheless be preferred in hiring decisions.

Many supporters of affirmative action justify their support for preferential treatment by race on what is sometimes called "institutional racism." By focusing on the *outcomes* of routine institutional and organizational practices, this type of racism divorces individual intent from responsibility. Racism in this sense is caused not so much by individual behavior as by abstract institutions. To Feagin, for example, institutional racism is any action "carried out by members of dominant groups, or their representatives, that have a differential and harmful impact on members of a subordinate group."[88] It essentially entails any institutional practices such as qualifying examinations that may be neutral and fair on their face but that have the effect of benefitting whites disproportionately. The putative racist may not even comprehend his (or her) culpability in today's America, caught up as he is in the institutional norms and values. That blacks often face various competitive handicaps over and above any discrimination is routinely denounced as "racism" or "blaming the victim," even when the competition is obviously open and fair (as in civil service examinations).

In large part the concept of institutional racism rests on a critique of objective testing for employee selection. Intellectuals and race relations authors assert that tests discriminate against minorities in that they are allegedly culturally biased. When pressed, however, to explain precisely how the tests are biased, they invariably cite the fact that minorities on average do less well than whites and Asians. Yet this criticism is far less telling than we may assume, since a low score is only biased when it underestimates the school and job performance of minority group members. In reality, as Schmidt and Hunter have amply documented, the tests are equally predictive for majority and minority performance alike.[89] Hence, they are fair in the sense that employers (and schools) use them to select the prospects more likely to succeed.

In its implication that blacks are unable to compete on an equal footing with whites and Asians, the accusation that these tests are biased is upon reflection highly insulting to minorities. By rejecting objective measures, it implies that blacks will never reach the performance levels of whites. Hence, it seems to follow that formal standards of equality must be severely restricted if black advancement is to become a reality. Blacks, it insinuates, cannot develop skills useful in the marketplace.

Given a mind-set in which market phenomena are presumed to be influenced less by supply and demand than by the whims of powerful whites, support for affirmative action is a logical choice for public policy. The reader may recall that when we considered the split-labor or neo-Marxist views, we emphasized the unfortunate consequence of imagining "labor," inter alia, as a "whole," a unit, or even a small number of units sealed off from one another. Most strong advocates of affirmative action, whether they realize it or not, embrace similar holistic assumptions about the homogeneity of labor markets. To their way of thinking, employees are essentially movable objects on a chessboard, either to be manipulated for the social ends of well-meaning politicians and bureaucrats or to be protected from the greedy or bigoted designs of capitalists. As such, a holistic approach is quite limited if one wishes to understand how the supply of and demand for heterogeneous forms of labor are established in real markets where real employers produce real products, the relative demand for which determines the relative fortunes of the various kinds of labor.

Much as the cargo cultists in the South Pacific, supporters of affirmative action suppose that resources are more or less superabundant, lying there to be distributed at will. When they observe that the majority seems to benefit disproportionately because of its superior market position, they tend to assume that someone must be taking unfair advantage. With so much discrimination supposedly built into society's daily life, government-coerced affirmative action becomes an indispensable means for group advancement.

To summarize, advocates of affirmative action wish to divorce labor demand from market competition. Convinced that employers hire qualified individuals for positions to be distributed by group means, they sincerely expect that their efforts will have little detrimental effect either on the national output of goods and services or on other groups. As for the former, there is every reason to believe that future research will finally expose the precise economic costs of affirmative action quotas.[90] Another effect, seldom mentioned but about which we shall have much to say in a subsequent chapter, is to engender resentment and conflict. In their quest for racial quotas, or at least for a better "balance," apologists for affirmative action programs give short shrift to the realities of group relations in a pluralistic society. They steadfastly ignore the simple truth that any serious effort to base public policy on group preferences will not only foster interracial animosity but undermine the rule of law and ultimately the free market order upon which our prosperity depends.[91]

CONCLUSION

The weight of cumulative evidence argues that discrimination and white racism are no longer the primary sources for socioeconomic underdevelopment within the black community. To the contrary, the major source is a paucity of basic skills and knowledge, notably numeracy and literacy, which can ultimately be translated into marketable skills. Correcting these deficiencies will be no easy task, since disorganized family life and ineffective social controls have undermined and devalued a respect for learning.

Still, many social scientists do not accept the argument that much of black life is characterized by behavioral patterns that must be substantially altered before black poverty can be eradicated in any fundamental way. In their opinion, it is white society, not black society, that must first be reformed. Only when whites have finally come to acknowledge their racism can the way then be cleared for long-term solutions. In light of what we know about black skills, school failure, family breakdown, and community disorganization in a period when actual white discrimination has sharply declined, however, this argument is hardly convincing to many Americans.

NOTES

1. Among the sociology texts are the following: Joe R. Feagin, *Racial and Ethnic Relations* (Englewood Cliffs, N.J.: Prentice-Hall, 1989); Anthony Gary Dworkin and Rosalind J. Dworkin, *The Minority Report* (New York: Holt, Rinehart and Winston, 1982); John E. Farley, *Majority-Minority Relations* (Englewood Cliffs, N.J.: Prentice-Hall, 1988); Harry H. L. Kitano, *Race Relations* (Englewood Cliffs, N.J.: Prentice-Hall, 1980); and George E. Simpson and J. Milton Yinger, *Racial and Cultural Minorities* (New York: Plenum, 1985).

2. Joe R. Feagin and Clairece Booher Feagin, *Discrimination American Style: Institutional Racism and Sexism* (Englewood Cliffs, N.J.: Prentice-Hall, 1978), p. 9.

3. Dworkin and Dworkin, *The Minority Report*, p. 18.

4. Kitano, *Race Relations*, p. 127.

5. Feagin, *Racial and Ethnic Relations*, p. 37.

6. Edna Bonacinch, "A Theory of Ethnic Antagonism: The Split-Labor Market," *American Sociological Review* 37 (October 1972): 549–59.

7. Dworkin and Dworkin, *The Minority Report*, p. 30.

8. In particular, see the following works by William H. Hutt: *The Economics of the Colour Bar* (London: André Deutsch, 1964), pp. 58–67, 68–81; *The Strike-Threat System* (Arlington, Va.: Arlington House, 1973), pp. 163–95; and *Individual Freedom: Selected Works of William H. Hutt*, ed. Svetozar Pejovich and David Klingaman (Westport, Conn.: Greenwood, 1975), pp. 3–13.

9. Hutt, *The Strike-Threat System*.

10. Joel Steinberg, *The Ethnic Myth: Race, Ethnicity and Class in America* (Boston: Beacon, 1981), p. 52; also see Frances Fox Piven and Richard A. Cloward, *Regulating the Poor: The Functions of Public Welfare* (New York: Vintage, 1972).

11. For studies of the role of economic competition in modern societies, see in general Ludwig von Mises, *Human Action: A Treatise on Economics*, 3rd rev. ed. (Chicago: Henry Regnery, 1966); Joseph Schumpeter, *Capitalism, Socialism, and Democracy* (New York: Harper Torchbooks, 1950); and Milton Friedman and Rose Friedman, *Free to Choose* (New York: Avon, 1979).

12. Thomas Sowell, ed., *Essays and Data on American Ethnic Groups* (Washington, D.C.: The Urban Institute, 1978).

13. Pierre Van Den Berghe, *The Ethnic Phenomenon* (New York: Elsevier, 1981).

14. See Murray N. Rothbard, *Freedom, Inequality, Primitivism, and the Division of Labor* (Auburn, Ala.: Ludwig von Mises Institute, 1991), pp. 17–30; and Mises, *Human Action*, pp. 141–61.

15. U.S. Commission on Civil Rights, *The Economic Progress of Black Men in America* (Washington, D.C.: Government Printing Office, 1986), p. 13.

16. For a discussion of how unemployed black males spend their time, see Richard B. Freeman and Harry J. Holzer, *The Black Youth Employment Crisis* (Chicago: University of Chicago Press, 1986), p. 9.

17. Gordon Allport, *The Nature of Prejudice* (New York: Addison-Wesley, 1954), p. 9.

18. Feagin, *Racial and Ethnic Relations*, p. 1; Kitano, *Race Relations*.

19. U.S. Commission on Civil Rights, *The Economic Progress of Black Men*, p. 55.

20. See Reynolds Farley, *Blacks and Whites: Narrowing the Gap?* (Cambridge, Mass.: Harvard University Press, 1984), p. 117.

21. Simpson and Yinger, *Racial and Cultural Minorities*.

22. U.S. Bureau of the Census, *Statistical Abstract of the United States: 1992*, 112th ed. (Washington, D.C.: Government Printing Office, 1992), p. 267.

23. See Howard Schumann, Charlotte Steeh, and Lawrence Bobo, *Racial Attitudes in America* (Cambridge, Mass.: Harvard University Press, 1985), pp. 71–162.

24. Bureau of the Census, *Statistical Abstract of the United States: 1992*, p. 456.

25. Schumann, Steeh, and Bobo, *Racial Attitudes in America*, pp. 71–162.

26. U.S. Government Accounting Office, *Equal Employment Opportunity: EEOC and State Agencies Do Not Fully Investigate Discrimination Charges* (Washington, D.C.: Government Printing Office, 1988), p. 5.

27. Increasingly, the personnel area is dominated by minorities. See Sharon M. Collins, "The Marginalization of Black Executives," *Social Problems* 36 (October 1989): 317–31; and idem, "The Making of the Black Middle Class," *Social Problems* 30 (February 1983): 369–82.

28. James P. Smith, "Affirmative Action and Labor Markets," *Journal of Labor Economics* 2 (1984): 269–301; and idem, "Affirmative Action and Its Effects" (paper presented at the American Sociological Society meetings, Washington, D.C., August 1990).

29. Andrew Hacker, *Two Nations: Black and White, Separate, Hostile and Unequal* (New York: Charles Scribner's Sons, 1992).

30. Ibid., p. 110.

31. U.S. Department of Labor, Bureau of Labor Force Statistics, *Labor Force Statistics Derived from the Current Population Survey, 1948–1987* (Washington, D.C.: Government Printing Office, 1988), pp. 764–66.

32. Hacker, *Two Nations*, p. 102.

33. U.S. Commission on Civil Rights, *The Economic Progress of Black Men*, p. 41.

34. Hacker, *Two Nations*, p. 118.

35. Frank L. Schmidt and John E. Hunter have published many studies in which they have established the validity of cognitive ability tests. They summarize their findings in "Employment Testing: Old Theories and New Research Findings,"

American Psychologist 36 (October 1981): 1128–37. For a technical discussion, see John E. Hunter and Rhonda F. Hunter, "Validity Generalization and Utility of Alternative Predictors of Job Performance," *Psychological Bulletin* 96 (January 1984): 72–98; and John Hunter, "Cognitive Ability, Cognitive Aptitudes, Job Knowledge and Job Performance," *Journal of Vocational Behavior* 29 (1986): 340–62.

36. See Feagin, *Racial and Ethnic Relations*, p. 221.

37. For a study of white attitudes with regard to the Klan, see Schumann, Steeh, and Bobo, *Racial Attitudes in America*, pp. 71–162. Relying on reports from the Anti-Defamation League and the Southern Poverty Law Center, Dinesh D'Souza points out that Klan membership is about 4,000 and that of the Skinheads about 3,000 to 3,500. See his *The End of Racism* (New York: Free Press, 1995), p. 392.

38. Timothy J. Flanagan and Kathleen Maguire, eds., *Sourcebook of Criminal Justice Statistics 1989*, U.S. Department of Justice, Bureau of Justice Statistics (Washington, D.C.: Government Printing Office, 1990), p. 391; and Anthony R. Harris, "Race, Class, and Crime," in Joseph F. Sheley, ed., *Criminology* (Belmont, Calif.: Wadsworth, 1991), pp. 95–119.

39. This technique is central to many works on race relations. For instance, see Stanley Lieberson, *A Piece of the Pie: Blacks and White Immigrants since 1880* (Berkeley: University of California Press, 1980).

40. See Feagin, *Racial and Ethnic Relations*, p. 216.

41. Farley, *Majority-Minority Relations*, p. 73.

42. Herbert G. Gutman, *The Black Family in Slavery and Freedom, 1750–1925* (New York: Vintage Books, 1977), pp. 32, 45; Eugene D. Genovese, *Roll, Jordan, Roll: The World the Slaves Made* (New York: Pantheon, 1974).

43. For a discussion of the disincentives of welfare, see Charles Murray, *Losing Ground: American Social Policy 1950–1980* (New York: Basic Books, 1984).

44. On black family life, see Simpson and Yinger, *Racial and Cultural Minorities*; and Charles Willie, *A New Look at Black Families* (Dix Hills, N.Y.: General Hall, 1988).

45. Edward W. Jones, "What It's Like to Be a Black Manager," *Harvard Business Review* (May-June 1986): 84–93.

46. See Feagin, *Racial and Ethnic Relations*, p. 228.

47. William R. Beer, "Sociology and the Effects of Affirmative Action: A Case of Neglect," *American Sociologist* 19 (Fall 1988): 218–31.

48. David Johnston, "Study Finds Job Complaints Are Widespread at F.B.I.," *New York Times*, June 19, 1991, p. A12.

49. See Aaron Wildavsky's rather amusing comments in his *Rise of Radical Egalitarianism* (Washington, D.C.: American University Press, 1991).

50. Simpson and Yinger, *Racial and Cultural Minorities*, p. 44.

51. Ibid.

52. Hacker, *Two Nations*, p. 80.

53. Virtually all examinations, including the Scholastic Aptitude Test, Armed Forces Qualifying Exam, The Weschler Adult Intelligence Scale, the National Assessment of Educational Progress, and the Civil Service Examination, report differences between 0.8 and 1.2 standard deviations. Obviously, these are substantial differences, since a one standard deviation difference means that 50 percent of

whites score above the median whereas only 16 percent of blacks attain that level. See D'Souza, *End of Racism*; and for a review of the test results, see the U.S. Commission on Civil Rights, *The Economic Progress of Black Men*.

54. Feagin and Pettigrew see little decline in the negative effects of prejudice. See Joe Feagin, "The Continuing Significance of Race: Antiblack Discriminations in Public Places," *American Sociological Review* 56 (1991): 101–16; Thomas Pettigrew, "The Ultimate Attribution Error: Extending Allport's Cognitive Analysis of Prejudice," *Personality and Social Psychology Bulletin* 5 (1979): 461–76.

55. James S. Coleman, Ernest Q. Campbell, Carol J. Hobson, James McPartland, Alexander M. Mood, Frederic Weinfeld, and Robert L. Yonk, *Equality of Educational Opportunity* (Washington, D.C.: U.S. Government Printing Office, 1966).

56. Robert Rosenthal and Lenore Jacobson, *Pygmalion in the Classroom* (New York: Holt, Rinehart and Winston, 1968).

57. Samuel S. Wineburg, "The Self-Fulfillment of the Self-Fulfilling Prophecy," *Educational Researcher* 16 (December 1987): 28–37.

58. Lee J. Jussim and Jacquelynne Eccles, "Are Teacher Expectations Biased by Students' Gender, Social Class, or Ethnicity?" in Yueh-Ting Lee, Lee J. Jussim, and Clark R. McCauley, eds., *Stereotype Accuracy: Toward Appreciating Group Differences* (Washington, D.C.: American Psychological Association, 1995), pp. 245–71.

59. Jere Brophy, "Teacher Behavior and Student Achievement," in M. C. Whittrock, ed., *Handbook of Research on Teaching* (New York: Macmillan, 1986).

60. The results of the Harris poll are reported in Tamara Henry, "Teachers' Crash Course in Reality Spells Burnout," *USA Today*, December 11, 1992, 1D.

61. James S. Coleman, Thomas Hoffer, and Sally Kilgore, *High School Achievement: Public, Catholic, and Other Private Schools* (New York: Basic Books, 1982).

62. Dworkin and Dworkin, *The Minority Report*, p. 55.

63. Schumann, Steeh, and Bobo, *Racial Attitudes in America*, pp. 71–162.

64. Coleman, Hoffer, and Kilgore, *High School Achievement*, pp. 88–121.

65. See Oscar Lewis, "The Culture of Poverty," *Scientific American* 15 (October 1966): 19–25.

66. U.S. Civil Rights Commission, *The Economic Progress of Black Men*, p. 41.

67. Farley, *Blacks and Whites*, p. 164.

68. Willie, *A New Look*, p. 8.

69. Harris, "Race, Class, and Crime," p. 105.

70. Marc Mauer, *Young Black Men and the Criminal Justice System: A Growing National Problem* (Washington, D.C.: The Sentencing Project, February 1990), p. 3.

71. See Harris, "Race, Class, and Crime," p. 100; and Anthony Harris and G. D. Hill, "The Social Psychology of Deviance: Toward a Reconciliation with Social Structure," *Annual Review of Sociology* 8 (1982): 161–86.

72. For a discussion of the central role of values in culture, see Ann Swidler, "Culture in Action: Symbols and Strategies," *American Sociological Review* 51 (April 1986): 273–86; and William A. Kelso, *Poverty and the Underclass: Changing Perceptions of the Poor in America* (New York: New York University Press, 1994), p. 170.

73. Quoted in D'Souza, *End of Racism*, p. 198.

74. For example, see David Featherman and Robert Hauser, *Opportunity and Change* (New York: Academic Press, 1978); Reynolds Farley, "Trends in Racial Inequalities: Have the Gains of the 1960s Disappeared in the 1970s?" *American Sociological Review* 42 (1977): 189–208; and Thomas Boston, *Race, Class and Conservatism* (Boston, Mass.: Unwin Hyman, 1988).

75. Irwin S. Kirsch and Ann Jungeblut, *Literacy: Profiles of America's Young Adults* (Princeton, N.J.: Educational Testing Service, 1986); and Audrey Pendleton, *Young Adult Literacy and Schooling* (Washington, D.C.: U.S. Department of Education, Office of Educational Research and Improvement, 1989).

76. For example, see Boston, *Race, Class and Conservatism.*

77. Larry Mikulecky, "The Mismatch between School Training and Job Literacy Demands," *Vocational Guidance Quarterly* 30 (December 1981): 174–80.

78. Schmidt and Hunter, "Employment Testing."

79. Kirsch and Jungeblut, *Literacy.*

80. June O'Neill, "The Role of Human Capital in Earnings Differences between Black and White Men," *Journal of Economic Perspectives* 4 (Fall 1990): 25–45.

81. For example, see Margery Austin Turner, Michael Fix, and Raymond J. Struyk, *Opportunities Denied, Opportunities Diminished: Racial Discrimination in Hiring* (Washington, D.C.: The Urban Institute Press, 1991). We discuss the misleading nature of this study in the next chapter.

82. U.S. Department of Labor, Bureau of Labor Statistics, *Employment and Earnings*, vol. 36 (Washington, D.C.: Government Printing Office, January 1988), pp. 183–88.

83. Christopher Jencks, *Rethinking Social Policy* (Cambridge, Mass.: Harvard University Press, 1992).

84. See Andrew Greeley, "The Ethnic Miracle," *Public Interest* 45 (1975): 20–36.

85. For example, see "Rich Man, Poor Man: The Gap between High Earners and the Lowest Paid Has Widened: Why?" *The Economist*, July 24, 1993, p. 71; also "Europe and the Underclass: The Slippery Slope," *The Economist*, July 30, 1994, pp. 20–21.

86. A very good summary of this problem may be found in Stephanie Flanders and Martin Wolf, "Haunted by the Trade Spectre," *Financial Times*, July 24, 1995.

87. Ibid. The theory and debate behind this argument have also been neatly summarized in "Schools Brief: Workers of the World Compete," *The Economist*, April 2, 1994, pp. 69–70.

88. Feagin, *Race and Ethnic Relations.*

89. See note 35.

90. For example, see Peter Brimelow and Leslie Spencer, "When Quotas Replace Merit, Everybody Suffers," *Forbes* 152 (February 15, 1993): 80–102. Their estimate of the total cost to the gross domestic product (GDP) is 4 percent.

91. Two of the best accounts of the nature of the rule of law are Michael Oakeshott, *On History, and Other Essays* (Oxford: Basil Blackwell, 1983); and Friedrich A. Hayek, *Law, Legislation, and Liberty: Rules and Order*, vol. I (Chicago: University of Chicago Press, 1973).

APPENDIX 3.1
EDUCATION AND THE BLACK-WHITE INCOME GAP

This study of the sources of the racial divide in average income uses the National Assessment of Educational Progress (NAEP) findings of large differences in the skills of blacks and whites to correct for differences in the quality of education the races acquire. It separates human capital into two components—highest degree attained and an estimate of broad general skills (e.g., literacy and numeracy). Our focus is on the extent to which these education-related variables can explain more of the income gap than the more commonly used variable—years of education.

METHODS

In order to assess the impact of education across the life course, we employed a nationally representative sample with data from subjects in all age groups. Unfortunately, none of the available data sets provides data on the general skills of individuals for a nationally representative sample of workers age 25 to 64. The most appropriate data set with individual level data—the National Longitudinal Survey of Youth (NLSY)—only contains respondents up to age 32.[1] Therefore, because we lacked measures of the general skills of older workers, we had to estimate black-white skill differences.

Data are from the National Survey of Families and Households, a nationally representative survey conducted by the University of Wisconsin and Ohio State University in 1987 and 1988. We selected all males age 25 to 64. There were 3,523 subjects, but we excluded those who earned less than $150 in the previous year, which left 3091 subjects—544 blacks and 2,547 whites.[2] Our analysis uses responses from males age 25 to 64 and employs these variables: age in years, annual income, race (black/white), years of education corrected for quality, and highest degree attained (high school, bachelor's, master's, or terminal). We focus on males, as gender differences in income are not as easily attributable to either skill disparities or race discrimination.

As noted, our estimate of relative black-white quality of education was derived from the 1985 NAEP study of literacy, which had a nationally representative sample of respondents 21 to 25 years old (1,997 whites and 957 blacks).[3] On all three measures of literacy, black young adults scored significantly below white young adults, with an average difference in test scores greater than one standard deviation. The disparities remained large even after educational attainment in years was taken into account. The

NAEP reported scale scores for blacks and whites in four educational categories: less than high school, high school, some college, and college graduation. Averaging the three literacy scales in each educational category, blacks, even when possessing the same number of years of education as their white counterparts, ranged from 44.8 to 47.2 points below whites in each category of education. The standard deviation on each test was 50 points. Thus, the average black college graduate was .90 standard deviation below the average white college graduate, and the average black high school graduate who did not attend college was .94 standard deviation below the average white high school graduate who did not attend college.[4] In sum, while the skills of blacks and whites similarly advanced with each increase in educational attainment, the black-white skill divide stubbornly remained about the same.

We believe we can translate the gap in standard deviations as measured by the NAEP into a gap that takes skill differences into account, because the NAEP found that blacks were similarly behind whites at each level of educational attainment. (Moreover, the NAEP result is similar to one in the NLSY, which found that blacks were one standard deviation behind whites in verbal and mathematical skills despite having the same average years of education.)[5]

Overall the measured differences in acquired skills equates to about a 3.19 year lag in skills between the average black and the average white with the same years of education. In our sample the mean years of education of our black respondents age 25 to 29 is 12.91. Taking the mean lag of 3.19 and dividing it by 12.91, it appears that for each year of education blacks completed, they fell further behind their white counterparts by .247 years.

Several studies have demonstrated that over the course of the last 50 years, black students have narrowed the skills gap.[6] Therefore, we expect that 3.19 years is the minimum difference in skill attainment between the races in the various population cohorts. Since the NAEP has not measured the gap in skills for cohorts other than that in the 21-to 25-year-old group, we estimated the gap by multiplying the .247 year lost per year of education by the mean number of years of education in each of our age cohorts (25–29, 30–39, 40–49, 50–59, 60–64). This figure is then subtracted from the actual years of education of each black respondent in the appropriate cohort. The mean years of education and the setback computed for each cohort are presented in Table A.1. We call the resulting estimate of black versus white skill levels (i.e., quality of education) NEWED.

This technique assumes that high and low estimates of general skill for individuals as gauged by years of education for whites and corrected years

Table A.1
Mean Years of Education for Blacks and Years Subtracted by Cohort

Cohort	Mean Years of Education	Years Subtracted
25–29	12.91	3.19
30–39	13.09	3.23
40–49	12.57	3.11
50–59	10.59	2.62
60–64	8.37	2.07

Source: James Sweet, Larry Bumpass, and Vaughn Call. "The Design and Content of the National Survey of Families and Households." (Working paper NSFH-1). Center for Demography and Ecology, Madison, Wis., 1988.

Table A.2
Mean Income with and without Controls for Education

Model	Black	White	Income Gap	P
No Control	20,466.41	26,696.44	6,230.03	.000
With Years of Education	22,630.38	26,250.81	3,620.43	.000
With NEWED	24,832.77	22,330.09	−2,502.68	.02

Source: James Sweet, Larry Bumpass, and Vaughn Call. "The Design and Content of the National Survey of Families and Households." (Working paper NSFH-1). Center for Demography and Ecology, Madison, Wis., 1988.

of education (NEWED) for blacks balance out across the sample. While it improves on the use of years of education as a measure of basic human capital, it is only an estimate of relative levels of group differences in level of human capital.

FINDINGS

Our hypothesis states that the observed difference in earnings between blacks and whites is a function of the quality of education each group receives; thus once quality of education is taken into account, the gap in earnings should diminish substantially. Table A.2 shows that annual mean income for black males age 25 to 64 ($20,466.41) is 76.6 percent of annual mean income for white males age 25 to 64 ($26,696.44). A significant black-white earnings gap of $3620.43 remains after number of years of education is taken into account (see Table A.2). But, when black education is corrected for quality of education (NEWED), the black-white earnings gap becomes a $2,502.68 advantage in favor of blacks. Thus, after correcting for quality of education, blacks earn more than comparable whites.

This finding supports our hypothesis but is counterintuitive. The problem is that NEWED does not take into account the credential effect of having a high school, college, or advanced degree. For example, if a black respondent possesses a bachelor's degree but has three years of education subtracted from his years of education, he is compared to a white who has not earned a college degree. In other words, the observed difference in income ignores the likely possibility that blacks benefit from acquiring credentials.

To address this problem, we examined earnings differences with analysis of covariance. Our design (Table A.3) included two main effects, race (black or white) and highest degree attained (no degree, high school, college, and post-college). (We collapsed master's and terminal degree because only 16 blacks had a terminal degree.) The covariate NEWED was then fitted within each cell. We are using ANCOVA, because regression could smooth over the variance specific to each category of race and highest degree held, which in turn could diminish the impact of race or any of its interactions. In addition, ANCOVA controls for potential bias in NEWED. It is also appropriate for our data, which are cross-sectional and static.[7] That is, ANCOVA is the more conservative methodology. The results are presented in Table A.3.

Table A.3
Analysis of Covariance: Income by Race, Highest Degree and NEWED

Source of Variation	Sum of Squares	DF	Mean Square	F	Sig of F
Covariates					
NEWED	93445274773	1	93445274772.6	546.843	.000
Main Effects	7293797794	4	1823449448.61	10.671	.000
Race	32242202	1	32242201.998	.189	.664
Highest Degree	55633644195	3	1854421398.17	10.852	.000
2-way Interactions					
Race Highest Degree	1040527594	3	346842531.370	2.030	.108
Explained	101779600161	8	12722450020.1	74.452	.000
Residual	449759727939	2632	170881355.600		
Total	551539328100	2640	208916412.159		

Covariate	Raw Regression Coefficient			
NEWED	1838.718	Multiple R2	.183	

Note: 2641 cases were processed; 0 cases (.0 percent) were missing.
Source: James Sweet, Larry Bumpass, and Vaughn Call. "The Design and Content of the National Survey of Families and Households." (Working paper NSFH-1). Center for Demography and Ecology, Madison, Wis., 1988.

With highest degree in the model, there is no significant race effect, either as an interaction term or as a main effect. Highest degree attained is significant, as is the coefficient for our indicator of skills, NEWED. These findings suggest that the use of the variable—years of education—as a control or proxy for wage-relevant skills when studying racial differences in income is methodologically as well as theoretically unsound. Therefore, future research on black-white income differences ought to employ the highest degree attained in conjunction with a measure or estimate of skill levels. That is, it ought to take the proven existence of significant gaps in the relative amount of skills the races acquire into account when assessing the sources of income differences.

NOTES TO APPENDIX

1. See George Farkas, Paula England, Keven Vicknair, and Barbara Stanek Kilbourne. "Individual Cognitive Skill, Occupational Skill and Wages Among Subordinated Ethnic Groups." Paper presented at the American Sociological Society meetings in Pittsburg, Pa., August 1992.

2. James Sweet, Larry Bumpass, and Vaughn Call. "The Design and Content of the National Survey of Families and Households" (Working Paper NSFH-1). Center for Demography and Ecology, Madison, Wis., 1988.

3. Irwin Kirsch and Ann Jungeblut. *Literacy: Profiles of America's Young Adults* (Princeton, N.J.: Educational Testing Service, 1986).

4. Audrey Pendleton. *Young Adult Literacy and Schooling* (Washington, D.C.: U.S. Department of Education, Office of Educational Research and Improvement, 1989).

5. June O'Neill. "The Role of Human Capital in Earnings Differences Between Black and White Men." *Journal of Economic Perspectives* 4 (1991):25–45.

6. Charles Murray and Richard Herrnstein. "What's Really Behind the SAT Score Decline?" *The Public Interest* 106 (1992):32–56.

7. John Neter, William Wasserman, and Michael Kutner. *Applied Linear Statistical Models* (Boston: Irwin Publishing, 1990).

4

Stereotypes and Contemporary Race Relations

In the preceding chapter, we observed that in racial matters scientific truth often falls prey to ideology. We demonstrated that, on average, black Americans earn incomes roughly corresponding to the particular skills they bring into the marketplace. Yet the image of the black American as hostage to a virulently racist society persists, obsessively resistant to facts. A major consequence is a growing alienation among the American intelligentsia from important political and social institutions and an inclination to justify or rationalize high crime rates, low educational achievement, and inadequate occupational skills among many blacks as somehow a natural outcome of racism. Given that America is apparently believed to be awash with anti-black sentiment, one is not surprised that virtually all problems are said to be caused by racism.

Whereas old-fashioned, state-imposed separation of the races no longer exists as an impediment to black progress, many commentators seem to agree that a new sinister and covert racism has arisen that presents, if anything, a greater barrier to social harmony and justice. This covert racism is much more difficult to detect and extirpate, but it presumably expresses an enduring white hostility no less inimical to black interests than was the older, legally imposed discrimination. In indirect and subtle ways too numerous to consider in full, whites are thought to place their fellow blacks at a disadvantage by belittling them, by stimulating their feelings of inferiority, and generally by making them feel less worthy as human beings.

Thus, it is said that the majority foists a badge of inferiority on the minority that in effect denigrates black cultural achievements and behavioral norms. One means of accomplishing these destructive ends is presumably by the widespread use of racial "stereotypes."

Sociologically speaking, stereotypes may be thought of as the expectations held by one group about the attributes of another group. These expectations can be positive, negative, or neutral. However, within the context of racial and ethnic rivalry for status and group power, stereotypes, it is argued, take on a more ominous aspect, since their expected consequence is to marginalize a minority socially, politically, and materially. To stereotype, many believe, is to label minorities as somehow less worthy than majorities of respect and consideration. Viewed as weapons in a struggle for status and social standing, stereotypes are said to distort rather than describe reality.

In this chapter, we dissent from the conventional account of the nature and use of stereotypes. As the Marxians sometimes put it, we shall "demystify" the role of stereotypes in race relations. We begin with the well-documented fact that many negative stereotypes appear to be true, which is to say that in some rough sense they more or less represent social reality. While of course no stereotype describes all blacks or all whites, many of them do accurately identify *differences* between groups that can be shown to exist empirically (i.e., the average Asian does better at mathematics than the average white; the average white is more literate than the average black; young black males are more likely to commit street crimes than are their white counterparts). Oddly, the degree of stereotype accuracy has been ignored. Given that stereotypes appear to capture group differences, should not their nature and use in race relations be a legitimate area of scholarly study? Indeed, how can we comprehend race relations without addressing the nature and accuracy of stereotypes?

To ask these questions obviously gives one pause, given the controversial nature of the subject. Perhaps, however, if the social scientist is true to his or her mission, he or she has little choice in the matter. As it is, many stereotypes may be both unflattering and untrue, which many assume is the norm. Yet some may be both unflattering and true, which naturally raises controversy. Just how morally and scientifically complex this problem can become is immediately apparent once we seek to sort out the various aspects of stereotypes.

Nevertheless, we must make an effort to comprehend their role and function in both race relations and the contemporary debate over racism. Accordingly, we ask the reader to consider three typical and admittedly simplified situations in which blacks and whites use stereotypes when interacting with one another: Chance encounters on the street; service to minority customers; and employer hiring practices. As pictured in our vignettes, blacks and whites routinely bring to their interracial encounters expectations that can be dubbed negative stereotypes. If, as we believe, these cases of interracial contact illustrate the use of stereotypical expectations in everyday life, it is easy to see why race relations are often characterized by mistrust and embarrassment, as well as much awkwardness and resentment.

Vignette 1

A young white woman is walking down a deserted central city street to visit a friend. It is 7 P.M., and the shops are closed for the night. Her friend lives on the side of the street she is presently walking on. Walking in her direction about a hundred feet ahead is a young black man dressed in jeans, sneakers, and a T-shirt but who is otherwise unremarkable in his appearance. He makes no threatening gestures, he does not stare menacingly at her, nor do his movements suggest that he has the least intention of doing so. Nevertheless, she is gripped by a sense of fear. Clutching tightly at her pocketbook, she crosses quickly to the other side of the street.

Once across the street, she feels a twinge of self-consciousness and not a little embarrassment, although she tells herself that under the circumstances her action was justified. She thinks almost aloud: "Most black men are certainly not criminals—I just passed two black men in business suits without a thought—but this particular individual might well have been a mugger. Better safe than sorry."

The black man notices her discomfort and is understandably annoyed by her effort to avoid him. He has often observed such behavior by whites, especially when walking with his friends. Although he has never robbed or attacked anyone, he feels branded as a dangerous criminal to be carefully avoided. The woman, he believes, is undoubtedly prejudiced, perhaps downright racist.

Vignette 2

A young, well-groomed black woman, dressed casually in an inexpensive outfit, enters a store specializing in expensive designer clothing popular with older college-educated career women. Two white sales clerks are present, one of whom is attentively waiting on a white customer who is herself attired in much the same way as the black woman. The second clerk makes no effort to greet the new customer but continues arranging scarves on the shelves behind the counter. She has observed the black woman entering the store but continues with her work. While the black woman looks at a skirt display, she speaks briefly with the other clerk. Finally, she approaches her potential customer, inquiring if she might be of any help. When the black woman responds that she is "just looking," the clerk retreats a few steps. She does, however, continue to observe the customer from the corner of her eye—as does the other clerk—but she makes no effort to be of further assistance.

The black woman feels unwelcome, even rebuffed by the clerks. She has at other times noticed the cold stares of suspicious clerks in such white people's stores, as she calls them. She notes the solicitude displayed by the clerks for the white customer's business and is convinced that an implicit "white's only" policy is being applied in her particular case. On the other hand, she does not know that from practical experience the clerks have learned that relatively few blacks are interested in purchasing the line of clothing they sell. From their perspective, a sale is unlikely to be consummated, so they feel little incentive to offer their services. True, some older black women patronize the store, but they comprise mainly professionals whose more expensive wear makes them obvious targets for attention from the clerks.

Consequently, given her age and appearance, the clerks immediately conclude that this particular black woman affords them little prospect for a sale. At the same time, they believe, she does pose some threat as a potential shoplifter. Shoplifting is a common occurrence, and this young woman readily fits one of the profiles of a typical shoplifter. Thus, the clerk who initially approached the black customer is wary but relaxes somewhat as the latter takes an interest in the displays. After a few minutes, the clerk asks a second time if she might be of service, but by this time both clerk and customer are ill at ease with one another. The latter soon departs without making a purchase.

Once the black woman leaves, the clerks cast knowing glances at each other. That no sale was consummated hardly surprises them, nor do they feel guilty for having kept a watchful eye on a shopper they believe might have been a shoplifter. The customer, however, saw the episode differently. Thinking about her recent experience as she walks down the street, she believes the clerks were at best cold and distant, at worst antiblack. After all, the only difference between the white customer and her, she reasons, was the color of their skins.

Vignette 3

Mr. Mason, the owner of a small brick manufacturing plant, is in the market for new employees. Fifty percent of his applicants are black, but only about 20 percent of his workforce is minority. He often employs blacks, but for some reason, they frequently resign or are fired for poor performance, absenteeism, or tardiness. Since many of his better workers are black and since, in addition, he worries about the possibility of discrimination lawsuits, he is quite eager to find capable black workers.

Forty individuals—20 whites and 20 blacks—have applied for 10 positions in production. Mason's personnel clerk wishes to administer a test to each prospect and subsequently employ the 10 highest scorers. However, since the average black candidate does less well than does the average white candidate on such tests, Mason fears that he may be inviting a lawsuit. He ardently desires to hire the best possible aspirants. At the same time, he cannot be absolutely confident as to who his best future employees are likely to be, although previous experience suggests that unemployed men, men with no record of steady employment, or individuals from the local black high school make poor prospects in that they are often unreliable and possess few basic reading skills. Mason has greater confidence in black applicants who have graduated from Catholic parochial schools as well as from the suburban or predominantly white ones. Graduates from these institutions are more likely to be diligent workers and to follow directions well, perhaps because they can read the shop manuals and, in addition, are more willing to cooperate with authority figures. At a minimum they are able to complete the application forms correctly, which cannot be said for most applicants from the local high school.

One of Mason's black employees, who graduated from a Catholic high school, is now a production foreman who has been absent from work on only three occasions in five years of employment. If only all applicants were so dependable, Mason sighs. Unfortunately, within the past two months, 50 percent of his black employees have quit or were dismissed for poor performance, whereas only 20 percent of his white employees have departed under similar circumstances. On the other hand, those blacks who previously attended parochial or suburban high schools have track records similar to his white applicants'.

After having assessed his pool of candidates, Mason hires seven whites and three blacks. Two of the blacks were educated at parochial schools; the third black was a graduate of the local black high school but possessed a steady work history and was able to fill out the application form. Mason was particularly impressed when it came to his attention that the latter had worked six consecutive months as a cook at a fast-food restaurant. Conversely, none of the remaining black applicants had established steady work histories or had attended a school Mason trusted. Ultimately, 15 percent of the blacks and 35 percent of the whites were hired.

Mason is aware from the outset that fewer of his black applicants are likely to prove employable. Furthermore, he realizes that he is rejecting capable and responsible people, white and black alike, whom he would willingly employ were he able to identify them. Unfortunately, he cannot do so, and training costs are simply too dear, as he is in need of workers he can count on from the outset.

He considered hiring Jimmy Smith. But Smith, age 20, is unemployed at present. Moreover, after attending the local predominantly black high school, he has jumped from job to job for various reasons—low pay, layoffs, disagreeable hours, or conflict with a supervisor. Smith knows nothing of Mason's reasons for not hiring him. But convinced that he is qualified for a position, he talks with his friends in the neighborhood, several of whom were themselves unsuccessful applicants. He and his friends conclude that Mason discriminates against blacks.

Before we dismiss these vignettes too hastily as examples of white malevolence, we would do well to consider them from the standpoint of the white majority. Various questions immediately arise: Do whites treat all blacks according to stereotypes? Or, to the contrary, are they capable of finding real individuals beneath the superficialities of race? Similarly, given the particular positions in which our imaginary whites find themselves, does it still make much sense to describe their behavior toward blacks as irrational? In general, are their attitudes based on race or do other, more complex realities intrude? Is racism a problem when other characteristics such as age, dress, general demeanor, literacy, occupational performance, dialect, and langauge exercise such a substantial impact on white attitudes and behavior that they overwhelm the race factor? At what point do we stretch such terms as *racist* or *prejudiced* beyond all meaning, especially when white behavior seems to be governed by considerations having to do with pecuniary interests, divergent cultural styles and values, different orientations to time, class distinctions, and so on? To describe whites motivated by nonracial factors associated with race, but not reducible to race, as bigoted may be useful for the status struggle but quite irrelevant to scientific analysis.

Our three vignettes illustrate the dynamics of race when the races come into contact. In each instance, members of the two races interpret the motives of the other race differently. In none of the vignettes do blacks and whites seem to anticipate pleasant exchanges, in all probability because they approach each other across a number of divides in addition to race:

linguistic, stylistic, social, and cultural.[1] Blacks tend to interpret these distinctions as race related, but in reality, the differences are more likely to be rooted in social and cultural experiences.

As is said so often nowadays, both races are engaged in racial stereotyping. Yet neither race bases its opinions and behavior solely on racial stereotypes. The female pedestrian, for instance, is less concerned about race per se than about the young man's age and dress. It is thus the combination of race, dress, and age that evokes so much fear. Indeed, she had previously passed well-dressed black professionals without the slightest trace of anxiety. Similarly, it is mostly dress and age that determine the actions of the white clerks when the young black woman enters the store. In both instances, the whites are distinguishing between types of blacks and not responding to race alone. The white businessman is concerned first and foremost with the challenge of finding and keeping good, dependable employees. He develops expectations (i.e., stereotypes based on his experiences with the blacks and whites who have worked for him in the past) that favor black graduates of Catholic and suburban high schools. However, he uses other stereotypes as well—those with established work records like the young man who worked the previous six months as a cook are likely to be good workers; those who are unemployed or have checkered work histories are ranked lower as likely prospects for successful employment. Of course, most black job applicants do not share his evaluation of work continuity. In fact, they see it as another sign of the ill effects of racism, believing that if white employers did not discriminate, black job applicants would have better work records. And, of course, job seekers for machine operator positions cannot see the relevance of the type of school attended for job performance.

We believe it is not unusual for whites in general, like the whites in our vignettes, to base their decisions on expectations associated with race. But it would be unusual for them to employ race *alone* as the basis of an assessment of a black person. Human action always depends on expectations about the likely behavior, inclinations, skills, styles, and motives of others. The behavior of the whites in the vignettes was not racist in any meaningful sense because their expectations were rooted in experience and involved legitimate concerns. We cannot expect people to expose themselves to danger or theft or to hire less productive workers.[2]

In the remainder of this chapter, we present a theory of modern race relations rooted in a large, if often neglected, body of social science literature. The major discovery of this research is that in the shops and workplaces where the races customarily meet, whites, for the most part, react to black people as individuals, recognizing their unique attributes and abilities. We demonstrate that white Americans largely interact with minority group members in a pragmatic and reasonable manner by taking all available knowledge about a person into account and that even when whites subscribe to negative stereotypes, they are rarely slaves to them, treating black people with appropriate courtesy and respect. By no means do they let stereotypes solely dictate their response to the blacks they meet in public or with whom they work.

Our approach to race relations is "rational" in the sense that we begin with the commonplace observation that human beings are thinking creatures, capable of using the gifts of reason and language in subtle and complex, yet mostly accurate, ways. Consequently, a theory of racial stereotypes and their use in everyday affairs must pay heed to the manifold capacities and powers of human cognition. To treat stereotypes in the conventional manner as inaccurate depictions of reality, which are applied to all or most individuals within a group, underestimates the capacity of most people to grasp complex realities by making fine and subtle distinctions between categories. In truth, it disallows all distinctions between groups, insisting that differences between groups are marginal or nonexistent.

Yet as we pointed out in the previous chapter, there are cultural and educational differences between blacks and whites. Quite appropriately, these give rise to stereotypes, since human beings are endowed with an ability to make distinctions and place people and objects in "appropriate" categories. Given their capacity for categorization, they can construct relatively accurate stereotypes in line with their own experiences and the known facts as they perceive them. These stereotypes are generalizations, of course, but, as we will demonstrate, most whites comprehend that a particular stereotype does not accurately describe all, or even most, of those individuals in a specific group. Rather, they merely tell us that the members of a group under consideration are more likely than the members of another group to possess a particular characteristic.

Our central insight into race relations and the use of stereotypes is that whites, not least white employers, cannot afford to apply negative stereotypes inflexibly to all blacks. They must take into account the fact that blacks, as whites, are concrete individuals who differ in a variety of ways. Some blacks are criminal, but most are law-abiding; some are work-shirkers, but most are productive, dependable employees. While some blacks are shoplifters, the vast majority are good, honest customers. But by the same token, whites cannot ignore important differences in the distribution of traits among the members of other groups inasmuch as the races do behaviorally diverge in important ways for a variety of reasons having to do with culture, history, and socialization. In this historical period, for example, blacks are more likely than whites to commit robbery and less likely to study effectively and acquire vital skills. Therefore, whites must make distinctions, which in practice means they must place blacks in categories—those with a specific trait and those without it. This, however, is not as difficult as it seems since whites also must categorize whites. The key distinction resides in the relative number of each group placed in a given category.

As we shall demonstrate, stereotypes are essentially *expectations* about which group as compared with another group or groups is more likely to possess a given trait. Following the work of Alfred Schutz, a social theorist and philosopher, we will designate the stereotype as a "type" and argue that what are routinely dismissed as white stereotypes of blacks are often no different from other types (e.g., they need not be any more irrational or inaccurate than the types—i.e., stereotypes—ordinary people, including "progressive" social scientists, construct in order to distinguish between, say, "typical" Democrats and "typical" Republicans or "typical" Catholics and "typical" Protestants). In other words, thinking stereotypically is part and parcel of human thought processes, not some kind of cognitive aberration that can be expunged from the consciousness of the ordinary white American. Categorization could not be eliminated, even if we wished, for categorizing or typing is simply fundamental to all human thinking, although it can be driven underground.[3]

Indeed, the process of typing often entails the specification of ever more refined categories. We necessarily see the objects in the world as composed of types or categories and notice the differences as well as the similarities between the members of a category. Hence, most objects in a type can be divided into subtypes. In the type "fruit," for instance, we may include the various subtypes—oranges, apples, bananas, and so on—useful for the purpose of making further, more accurate, refined, and/or delimited subtypes.

HUMAN ACTION AND STEREOTYPES

Although too many social scientists forget this elementary truth, human beings are best conceptualized not as more or less passive robots subject to abstract historical forces but as intentional and rational creatures who necessarily employ their minds in unique ways to make sense of events and situations encountered in everyday life.[4] Indeed, it is an undeniable fact, if one excludes purely knee-jerk behavior, that all human action is purposive. We must of necessity think before we act without necessarily knowing what the ultimate outcome portends. Since the actions of individuals take place through time, it follows that the future is clouded in varying degrees with uncertainty. Therefore, we must rely on hazy expectations about unfolding events. After all, our own plans are likely to diverge from those of our fellow beings, who are themselves making and carrying out their own plans. In practice, each individual makes plans for future actions as if he or she already knows the outcome, when in point of fact we can seldom be sure with absolute certainty that events will unfold as expected. In social science jargon we say that an individual's actions include initial plans, which are imagined as having already been accomplished as "acts" prior to their actual completion.[5]

What is meant by the individual *plan*? Basically, it is a welding together of means, ends, and obstacles to be faced in settings where uncertainty necessarily exists. In the words of the late economist Ludwig Lachmann, "The plan [is] the coherent design behind the observable action in which the various purposes as well as the means employed are bound together." Thus, before we act we must craft a mental design. "When men act they carry in their minds an image of what they want to achieve. All human action can be regarded as the carrying out of projects that are designed to give effect to imagined ends."[6]

It is important to understand that planning and the formation of *expectations* are inseparable from one another. Expectations for their part heavily depend on past experiences as guides to future behavior, since the future cannot be known before it has arrived. Those prior experiences that are believed to be useful for future success will be drawn on in the process of making plans. As a general rule, we tend to assume that if an event occurred in the past, it is likely to occur again in the future.

In a word, we perforce typify events and objects, categorizing and grouping them in our minds for subsequent action. We thus experience the behavior of our fellow humans, various events in our lives, and objects in our environments as typical of previous occurrences, quite likely to be repeated under more or less similar conditions. In other words, the matching of expectations among people is built on typically performed prior acts. In observing that other individuals and occupants of particular roles have previously behaved in rather predictable fashion, we reasonably anticipate that they will behave in a familiar way in the future when faced with a similar situation. That is to say, the typification of experiences and the formation of expectations are inseparable from one another. Therefore, every action is a speculation.[7] Indeed, insofar as certainty is impossible, "the most that can be attained with regard to reality is probability."[8] Thus, our plans of necessity are provisional, as the mind cannot know with certainty what unfolding events will bring. As a result, we must continually revise our plans in light of new information.

In pursuing our goals, we frequently change our plans and the expectations on which they are based, as events present new possibilities to us. In other words, to reach our ends successfully, we must be willing to abandon chosen means and ends when they appear to us as wrong or ineffective. In short, human life and thought have an open-ended, contingent, and tentative quality—with the objects we encounter, including other people, being interpreted in light of their relevance to the plan. As unexpected obstacles present themselves or as errors in the plan employed become manifest, individuals alter their plans or devise new ones. At all times, however, behavior is purposive and flexible.

It is obvious that the notion of typicality is inseparable from thinking. Typification, categorization, classification, or whatever term one wishes to employ when describing these cognitive processes is simply inherent in the way we think. Given the unique qualities of each individual experience, it goes without saying that the manner in which these experiences are interpreted differs widely among individuals, which is why our plans often go awry and why overall coordination of plans presents so many obstacles for us in the real world. Moreover, as Schutz, that outstanding student of this problem put it, "the concreteness of the individual type is inversely proportional to the level of generality of the past experiences out of which it is constructed."[9] That is, the more general the experiences the type must seek to encompass, the more abstract it becomes and the less accurate it may prove to be in describing particular objects and events—which is not the same thing as saying that a particular category, broadly encompassing, has failed to describe reality, as that elusive term is commonly understood. Instead, it is more accurate to say that it has approximated reality. Specific attributes of the members in the particular category in question usually diverge to some extent from the type. For instance, an individual's typification of a "house" will not include all the attributes of any specific house. Nonetheless, although his or her understanding of the term may well be somewhat abstract or general, it is quite adequate to the task of interpersonal communication. If, for instance, the individual contracts with a carpenter to have a house constructed, he or she need not specify that it must have a roof, since it is understood by all parties, including the judge whose duty it is to enforce contracts, that the typification of a "house" includes a roof. The point is that while typifications are abstract and do not exactly match the concrete instances that actually exist, they do tend to capture *common* features of the members of the category around which a consensus regarding the type can emerge.

While the terminology used by Schutz and other students of "everyday life" is abstract, it does refer to commonplace practices in which people engage in order to cope with the ordinary demands and predicaments of daily existence. Types, in fact, are the building blocks of individual plans. Each of us can draw on an almost limitless supply of types in the construction or revision of our plans. We view this supply of types as a stock of knowledge, consisting of techniques or recipes we and others acquire for mastery of routine problems in daily life.[10] With a storehouse of useful types, we strive to devise effective plans in order to meet our ordinary needs and to handle the inevitable exigencies that arise. If, for example, a woman's car does not start, she can refer to a stock of knowledge about automobiles, repair services, alternative methods of reaching work, and so on. She assesses the situation by placing it from her standpoint into an appropriate category or type. She knows the car will not start because once the ignition was turned, she did not hear the typical sound a car makes when the ignition is engaged. Her next thought may conceivably be that when a similar event occurred in the past (either experienced directly or indirectly), the battery was not charged. She then categorizes the situation as one involving a "dead" battery and not a major repair. If she is correct, then she may draw further upon her stock of knowledge by using the jumper cables in her trunk to get her car on the road. She expects to get help from her neighbor, whom she assumes is still at home since, after all, he typically is there if his car is in the driveway at this time of day. Note the number of typifications that she has applied in devising a suitable plan for solving her transportation problem.

Our mental processes thus entail the creation, application, and revision of such types as the typical employee, the typical cause of ignition failure, and the typical behavior of a neighbor.[11] Types are constructed and objects are placed within categories and endowed with certain attributes in the course of our daily affairs. "The world, the physical as well as the socio-cultural one," says Schutz, "is experienced from the outset in terms of types: there are mountains, trees, birds, fishes, dogs."[12] There are also subtypes—types of mountains, trees, birds, fishes, dogs. The more effectively these types describe the reality to which they refer, the more useful they are likely to be for the construction of our plans and projects, although the more general and encompassing, the less reliable they may prove to be in particular cases.

Because people require types that are appropriate to the situations in which they hope to bring their plans to fruition, they are inclined to display much flexibility and tentativeness in the creation and application of the types they construct. Rather than being mere prisoners of their typifications, they must necessarily check them against the details of their experiences in order to ascertain their validity or applicability in a given situation. "Actual experience will or will not confirm our anticipation of the typical conformity of these other objects [to the type]."[13] Thus, individuals appear to assume that their typifications are "valid until counter-evidence appears,"[14] for "every empirical idea of the general [i.e., the type] has the character of an open concept to be *rectified or corroborated by supervening experience*."[15] Sensitive to the contingent, open-ended character of human action, Schutz argues that "our everyday thoughts are less interested in the antitheses 'true-false' than in the sliding transition 'likely-unlikely.' "[16] In other words, the cognitive process fits the contingent nature of the human condition in that individuals quite appropriately construct tentative typifications, which they perceive as approximations of reality and which, when necessary, they will eliminate or modify in order to realize the ends for which their plans were initially constructed. When people change their plans as new facts in a situation arise, they must change their typifications as well. They are "retyping," as it were.

How is our discussion of types related to the study of race relations? To begin, it alters our understanding of the nature of stereotypes and their effects in interracial encounters. Properly understood, a stereotype is a type applied to a group. People type groups in much the same way as they type other objects. While we may disapprove of this inclination to place people into categories, we have little choice but to see typing for what it is, namely, fundamental thought processes in action. Fortunately, we need not demonize the typification process, for its consequences are rarely as deleterious as the reader may assume. As is true of other types, stereotypes are for the most part tentatively held, subject to revision if they fail to match experience.

Nor are stereotypes generally applied to all members of a particular group. Most of us acquire diverse kinds of information about a variety of people within any group. In the process, we utilize such knowledge in order to distinguish subtypes within the minority in question. These subtypes of the categories "black" and "white" may serve to render particular stereotypes more "accurate" in an empirical sense than would otherwise be possible.

For instance, rather than suggesting that all blacks possess a singular negative trait, whites may sometimes stereotype by saying that blacks are more likely than whites to behave "irresponsibly." These whites implicitly create four subtypes—namely, responsible whites, responsible blacks, irresponsible whites, and irresponsible blacks. In this manner, stereotypes are to be seen as expectations about which group is relatively more likely to possess a given trait. It is not necessary that the trait be applied to all or even to a majority of a group in order to qualify as stereotypical. It need only be one that makes a useful distinction between the groups in question. In stereotyping blacks generally as somehow irresponsible, the individual may well believe that only 20 percent of blacks and 10 percent of whites possess the particular trait. Thus, the former may be stereotyped as irresponsible in much the same way as smoking cigarettes is said to "cause" lung cancer. Most blacks are certainly not irresponsible, nor do most smokers develop lung cancer.

Just as all sorts of types enable us to cope with the realities of daily living, categorizations of groups may be useful for apprehending the essential characteristics that may be pertinent to our plans. Even negative stereotypes, as when our imaginary store clerk kept a wary eye on a person she regarded as a potential shoplifter, are rarely constructed for the purpose of degrading or insulting an out-group. Rather, their primary function is to grasp reality as it is perceived by the individual—a function that is presumably enhanced by types that describe the attributes of majority and minority members alike. Depending on one's perception, such comparisons of groups may be harmful or harmless, true or untrue, or significant or insignificant. Much depends on time, place, circumstance, taste, or ideology. In other words, labeling something as "racist" is a relatively easy task at the extremes where fanatics dominate the debate. It is in the disputed terrain, where legitimate personal, pecuniary, or ideological interests are involved, that name-calling is inappropriate.

This is not to say a negative attribution cannot cause anguish to innocent individuals within the out-group. But it does imply that in-group perceptions are quite malleable, depending as they do on the circumstances in which they occur.

Whites by no means carry perfectly accurate estimates in their heads about all possible differences between the two races. To be sure, that would be an impossible task. We do assert, however, that they categorize both whites and blacks, translating the types, if need arises, into *rough distributions of the traits* in each group. This tendency ought not be surprising in the least, for we can generate rough estimates with virtually all social categories. For example, people know that the average man is taller than the average woman, but they are also aware that some women are taller than some men. Certainly few of us know the precise distribution of heights, say, the exact percentage of men who are taller than 5'10". Yet we can surely offer estimates that would place a larger percentage of men than women over that height. Such estimates cause no difficulties. In all likelihood, we would base our calculations on a few basic types such as the man of average height, the woman who is much taller than average, and so on.

To summarize, while a stereotype is indeed a generalization about a group, the argument does not end there. In addition, stereotypes are often held tentatively, open to revision, as people continually seek to construct more accurate ones in order to improve their chances for grasping reality and, as a consequence, carrying out their plans. When an employer, for example, tests applicants for their basic reading abilities, he may be said to perpetuate a stereotype since he is already aware that blacks do not usually score as well on average on these kinds of tests as do whites. The stereotype may be confirmed by his own experience if black scores do not match those of whites. Multiply such experiences not only among employers but among the larger public as well. It is then a relatively easy matter to see how white anticipations are derived from prior knowledge gleaned from any number of sources. It is this kind of information that leads to the formation of what are ridiculed as generalizations and stereotypes in the first place. Or, to take a better-known example, when most white Americans tend to avoid certain urban neighborhoods, they may surely be accused of stereotyping; however, if avoiding high-crime neighborhoods is an effective strategy for reducing their victimization, these whites may be said to benefit from useful, though invidious, stereotypes.

In general, our discussion is pertinent to an understanding of white behavior. Although the latter may typify blacks as potentially less productive on average for certain kinds of work, the typical white will probably assume that some percentage of blacks are quite proficient at the job. Therefore, he or she will likely search for signs of competence such as high test scores, grades, diligence, enthusiasm, previous or current job performance, or letters of recommendation. Consequently, negative stereotypes that may be applied to a subset of a minority in general do not automatically trigger prejudice and discrimination. It will be recalled, for example, that Mr. Mason, our factory owner, had a number of valued black employees despite his pessimism about the potential value of many of his black applicants. But he nonetheless employed blacks, since more specific subtypes were also readily available to him as data. From his experience, he has concluded that the typical black graduate of a Catholic school is more likely to succeed at the job than is the typical graduate of an all-black public school or that the typical black applicant with an established work history will more likely become a productive employee than the typical applicant with a checkered work history. Hence, by setting aside all-inclusive generalizations to call on subtypical information gained from real-world experiences, the Mr. Masons of this world increase the probability of obtaining "correct" information about their workers.

Our reconceptualization of stereotypes of minorities as expectations about which group is more likely to possess given traits has important implications for our knowledge about race relations. It suggests that white typifications about blacks (i.e., white stereotypes) do not necessarily determine white evaluations of individual blacks in concrete situations, which is to say that whites rarely make decisions on the basis of race alone. Rather, they take a variety of factors about a specific individual into account. Depending on the concrete circumstances in which they find themselves, they may draw distinctions, other things being equal, between particular blacks. That is, they are likely to assess blacks according to whether or not the latter possess the attributes supposedly indicative of membership in a particular subtype. Employers, for instance, who believe that blacks are on average less mathematically adept than whites may base their decision on the subtypes—numerate blacks, innumerate blacks—and look for indicators of the category in which a specific black applicant ought to be placed. In other words, whites, as others, exhibit flexibility in the utilization and construction of typifications, which are checked against the facts of concrete situations in order to see if the specific type is applicable to the individual or individuals in question. This contingent and flexible approach to minority individuals is not surprising. We can rarely categorize without giving our attention to an individual's attributes, since we know from experience that there are in fact a great variety of types of people to be found within all ethnic and racial groups. Thus, we may believe that whites as a group are more literate than blacks as a group, while knowing that some blacks are more literate than some whites in much the same way we know men as a group are physically stronger than women without forgetting that some women are stronger than some men.

Since most whites are aware that stereotypes apply only to a certain proportion of a group rather than all of it, racial stereotypes alone may rarely determine behavior. After all, it makes little sense to discriminate against an entire group when only some of its members possess an undesirable characteristic. Hence, white behavior (e.g., the employment decision) will depend on the subtype in which a particular black is placed. For instance, employers, it goes without saying, look for indicators of whether or not a specific individual has the motivation and ability to produce. Blacks with adequate credentials and work records no doubt can and do secure desirable employment. Hence, racial discrimination in hiring is most likely to occur when employers typify blacks as less qualified but have no available signs of motivation and ability apart from race (e.g., no previous work histories, test scores, letters of recommendation, samples of previous work, etc.). Since most job applicants can present evidence of previous achievements, they can locate suitable employment.

Following this line of thought, it is useful to view stereotypes as other types, namely, as mental constructs useful to the formation of plans, projects, or fantasies. Based as they are on anticipations and speculations about group values, attitudes, and behaviors, these categorizations, which we sometimes dismiss as merely stereotypical, are constitutive of individual plans. If a specific stereotype fails to conform to reality—that is, if it imposes a barrier to the success of the plan from the standpoint of the planner—the individual, when faced with external and internal pressures, is likely to revise his or her plans as new information presents itself. Otherwise, over time the individual would be seen by others as uninformed, stupid, a nuisance, misguided, mad, irresponsible, or in the context of this book, a bigot and a racist.

In practice, therefore, a negative stereotype is likely to be applied to a subset of its members rather than to all in a minority group. Like other typifications, stereotypes are likely to be realistic or roughly accurate estimates of how groups differ. In any event, we are not prisoners of our stereotypes. In their everyday interaction with individual blacks, whites may often ignore stereotypes or create noninvidious subtypes. Given this willingness to set aside negative stereotypes—at least temporarily or under special circumstances—the connections between stereotypes and prejudice or discrimination are relatively weak. So whites rarely respond to blacks as mere members of a racial category, especially when they are armed with specific information about the individual blacks with whom they interact.

Moreover, many negative stereotypes at bottom are related more to social class than to skin color. In all probability they arise from the fact that 33.4 percent of all blacks rely on government welfare subsidies.[17] Lastly, in modern, market-oriented democracies such as the United States, employers who treat minorities unfairly in their evaluations of prospective and current employees are likely to pay any number of monetary, psychic, or social costs. As much theory and research have demonstrated, by turning away more qualified minorities in order to employ "their own kind," many of whom may well be less productive, employers can end up costing themselves as well as the minorities against whom they discriminate. The critical insight here from theory is that when government edicts do not prevent groups that are despised or discriminated against from discounting the value of their services, markets can exercise a benevolent discipline over bigoted employers. Finally, let us remember that social pressures and altered social attitudes can play important roles in the erosion of employment discrimination.

STEREOTYPES, DISCRIMINATION, AND THE VICTIM VISION

The Victim Vision of race relations was first articulated in the 1940s. To this day, it carries the intellectual baggage of the social science of that era, especially in its assumption that human beings passively absorb the attitudes and beliefs of their surrounding cultures, which are said to largely determine individual behavior even when they have little or no relationship to objective reality. In that period (and to a lesser extent today) it was naively assumed that culture directly causes our behavior more or less independently of our personal experiences and self-interests. In that it was and is influenced currently by methodological holism or cultural determinism, this form of social science had little respect for individual will and reason. By following the doctrines of traditional anthropologists, it tended to shackle the individual to the bonds of tradition.[18]

Today's students of race relations similarly view human action as a product of cultural forces. Convinced that negative and false stereotypes largely dictate the behavior of whites toward blacks, these intellectual descendants of the cultural determinists continue to see blacks mainly in the same mold, namely, as passive victims of the racist attitudes of whites. They tend to believe, moreover, that whites subscribe to beliefs largely unrelated to the facts at hand, applying their biases indiscriminately to the individual blacks with whom they come into contact.

If stereotypes invariably lack factual foundations, then how are they derived? Social scientists usually tend to assume that stereotypes and prejudice are learned from parents and friends. That is, they are a form of ignorance. Let us consider the words of social scientists Anthony Dworkin and Rosalind Dworkin for whom the terms *prejudice* and *stereotype* are in essence interchangeable: "Prejudice is formed either in the absence of the target group or with limited contact with that group. . . . [I]ndividuals learn prejudiced attitudes about minority groups, not from contact with the minorities but from contact with others who have prejudiced attitudes toward the minority group."[19] Since stereotypes cannot apparently be based on real experiences, their ultimate source must be hidebound traditional culture or, to be blunt, white culture.

These inaccurate and irrational stereotypes, learned from parents, peers, the media, and public opinion, are said to predispose whites to discriminate against minorities. That is, a direct connection is posited between stereotypes and behavior, which predicts that whites who hold negative opinions of blacks will proceed to use their beliefs and attitudes as guides to action in concrete cases. A white employer, for instance, who believes that blacks in general are less responsible than whites, will be predicted to hold steadfastly to his prejudice and refuse employment to the minority race. In this way stereotypes are said to play a destructive role in race relations. Being false, they may be said to initiate processes that culminate in irrational discrimination.

In other words, the Victim Vision concept of stereotypes posits a radical disjunction between one's beliefs about a group and the real attributes of that group. This notion that stereotypes are divorced from reality is to be found in most discussions of stereotypes, including Walter Lippmann's early classic, *Public Opinion*, in which "the pictures in our head" are to be distinguished from "the world outside."[20] In his opinion, we do not respond directly to external reality so much as to a "representation of the environment which is in lesser or greater degree made by man himself." He argued that our representations differ from reality and may well determine our assessment of the world outside. Culture, not reason and experience, is the source of the stereotype: "In the great blooming, buzzing confusion of the outer world, we pick out what our culture has already defined for us, and we tend to perceive that which we have picked out in form stereotyped for us by our culture."[21] Subsequently, race relations scholars would also claim that stereotypes are only tangentially connected to the experience of the individual who holds them. Particularly in the case of racial stereotypes, a divorce is said to occur between an individual's description of the traits that characterize blacks and the actual attributes of that group. The absence of substantial, if any, correspondence between stereotypes and reality renders them false or at least grossly inaccurate.

Lippmann, as many intellectuals of his era, conceptualized culture as a set of internalized stereotypes, attitudes, and values that mold human action. People were said to respond not to the world as encountered but to one that is prepackaged by culture. Surely the radical proposition that our ideas about the world do not tend to reflect our experiences of the world ought long ago to have called forth an outpouring of empirical studies about the accuracy of stereotypes. Instead, the social science community ignored the issue or defined it away. In a review of the stereotype literature up to the early 1970s, for example, Marlene Mackey found that no effort had been made to test the hypothesis that stereotypes are inaccurate or invalid.[22] For the most part, researchers just assumed that stereotypes are wrongheaded or gross overgeneralizations. They justified this opinion by maintaining that stereotypes are acquired by majority individuals either from conversation within the majority group itself or from limited contact with members of the minority group.[23]

Historically, most students of race and ethnic relations have evinced little or no interest in researching the relative validity of stereotypes. Moreover, those social scientists who did have such interest were hampered by the way in which the concept was customarily measured or, in the language of research, how stereotypes were "operationalized." The most common technique was pioneered by social psychologists Daniel Katz and Kenneth Braly in 1933.[24] In their studies, subjects were given a long list of traits and then asked to select those traits that describe the typical member of a specific ethnic group or race: intelligent, lazy, musical, industrious, humorous, argumentative, and so on. Most people generally cooperate with researchers by selecting some traits that they presumably believe are characteristic of each group.

Although the Katz and Braley technique identifies which traits or stereotypes are associated with each group, it has one great flaw: It fails to allow subjects to specify the percentage of the particular group that is said to possess a given characteristic. Nor does it ask subjects to compare the percentage of the group supposedly possessing a particular trait with that of another group in order to see the extent to which groups are thought to differ with regard to the particular attribute in question. It merely asks people to indicate which traits are thought to be typical for the members of the chosen group. Moreover, no effort is made to ascertain just what people mean by *typical*. For example, is it a trait thought to describe more than 50 percent of the group in question? Or just more than what is typical of a comparison group (e.g., 20 percent of blacks have it versus 10 percent of whites)? Or even as what they believe other people (but not themselves) view as group typicality?

For victimologists, however, the Katz and Braly technique does have a signal virtue in that it obtains results consistent with their own notions about stereotypes. Scholars may indeed use it to demonstrate that about 80 percent of a white sample stereotype blacks in some manner—that is, as irresponsible, musical, impulsive, unintelligent, et cetera. And since the vast majority of blacks do not in fact possess such traits, social scientists were easily led to the conclusion that blacks are inaccurately depicted in the stereotypes of whites, which can be described therefore as ignorant and divorced from reality.

The basic weakness of this particular approach lies in its assumption that a white who selects a particular trait, say, "laziness," believes that many more blacks than whites exhibit the behavior commonly referred to as laziness. It is quite possible that most respondents in any particular study believe that what is typical for a group is not necessarily that which describes more than 50 percent of its members so much as that which merely distinguishes in some diffuse, general way the group in question from other groups. Hence, when Katz and Braly found that 78 percent of their sample of college students stereotyped Germans as "scientifically minded," the students did not necessarily believe that more than 50 percent of Germans are interested in science (if that is what that phrase means). There is a more simple explanation of what the students believed. They may have been saying, to wit, that, as compared with other groups, Germans are relatively more likely to be interested in science. In this particular case, the respondents may just as well have believed that 15 percent of Germans but only 5 percent of Americans are likely to take an interest in science.

But before we turn to the available evidence supporting our interpretation of the nature and use of stereotypes, we must adumbrate the implications of our analysis for the conventional wisdom on race relations. In contrast to our approach, conventional assessments as a rule take what can only be called an extreme position, depicting whites who hold stereotypes as simpleminded bigots who view all blacks in a stark, negative light. In other words, many simplify the study of race relations by dividing whites into two groups: the good ones who do not stereotype and the evil ones who do. Alas, we do not live in a simple world, and the race dilemma cannot be reduced to a morality play with bad guys who stereotype and good guys who do not.

HOW ACCURATE ARE WHITE STEREOTYPES OF BLACKS?

What little social science research we possess about the accuracy of stereotypes finds that people construct and employ them in a manner consistent with known behavioral differences between the races. Most of this work, developed primarily by social psychologists, is informed by a cognitive model of human action. Researchers in this tradition argue that stereotypes perform a knowledge function in that they reflect the basic cognitive structures of human thought processes. More specifically, humans simplify incoming information by categorizing, or typifying, it. If we did not do so, our mental and emotional worlds would become completely unmanageable.[25] Hence, stereotypes are usually related to our own direct experiences or to conversations with trusted sources. They are certainly not inevitably immoral, invariably inaccurate, and overgeneralized attitudes, although on many occasions they may surely be so described. In fact, we use what are sometimes casually referred to as stereotypes for no other purpose than making appropriate distinctions, which may be used for decision making in conjunction with other pieces of information. Thus, an individual who plans a dinner party for Mormon guests may reason that since Mormons typically do not drink, it is probably inappropriate to serve alcoholic beverages. Or, to take an example pertinent to our study, when one enters an unfamiliar neighborhood, the event may bring to mind a type containing the attributes of a dangerous neighborhood. If this is the case, he or she will in all probability quickly assess the area, draw an appropriate conclusion based on the type created within his or her mind, and either leave the area or take suitable precautions. By categorizing, by typing, we cope with the demands of daily life.

In addition, the research data clearly show that people who stereotype do not assume that all or even most of a given group necessarily possess the particular trait in question.[26] Social psychologist John Brigham found that whites, so far as their common stereotypes of blacks are concerned, estimate that relatively low percentages within the black population display undesirable traits. In a recent review of the research following Brigham's initial work, the editors of an American Psychological Association book conclude, "Although people often perceive differences among groups, we are not aware of a single study identifying a single person who believed all members of a social group had a particular attribute."[27] By assuming that a particular trait applies to some, but hardly all, blacks, most whites would seem to stereotype in a manner that more closely reflects the world as it is experienced.

Strange as it may seem, as these words are being written, only one publication has appeared that tests the hypothesis that white stereotypes of blacks are grossly inaccurate, although this particular study suggests that white estimates of the percentages of blacks who complete high school, who are born illegitimate, who are on welfare, who have four or more children, who live in a female-headed family, who are unemployed, and who were the victims of crime are startlingly accurate. The participants in the study were asked by social psychologists Clark McCauley and Christopher Stitt to estimate the percentage of whites and blacks in each of these categories. White estimates were subsequently compared with official statistics. The authors concluded that stereotypes tend to be accurate. Moreover, they observed *no* instance in which the stereotype ratio (the ratio of the estimate of percentage of blacks to that of whites) was greater than the actual ratio of blacks to whites taken from official government statistics. In fact, whites often underestimated the true difference in the direction favorable to their fellow black citizens![28] Although most whites held some negative stereotypes, they could hardly be labeled as necessarily antiminority.

A similar study at Transylvania University extended the McCauley and Stitt technique to the more negative traits. One hundred and thirty-six white students were asked to estimate the percentage of whites, blacks, and Asians having the traits shown in Table 4.1. The question wording and the average percentages estimated for each trait or characteristic are also presented. So far as this particular study is concerned, the results suggest three

Table 4.1
Average Student Estimate of Percentage of Racial Group with Trait

1.   What percentage of each group is on welfare?

        Blacks 35.8%   Asians 12.7%   Whites 20.7%

2.   What percentage of each group has low intelligence?

        Blacks 24.09% Asians 12.8%   Whites 16.9%

3.   What percentage of each group has a tendency to steal?

        Blacks 29.3%   Asians 15.2%   Whites 20.3%

4.   What percentage of each group has a tendency to drink too much?

        Blacks 29.2%   Asians 15.1%   Whites 28.9%

5.   What percentage of each group has a tendency to take illegal drugs?

        Blacks 29.4%   Asians 13.6%   Whites 22.9%

6.   What percentage of each group has a tendency to be violent?

        Blacks 31.9%   Asians 14.2%   Whites 22.8%

7.   What percentage of each group has a tendency to act impulsively?

        Blacks 32.4%   Asians 16.7%   Whites 27.3%

8.   What percentage of each group has a tendency to be illiterate?

        Blacks 28.5%   Asians 10.7%   Whites 18.2%

9.   What percentage of each group has babies born to unwed mothers?

        Blacks 35.3%   Asians 11.6%   Whites 21.7%

10.   What percentage of each group has been convicted of a violent crime?

        Blacks 27.8%   Asians 11.4%   Whites 18.5%

11.   What percentage of each group are racist?

        Blacks 48.8%   Asians 32.4%   Whites 47.9%

Source: Based on original research by authors.

basic conclusions about the nature of stereotypical beliefs. First, whites attribute negative traits only to a minority of blacks. Second, their estimates are in line with the known facts about the particular traits in question, but they also tend to underestimate the size of the gap between the races. For example, government statistics tell us that 9.1 percent of whites and 33.4 percent of blacks are on some form of means-tested welfare, which is more pronounced than the student estimates of 20.7 and 35.8 percent in our study. With regard to the problem of criminality, Greenfeld reports 3 percent of white males will serve time in jail or prison, whereas the comparable figure for black males is 18 percent. As for births to unwed mothers, the respondents likewise underestimated the actual difference between the races. In fact, in 1988 it was approximately 45 percent rather than 15 percent.[29] Similarly, larger gaps are found in the official records of test score performances for literacy, intelligence, and so on, than in the student estimates.[30] Third, the average gap between blacks and whites in the college sample is not very great. In other words, whites do not appear to perceive that marked differences between the races exist. It ought to be noted in passing that whites depict Asians more favorably than their own race, which also suggests that stereotypes tend toward accuracy.

A basic question arises in this connection: Is it just to denounce as racist, prejudiced, and/or irrational those citizens who hold negative typifications if their typifications describe an "appropriate" or "realistic" subset of the behaviors or values of the minority group in question and, moreover, if majority beliefs are consistent with a broad range of established evidence and personal experience? We think not, especially since both whites and blacks often reach similar conclusions—for instance, the finding that almost as many blacks (18 percent) as whites (21 percent) in a National Opinion Research Corporation (NORC) survey believe that blacks possess less desirable jobs, incomes, and housing on average because "blacks have less inborn ability to learn."[31] This willingness to subscribe to a painful stereotype suggests that what is generally considered the enlightened or compassionate view may be somewhat misplaced, especially when many individuals in each race tend to reach similar stereotypical conclusions. The willingness of so many black Americans to endorse negative stereotypes, of course, implies the deep psychological scars of historical experience, but it may also say something about the experiential source and accuracy of stereotypes. Indeed, blacks are more likely than whites to agree with negative statements. In the 1991 National Race survey, to take still another example, 34 percent of the whites and 39 percent of the blacks characterized blacks as being "lazy." In this case, the opinion gap was relatively small. In others, however, it can be rather large, as when 21 percent of the whites and 40 percent of the blacks described blacks as being "irresponsible."[32]

In other words, since we humans must of necessity employ typologies to apprehend reality, it is to be expected that both blacks and whites will often subscribe to similar types and that their types, furthermore, will roughly correspond to known differences between the races. It is no more racist to infer from the record of poor schooling that the average black is less cognitively skilled (less literate or numerate) than is the average white than it is to assume that, as based on reports of victims who saw the individual who robbed or raped them, the average black is more likely to commit these crimes than is the average white. A similar logic applies to other racial disparities, including income and family differences.

It ought to go without saying that this discussion leaves aside the *source* of differences in cognitive skills. The NORC survey found that some whites and blacks believe that the differences are due to hereditary or genetic factors. Most members of both races, however, do not accept this interpretation. In fact, surveys show that many whites attribute skill differences to educational deficiencies, which, of course, can be remedied.

In sum, as our approach to race relations predicts, few whites apparently believe that stereotypes are applicable to a majority of blacks. On the other hand, whites do have some empirical grounds for a variety of the negative opinions that they have formed. Nevertheless, they do not ordinarily attribute these differences to race as such. Hence, when important differences in skills and culture begin to recede, their attitudes will also undergo a transformation. So long as real disparities remain, however, they will in all likelihood take them into account and draw the inevitable distinctions.

This discussion poses a sobering challenge to advocates of the conventional wisdom, convinced as they are that race relations can be manipulated by indoctrinating whites with "correct" thinking. To the extent that stereotypes are consonant with perceived reality, attempts to reform the public, however well meaning, will simply meet resistance. Neither media propaganda nor sensitivity training on college campuses and in corporations will prevent most individuals from developing typologies that more or less reflect the realities of their environments as they perceive them to be.

Nothing said so far is intended to deny the harmful consequences that stereotypes can produce. Indeed, to some extent, they may contribute to the very problems that give rise to them in the first place. Using as their subjects black undergraduates with well-above-average verbal aptitude scores on their SATs at Stanford University, social psychologists Claude Steele and Joshua Aronson observed that average black performance on standardized items of verbal aptitude was lower if their black subjects were initially informed that their mental abilities were being measured. Conversely, black students did much better on the same items if they were told prior to the examination that the test measured another kind of attribute. The scores of comparable white students were not affected by the manner in which the test was described.

It seems that the mere possibility of doing poorly on tests of cognitive ability creates anxiety and fear sufficiently strong to impair intellectual performance. Steele and Aronson speculate that self-doubts and fears associated with stereotypes about the relative abilities of the two races "[contribute] powerfully to the pattern of group differences that have characterized these tests since their inception."[33] It is indeed probable that such fears exert a negative influence on the average black score. But the solution they so clearly prescribe seems rather utopian. In attributing black fears to a white propensity to subscribe to stereotypes of black inferiority, they ask that the majority eliminate their negative assessments.

A fundamental problem remains, at least in the near future—namely, how is it possible to abolish undesirable stereotypes if discrepancies in performance exist and if the general public is aware of these differences? So long as such differences persist, the public—black and white alike—is likely to see them as evidence of significant gaps in ability. Many in each race will suspect that stereotypes are probably relatively accurate depictions of reality. As such, black announcements will often tend to be discounted, thereby fueling the present identity crisis within the black community.

Thus, many black Americans will understandably experience status anxiety whenever cognitive abilities are open to view. But how is it possible to address in any realistic manner an anxiety rooted in what is widely thought to be the measureable "reality" of scientific research? Must one not first close the perceived ability gap upon which stereotypes are based? In calling for the elimination of stereotypes without first eradicating the differences that sustain the types themselves, Steele and Aronson have unfortunately appealed more to effect than to cause and less to reality than to hopes.

ARE WHITES PRISONERS OF THEIR STEREOTYPES?

If whites and blacks often hold negative stereotypes about one another, it does not follow that our stereotypes automatically guide behavior. In fact, most studies find little or no connection between beliefs and behavior.[34] Simply put, people learn from their mistakes and seek better information when existing data prove inadequate to their current plans. Moreover, they are quite capable of changing or temporarily suspending their beliefs if the facts in a particular situation contradict their preconceptions. In other words, humans respond to a wide range of signals and are much more flexible in their attitudes and values than many social commentators like to admit.

Given the complex and subtle nature of human thought, a willingness on the part of the individual to abandon expectations that fail to conform to reality as he or she perceives it ought not to surprise us. Race-related thinking is no exception to the general rule that we respond to a variety of cues in specific kinds of settings. Whites, not surprisingly, will often alter their views and prejudices with regard to black Americans. Thus, they appear to look on their fellow blacks in much the same way as they view members of their own race, namely, as complex individuals who have any number of traits and abilities. A willingness to recognize blacks as unique individuals in their own right irrespective of race is evident in a variety of social science reports, running the gamut from studies about friendship preferences and interracial contacts to works on leadership behavior and majority feelings about blacks who possess skills. Whenever racially neutral attributes such as kinds of skills, similarities in attitudes and interests, and task performance come into play, whites are usually flexible and open to change in their response to minorities. In that prejudice, dislike, and social distance generally decline as minority groups acquire the culture of the dominant group, these findings roughly correspond to the historical record.[35]

Recognition by whites of the particular, or special, attributes of individual blacks is found in virtually all research on the so-called contact hypothesis of racial attitudes. This hypothesis holds that interracial contact—at work, in school, in the neighborhood, or in an apartment complex—reduces majority prejudice, in the process encouraging a respect for the minority group. To explore attitude change, research psychologists brought blacks and whites together within the same physical location and measured the changes in attitudes that followed interracial contact. In most research designs of this sort, researchers anticipated that social interaction under all conditions would produce more positive attitudes about minorities. On the other hand, in his initial formulation of the contact hypothesis, psychologist Gordon Allport stipulated "equal status contact" as a prerequisite necessary for a favorable shift in racial attitudes. By "equal status" he suggested that minorities must have characteristics similar to those of the majority group such as comparable occupations, social skills, literacy, and grades.[36] His assumption, of course, was that whites would be more likely to respond to those attributes that they themselves value more highly. And presumably, they would be able to assess the traits with some degree of accuracy.

Most researchers, however, observed contact under two stipulated conditions—namely, in those cases when the whites had superior status and when both races were of equal status. After hundreds of studies, the record overwhelmingly supports Allport's equal status hypothesis as a necessary condition if interracial contacts are to lead to positive changes in white attitudes.[37]

Conversely, when lower-status minority members interacted with higher-status whites, negative stereotypes persisted.[38] One study of white soldiers who worked with black soldiers during World War II illustrates the marked influence of status differences on the attitudes of whites. Only 5 percent of the white soldiers who worked with unskilled blacks had a favorable attitude toward blacks in general. Yet fully 64 percent of those soldiers who were acquainted or who worked with skilled black soldiers held positive opinions.[39] In other words, majority group members appear to evaluate blacks according to their perceived mastery of the styles, skills, and abilities valued by whites. To the extent that minorities display these desirable attributes, whites, it seems, evaluate them in a positive manner. We may safely conclude that the concrete attributes of minorities, as opposed to stereotypical preconceptions, are at the heart of white assessments of individuals from other races.

Whites do not only esteem skills. A perception of kindred values, interests, and beliefs also appears to influence their assessments of individual blacks. That is, whites prefer those blacks who appear to have values and interests similar to their own. Milton Rokeach, perhaps the foremost student of attitudes, has conducted a series of studies on preferences for work, friendship, and discussion partners. He consistently finds that people prefer to associate with those whose interests are similar to their own. Confronted with a choice of associating with a black who has similar attitudes and beliefs or with a fellow white with different values, whites overwhelmingly prefer the similar black to the dissimilar white.[40] These results support the general conclusion that whites do not view blacks as a monolithic group. To the contrary, they tend to see the latter as composed of individuals, each of whom is possessed with a unique combination of attributes and inclinations. Hence, much racial prejudice is apparently due to differences in values, attitudes, and norms.[41] These cultural roots of racial conflict, for instance, were observed in an experiment in which whites evaluated a black speaker. Whites rated him more positively if his diction was standard English as opposed to Black English.[42] Such findings suggest that culture, not race per se, resides at the heart of black-white tensions.

To be sure, there is little doubt that characteristics related to social class background contribute to the negative attitudes of white Americans. In several studies, whites attribute positive traits to blacks and whites alike, once they are perceived as belonging to the middle and upper classes. Conversely, negative traits are accorded to members of both races who are felt to be lower class. In fact, the portrait of the white and black lower classes painted by each race is much the same in that people on the bottom rungs of the status hierarchies of each race are seen as less responsible, more impulsive, more criminal, and less ambitious.[43]

In modern societies the possession of cognitive skills is probably the trait most esteemed in the population. We ought not to be astonished, therefore, that research on race relations finds that whites tend to set aside their negative stereotypes once blacks display competence in their tasks, particularly in the more demanding areas. In both natural and laboratory settings, whites have repeatedly altered their expectations, attitudes, and behavior once blacks were seen to be competent workers.[44] That they tend to evaluate blacks in a positive manner after exposure to experimental manipulations, for instance, in which whites on film were observed working on a project with a skilled black is hardly surprising. Such studies indicate that minority group members who can call on valued sorts of talents will win the respect of whites. That whites subsequently change their behavior (e.g., that they cede more initiative and decision-making authority to skilled blacks) suggests that in acknowledging black competence whites are willing to show them deference and respect. Even whites who joined the experiments with negative stereotypes changed their perceptions once they were presented with contrary evidence. So under experimental conditions, whites and blacks based their behavior not on racial stereotypes but on their assessments of the qualities of the individual, irrespective of his or her race.[45]

Taken in their entirety, these studies suggest that blacks as well as whites have relatively low expectations about black group achievements, which, given the former's historical record of relatively low average educational attainments, is to be expected. But once contrary information is presented, both races, by coming to accept the new facts at hand, either set aside or change their historical stereotypes.

Thus, contrary to the conventional wisdom found in so much of our contemporary race relations literature, it may just be possible that whites can ignore their own stereotypes and respond to blacks as specific individuals. Social psychologist Anne Locksley, in the abstract language of social psychology, provides an explanation for this apparent phenomenon that entertains the commonsense truth that people simply take the world as it presents itself to their minds subjectively. After all, adjustment to one's environment would compel normal people to bring their subjective worlds into some conformity with their "objective" ones over the long run. Otherwise, adaptability to one's surroundings would prove exceedingly difficult. "Research in the psychology of prediction," she argues, "has demonstrated that people often neglect prior probabilities (based on past experiences) when making predictions about individuals, especially when individuating information about the person is subjectively diagnostic of the criterion [behavior]."[46] In other words, people may readily set aside their negative typifications—or stereotypes and gross generalizations, to employ two terms much in use—if their experiences in a specific situation fail to confirm the stereotype. As we have said, they do this by placing the minority individual in an appropriate subtype.

Let us take an example from everyday experience. Assume that a white man enters a restaurant where he is served by a black waiter. The waiter proceeds to adopt an indifferent attitude toward his table. He fails to attend promptly to his guest's requests for water and coffee, unduly delays bringing the dessert following the meal, uses improper speech, and generally makes a poor impression on the patron. It is quite likely that the white man, if inclined to stereotypical thinking about race, may tell himself that the service he is receiving is only what he ought to have expected in the first place, reasoning perhaps that blacks are more likely to be "irresponsible." He has placed this waiter in the subtype "irresponsible blacks."

On the other hand, let us assume a different scenario; namely, that upon entering the establishment, our same white man is served by a black waiter who promptly sees to his needs, is extremely courteous and "well spoken," and in general gives every indication of being a diligent, ambitious person. In that event it is quite possible that the white man will proceed to set aside his prior unflattering stereotype, telling himself that this young man is a "responsible black." Moreover, even if he never completely conquers his tendency to "generalize," it by no means follows that he can be any less open-minded and receptive in his relations with individual black people than will those more upright whites who profess, let us say, "to be without stereotypes."

Are employers likely to be as flexible in the way they respond to the traits of individuals as social science research suggests? The little evidence we have implies that indeed they are. For instance, in a study of the recruitment strategies and decisions of Chicago-area employers, sociologists Kathryn Neckerman and Joleen Kirschenman found that employers who tested for skills with standardized tests recruited twice as many black employees as did employers who did not administer tests.[47] The authors concluded that employers who do not use objective indicators of ability tend to presume that blacks are less able than whites. Ironically, it was their fear of discrimination lawsuits that led them to abandon testing.

Conversely, employers apparently will ignore their negative views once ability can be demonstrated by evidence from tests. In fact, they tend to respond positively to a variety of indicators, including recommendations from trusted colleagues and the kinds of schools from which potential recruits matriculated (namely, graduation from Catholic or suburban high schools). Once they are in possession of what they see as pertinent information about their prospective employee's potential for success, they tend to revise their negative opinions (assuming they held them in the first place). In other words, they will alter the contents of their typifications, eliminate them altogether, or set them temporarily aside by creating subtypes. If it is the latter, they may rely on more specific kinds of data in their evaluations of black recruits, such as whether the prospect is a Catholic school graduate or whether he or she scores well on a job-related test.

ARE WHITE STEREOTYPES ERADICABLE?

If we mean by this question, Is it possible to eliminate stereotyping from the human mind? the answer is plainly in the negative. As we have attempted to demonstrate, the process of stereotyping is in essence no different from what Schutz called typing. The mind of necessity must categorize or group mental phenomena from a wealth of sense impressions and recollections, for categorization is inseparable from human thought and action. Accordingly, a stereotype may be benign or harmful in its effects on others. But once we label a type a stereotype, to be sure, we more or less automatically transform it into a construct potentially fraught with moral impact and social meaning. For by charging another individual with stereotyping, the accuser usually hopes to gain the moral high ground at the expense of the accused. If the accused expresses a particular gesture, attitude, or statement about a group in a manner another individual labels as stereotypical, and hence objectionable, the terms of discussion and the debate are changed. This process is less paradoxical than may be supposed at first glance in that each side, after all, is engaging in typifying, which is essential to thinking. From this standpoint, a stereotype is merely a type that we may dislike. Meaning and morality, as well as social and political power, naturally determine whether the charge of stereotyping will stick.

If, however, we were to ask whether it is possible to eliminate particular kinds of stereotypes thought to be false and invidious, then the answer is yes. We learn from past experience, and we can change our minds, although we do so in different degrees and with different frequencies. Be that as it may, experiences that contradict a negative stereotype about racial, ethnic, or religious groups may lead us to forsake it altogether, set it aside for particular purposes, or create subtypes, the effects of which are to undermine substantially the strength of the type itself. It is the latter process that we have stressed as crucial throughout this work.

Let us recall the young woman in our first vignette who crossed the street to avoid the young black man dressed in jeans and T-shirt. While this pedestrian is unlikely to know that blacks are 13 times more likely than whites to commit robbery, or 7.5 times as likely to commit rape, she is aware that blacks are more likely on average to commit such crimes than are whites. By censoring all news accounts, we could conceivably keep this knowledge from the general public, but by restricting access to information, we also violate the tenets of a free society. Moreover, were we able to keep this information from the media, we could hardly eliminate word-of-mouth transmission. Indeed, gossip might well encourage people to make even more invidious distinctions than already exist among the populace.

Perhaps in order not to offend the black pedestrian, we might insist that she suppress any inclination to cross the street. After all, if she continues her walk on the same side, she only increases slightly her chances of becoming a statistic. So in the interest of good race relations, perhaps she ought willingly to accept the risk. This advice is sometimes proffered by those well-meaning individuals in academia and the media who worry much about minority citizens being offended when ordinary whites take precautions out of what is regarded as an obsessive fear for their life and property.

This recommendation appears to be reasonable and productive of good race relations, but it ignores human psychology. By crossing the road, our pedestrian reduces her fear of unwanted aggression. If public officials and other elites insist that she ignore her fears and anxieties merely to save the young man embarrassment, will she not resent the greater solicitude for the black man's feelings than concern for her physical safety? And there is another reason to expect a backfire. As a general rule, the more fear we associate with a stimulus, the greater our dislike for it. Thus, when we seek to improve race relations by making others ashamed for what they regard merely as prudential attempts to preserve their own well-being, our opinion leaders run the risk of stimulating an even greater inclination to avoid blacks. (And by engaging in sophistical sleight of hand, for example, by quoting statistics to the effect that *total* black crime in America is less than *total* white crime, we will hardly reduce the propensity of whites to stereotype as long as they feel more threatened by the typical young black male than by his typical white counterpart.) In short, we cannot alter the young woman's stereotypes without making her even more aware of its source. In a similar vein, our store clerk knows from experience that young, casually dressed black women are relatively less likely to purchase merchandise but are more likely to shoplift than are their white customers. In the interest of eliminating situations that are potentially embarrassing to black customers, perhaps store clerks and managers ought to refrain from making such distinctions. But how do we compel them to abandon types that they not only believe to be true but also regard as helpful in the pursuit of their legitimate interests? As long as the typical white is perceived as less likely to steal than is the typical black, we can expect store clerks to construct stereotypes reflecting these "facts" as they see them.

Thus, efforts to coerce people into abandoning their stereotypes through social pressure may impose unacceptable costs on the targeted group. Resentments almost inevitably arise when people are pressured to forget what they in fact believe to be true. Many merchants and employees are convinced that they have a duty to protect their merchandise from theft by surveilling those whom they regard as potential thieves. Is not a defense of property a basic right? If that right is abridged in a manner regarded by whites as inimical to their fundamental rights in order to appease minority sensibilities, it is likely to exacerbate race relations over the long run.

One area of public policy in which minority demands and majority property rights are sure to collide with increasing frequency is affirmative action. Society may rightfully ask employers, say the proponents of racial preferences, to incur additional costs and risks by hiring employees many regard to be less qualified. It is said that even if race-neutral standards produce a more productive workforce, the social benefits of affirmative action would outweigh the economic costs. Leaving aside the highly questionable proposition that the social benefits of affirmative action exist, many intelligent people are sincerely convinced that race relations can be improved by government-imposed allocations of more desirable positions through quota schemes.[48] A rise in the number of prestigious positions held by black

Americans, it is argued with much sincerity, will enhance their social status. Additionally, it will provide appropriate role models for the young not only by raising black status and income but by strengthening social cohesion between the races. Stereotypes will simply wither away in the process.

Here we pose an obvious question, which we will address in more detail in the next chapter: Why should race-based preferences of any kind conduce to interracial harmony? Quota systems aimed against whites, however limited, increase the belief among the majority that they are the victims of "reverse discrimination" in that blacks are unjustly awarded positions for which they are either unqualified or at least less qualified than available whites. Not only is morale likely to suffer in the workplace when racial hiring is practiced, but marginal productivity will fall as inadequate workers must be eventually dismissed and their replacements trained (or, as is sometimes the case in white-collar occupations, shifted to less demanding or "make-work" roles so that employers can avoid government scrutiny).

Employers for their part are not completely helpless in the face of such pressures. The rising costs of racial hiring can only make them more sensitive to problems of the workplace once they are compelled to employ more inefficient or expensive labor. In fact, some even suspect that this sensitivity has encouraged employers to move plants and jobs to new locations away from areas populated by minorities. How the resulting unemployment will benefit blacks as a group is not clear, and how compulsion of employers to hire minorities with lower qualifications can eliminate the tendency to stereotype is never specified. But it seems very unlikely to change the attitudes of whites.[49]

In general, research and common sense alike tell us that white beliefs tend to improve when whites work with blacks of roughly equal status and competence. Conversely, white employees and supervisors who work with less competent blacks can be expected to have little respect for the beneficiaries of preferential hiring. Far from undermining the plausibility of stereotypes, these policies confirm in white minds the validity of forbidden beliefs.

CONCLUSION

Our approach to human action argues that the nature of stereotyping is much more complex than the conventional wisdom allows. Most certainly, whites (and blacks) do in fact regularly stereotype; but they do so in a manner that allows them to respond to blacks as individuals with unique combinations of traits. That is, few stereotype by placing all blacks in a specific category; rather, most place blacks (and whites and Asians, for that matter) in various subtypes. It is this subtyping that facilitates responding to members of out-groups as individuals and frees whites from servitude to stereotypes in everyday interactions with blacks.

Consequently, while stereotyping inevitably occurs, it need not lead to discrimination whenever individuating information is available. The tendency to assess blacks as individuals is reinforced in the workplace by a combination of social pressures, government regulations, and market forces, which operating together appear to have all but eliminated discrimination on the grounds of race. So racism is no longer a major barrier to black socioeconomic progress.[50]

One implication of our analysis of stereotyping and discrimination is that to the extent that stereotypes reflect empirically valid differences in the attributes associated with the races, we cannot expect to alter the attitudes of whites by simply denouncing them as stereotypical. If, for instance, blacks on average are in fact less numerate or literate, many whites will be cognizant of the disparity in skills. It is therefore futile to attempt to change white attitudes without first transforming the underlying realities that inform race-related beliefs in America today. Attacking the attitudes of whites in the absence of a marked improvement in the lifestyles and capacities of lower-class blacks is an unproductive endeavor, no matter how well intentioned the aims of the reformers. To put it in direct terms, since the white man's attitudes are not the problem, reform of those attitudes is not the solution.

We do not argue that prejudice, discrimination, and consciousness of race disappeared during the 1970s and 1980s. Apart from the public world of business, government, and commerce, race is a primary "social fact of life." That many whites oppose intermarriage and rarely socialize with blacks or attend interracial churches are not unimportant data. Eleven o'clock Sunday morning is now less segregated, but it still remains the most segregated hour of the week. Whites also continue to resist black entry into country clubs and other social organizations. But the public world in which impersonal and achievement-oriented criteria prevail to a much higher degree is more receptive to the interests of blacks than ever. After all, on-the-job relations are ultimately related to performance even in a less-than-perfect world.[51]

But in the final analysis, employers recruit fewer blacks proportionately than whites for more preferred positions and promote fewer blacks for the same reasons that Harvard and Berkeley graduate proportionately fewer blacks than whites and Asians. Simply stated, whether they are students or employees, blacks all too frequently lack the basic tools necessary for competition in school and in the marketplace.

Fundamental reforms must aim at preparing blacks to compete. Many leaders, of course, vigorously disagree. Given their assumption of an entrenched white racism, they envision a great moral struggle in which white America is purged of its irrational stereotypes and prejudice. Oddly enough, this moral crusade has already been waged and mostly won. Yet the civil rights establishment and its white allies insist that stereotyping whites are the fundamental source of ills in the black community.

This persistence in error is rooted in more than mere inertia. At the very least, the obsession with white attitudes is the seed bed that nurtures the spread of affirmative action. The reason for this is not hard to grasp. If it can be shown (or asserted) that stereotypes lead to discrimination, then victimologists can argue plausibly that only affirmative action can remedy the so-called underrepresentation of blacks in the better positions. And of course the attack on stereotypes by victimologists is an effective weapon with which to silence the critics of racial preferences, who perforce must argue that stereotypes do indeed capture real differences in black and white preparation. In this way, the Victim Vision of race relations is inextricably tied to the debate over affirmative action, a debate to which we now turn.

NOTES

1. One cultural practice relevant to manual work is the apparent racial difference in the use of tools at home. Homeownership statistics show 44.4 percent of blacks own a home and 67.8 percent of whites. U.S. Bureau of the Census, *Statistical Abstract of the United States: 1992*, 112th ed., (Washington, D.C.: Government Printing Office, 1992), p. 716. Thus, compared to blacks, whites are 52 percent more likely to own a home, but they are 247 percent more likely to own an electric saw, 182 percent more likely to own an electric drill, and 125 percent more likely to own a spray painter. Simmons Market Research Bureau, *1990 Study of Media and Markets—P8* (New York: Simmons Market Research Bureau, 1990), pp. 442, 446.

2. Research in the area of friendship and attraction finds consistently that people are attracted to others with similar attitudes and values. For a discussion, see Don Byrne, *The Attraction Paradigm* (New York: Academic Press, 1971); and David G. Myers, *Social Psychology* (New York: McGraw-Hill, 1990), chap. 13.

3. For an introduction to Schutz's work, see Alfred Schutz, *On Phenomenology and Social Relations*, ed. Helmut R. Wagner (Chicago: University of Chicago Press, 1970).

4. For example, see Francesca M. Cancian, *What Are Norms? A Study of Beliefs and Action in a Maya Community* (London: Cambridge University Press, 1975); and Ann Swidler, "Culture in Action: Symbols and Strategies," *American Sociological Review* 51 (April 1986): 273–86.

5. See, especially, Ludwig von Mises, *Human Action: A Treatise on Economics*, 3rd rev. ed. (Chicago: Henry Regnery, 1966); Murray N. Rothbard, *Man, Economy, and State: A Treatise on Economic Principles* (Princeton, N.J.: Van Nostrand, 1962); Schutz, *On Phenomenology and Social Relations*; and Bernard P. Dauenhauer, "Making Plans and Lived Time," *Southern Journal of Philosophy* 7 (Spring 1969): 83–90.

6. Ludwig M. Lachmann, *The Legacy of Max Weber* (London: Heineman, 1970), pp. 20, 30; also his "From Mises to Shackle: An Essay on Austrian Economics and the Kaleidic Society," *Journal of Economic Literature* 14 (March 1976):

54–61; and T. Alexander Smith, "A Phenomenology of the Policy Process," *International Journal of Comparative Sociology* 23 (March-June 1982): 1–16.

7. See Mises, *Human Action*, p. 106.

8. Ibid., 107.

9. As quoted in Fritz Machlup, "Homo Oeconomicus and His Class Mates," in Maurice Natanson, ed., *Phenomenology and Social Reality* (The Hague: Martinus Nijhoff, 1990), p. 135.

10. For an introduction to the concept of the "stock of knowledge," see Peter L. Berger and Thomas Luckmann, *The Social Construction of Reality* (Garden City, N.Y.: Doubleday, 1967).

11. For a discussion of the cognitive approach in academic social psychology to stereotype construction, see David Hamilton, ed., "Stereotyping and Intergroup Behavior: Some Thoughts on the Cognitive Approach," in David Hamilton, ed., *Cognitive Processes in Stereotyping and Intergroup Behavior* (Hillsdale, N.J.: Lawrence Erlbaum, 1981), pp. 333–53; and Richard Ashmore and Frances Del Boca, "Conceptual Approaches to Stereotypes and Stereotyping," in Hamilton, *Cognitive Processes*, pp. 1–35.

12. See Schutz, *On Phenomenology and Social Relations*, p. 119.

13. Ibid., p. 117.

14. See Alfred Schutz, *Collected Papers II: Studies in Social Theory*, ed. Arvid Brodersen (The Hague: Martinus Nijhoff, 1971), p. 286.

15. Our italics. See Schutz, *On Phenomenology and Social Relations*, p. 117.

16. Ibid., p. 134.

17. In contrast, only 9.1 percent of whites receive some combination of means-tested assistance (Aid to Families with Dependent Children [AFDC], supplementary security income [SSI], food stamps, Medicaid, housing assistance). U.S. Bureau of the Census, *Statistical Abstract of the United States: 1995*, 115th ed. (Washington, D.C.: Government Printing Office, 1995), p. 378.

18. For a good discussion of these problems, see Margaret S. Archer, "The Myth of Cultural Integration," *British Journal of Sociology* 36 (September 1985): 333–53.

19. See Anthony Gary Dworkin and Rosalind J. Dworkin, *The Minority Report* (New York: Holt, Rinehart and Winston, 1982), p. 69.

20. See Walter Lippmann, *Public Opinion* (New York: Free Press, 1965), p. 3.

21. Ibid., pp. 10, 55.

22. See Marlene Mackey, "Arriving at Truth by Definition: The Case of Stereotype Inaccuracy," *Social Problems* 20 (1973): 431–47.

23. For example, George E. Simpson and J. Milton Yinger, *Racial and Cultural Minorities* (New York: Plenum, 1985).

24. The classic study of stereotypes is Daniel Katz and Kenneth Braly, "Racial Stereotypes in One Hundred College Students," *Journal of Abnormal and Social Psychology* 28 (1933): 280–91.

25. In the language of cognitive theory, stereotypes are a "schema," an organized configuration of knowledge derived from past experience that people use to interpret their current experience. For extended discussions, see Hamilton, *Cognitive Processes*; also see P. J. Oakes, S. A. Haslam, and J. C. Turner, *Stereotyping and Social Reality* (Oxford, England: Basil Blackwell, 1994). Some writers even maintain that people use types in all activities in much the same way. Fritz Machlup,

for instance, refers to types as "ideal types": "There is no essential difference in the construction of ideal types as commonsense concepts of ordinary people and as scientific concepts of the historian or social scientist." See Machlup, "Homo Oeconomicus and His Class Mates," p. 135.

26. For example, studies finding that people tend to make percentage estimates include John C. Brigham, "Ethnic Stereotypes," *Psychological Bulletin* 76 (1971): 15–38; idem, "Ethnic Stereotypes and Attitudes: A Different Mode of Analysis," *Journal of Personality* 41 (1973): 206–33; and Clark McCauley and Christopher Stitt, "An Individual and Quantitative Measure of Stereotypes," *Journal of Personality and Social Psychology* 36 (September 1978): 929–40.

27. See the University of Colorado doctoral dissertation of John C. Brigham, *Ethnic Stereotypes, Attitudes, and Treatment of Ethnic Group Members*, No. 70-5822 (Ann Arbor, Mich.: University Microfilms, 1969); also see the comments of Lee J. Jussim, Clark R. McCauley, and Yueh-Ting Lee, "Why Study Stereotype Accuracy and Inaccuracy?" in Yueh-Ting Lee, Lee J. Jussim, and Clark R. McCauley, eds., *Stereotype Accuracy: Toward Appreciating Group Differences* (Washington, D.C.: American Psychological Association, 1995), p. 7.

28. See McCauley and Stitt, "An Individual and Quantitative Measure of Stereotypes."

29. See Bureau of the Census, *Statistical Abstract of the United States: 1995*. For births to unwed mothers, see Andrew Hacker, *Two Nations: Black and White, Separate, Hostile and Unequal* (New York: Charles Scribner, 1992), p. 80. For estimates of black and white rates of imprisonment, see Lawrence Greenfeld, *Measuring the Application and Use of Punishment* (Washington, D.C.: National Institute of Justice, 1981), p. 48.

30. June O'Neil, James Cunningham, Andy Sparks, and Hal Sider, *The Economic Progress of Black Men in America* (Washington, D.C.: U.S. Commission on Civil Rights, 1986).

31. National Opinion Research Corporation, *The General Social Survey* (Chicago: University of Chicago, 1986).

32. Survey results as reported in Paul Sniderman and Thomas Piazza, *The Scar of Race* (Cambridge, Mass.: Harvard University Press, 1993), p. 45.

33. See Claude M. Steele and Joshua Aronson, "Stereotype Threat and the Intellectual Test Performance of African Americans," *Journal of Personality and Social Psychology* 69 (November 1995): 810.

34. For a review of the literature on the connection between attitudes and behavior, see Richard J. Hill, "Attitudes and Behavior," in Morris Rosenberg and Ralph H. Turner, eds., *Social Psychology: Sociological Perspectives* (New York: Basic Books, 1981).

35. See Thomas Sowell, *Ethnic America: A History* (New York: Basic Books, 1981).

36. See Gordon Allport, *The Nature of Prejudice* (New York: Addison-Wesley, 1954), p. 9.

37. In two comprehensive reviews of the extensive research literature on the contact hypothesis, Amir concluded that equal status contact, which was usually defined in terms of similar type of skill or years of education, was an essential ingredient in positive attitudinal change. See Yehuda Amir, "Contact Hypothesis in Ethnic Relations," *Psychological Bulletin* 71 (May 1969): 319–42; idem, "The

Role of Intergroup Contact in Change of Prejudice and Ethnic Relations," in Phyllis Katz, ed., *Towards the Elimination of Racism* (New York: Pergamon Press, 1976), pp. 245–308.

38. D. Wilder, "Intergroup Contact: The Typical Member and the Exception to the Rule," *Journal of Experimental and Social Psychology* 20 (1984): 177–94.

39. See B. K. Mackenzie, "The Importance of Contact in Determining Attitudes towards Negroes," *Journal of Abnormal and Social Psychology* 43 (1948): 417–41.

40. See Milton Rokeach and Louis Mezei, "Race and Shared Belief as Factors in Social Distance," *Science* 151 (January 1966): 167–72; Jefferey Moe, Rupert Nacoste, and Chester Insko, "Belief versus Race as Determinants of Discrimination: A Study of Southern Adolescents in 1966 and 1979," *Journal of Personality and Social Psychology* 41 (1981): 1031–50; C. Hendrik, P. Stikes, E. Murray, and C. Puthoff, "Race versus Belief as Determinants of Attraction in a Group Interaction Context," *Memory and Cognition* 1 (1973): 41–46.

41. See Milton Rokeach, *Beliefs, Attitudes, and Values* (San Francisco: Jossey-Bass, 1968).

42. D. McKirnan, J. Smith, and E. Hamayan, "A Sociolinguistic Approach to the Belief-Similarity Model of Racial Attitudes," *Journal of Experimental and Social Psychology* 19 (1983): 434–47.

43. Studies more than 20 years apart show many, if not most, stereotypes are based more upon class than race. For example, James A. Bayton, L. B. McAlister, and J. Hamer, "Race-Class Stereotypes," *Journal of Negro Education* 25 (1956): 75–78; Joseph Smedley and James A. Bayton, "Evaluative Race-Class Stereotypes by Race and Perceived Class of Subjects," *Journal of Personality and Social Psychology* 36 (1978): 530–35.

44. See Elizabeth Cohen, "Expectation States and Interracial Interaction in School Settings," *Annual Review of Sociology* 8 (1982): 209–35; Elizabeth Cohen and Susan Roper, "Modification of Interracial Interaction Disability: An Application of Status Characteristic Theory," *American Sociological Review* 37 (December 1972): 643–57.

45. We have known for some time that an individual's assessment of another person can be quite accurate. For example, Richard Clarke and Donald Campbell in a 1955 study found that perceptions of the likely intelligence of black individuals were significantly correlated with the latters' classroom grades, whether the perceiver was white (r. = .56) or black (r. = .47). Richard B. Clarke and Donald T. Campbell, "A Demonstration of Bias in Estimation of Negro Ability," *Journal of Abnormal and Social Psychology* 51 (1955): 585–88.

46. Anne Locksley, Eugene Borgida, Nancy Brekke, and Christine Hepburn, "Sex Stereotypes and Social Judgement," *Journal of Personality and Social Psychology* 39 (November 1990): 821–31. Our ability to respond to such individuating information is well established. A recent review of the research concluded that "perceivers rarely completely disregard individuating information about a social category member." See Victor Ottati and Yueh-Ting Lee, "Accuracy: A Neglected Component of Stereotype Research," in Lee, Jussim, and McCauley, *Stereotype Accuracy*, p. 45. For a general consideration of the problem of "intersubjectivity," one ought to consult the works of Peter Berger and Alfred Schutz, previously cited.

47. Kathryn M. Neckerman and Joleen Kirschenman, "Hiring Strategies, Racial

Bias and Inner-City Workers: An Investigation of Employers' Hiring Decisions" (paper presented at the American Sociological Society meetings, Washington, D.C., August 1990).

48. For example, see James M. Buchanan, *Cost and Choice* (Chicago: Markham, 1969).

49. Christopher Jencks, *Rethinking Social Policy* (Cambridge, Mass.: Harvard University Press, 1992), p. 54.

50. Margery Austin Turner, Michael Fix, and Raymond Struyk, *Opportunities Denied, Opportunities Diminished: Racial Discrimination in Hiring* (Washington, D.C.: The Urban Institute Press, 1991), pp. 38, 57. This recent Urban Institute study seems to illustrate the relatively mild effects of discrimination. The institute sent out carefully matched pairs of black and white job applicants from similar educational backgrounds into the community to apply for the same advertised position. Each individual in a pair had the same credentials and work histories. They were also matched for physical size, interviewing skills, and so on. Twenty-nine percent of the white applicants and 19 percent of the black applicants were offered employment. There were no differences in starting pay. The relatively small amount of discrimination detected by the study probably extends the average employment search of black job seekers by a week or two, which means low wages and high unemployment have more fundamental causes. For a discussion with regard to the ability of minorities to compete and succeed, see Andrew Greeley, "The Ethnic Miracle," *Public Interest* 45 (1976): 20–36.

51. See, for example, William H. Hutt, *The Economics of the Colour Bar* (London: André Deutsch, 1964); also see idem, *The Strike-Threat System* (Arlington, Va.: Arlington House, 1973).

5

The Case against Affirmative Action

No public policy associated with race evokes greater controversy than what is called affirmative action. Unlike school busing, which began to recede into the background once its disruptive effects were felt by blacks and whites alike, the debate over racial preferences refuses to abate. To this day, middle-class blacks, white liberals, and not a few conservatives remain steadfast in their support for it, whereas the vast majority of whites are opposed although unable to resist its relentless advance.

Affirmative action is a perplexing issue for the social scientist. It certainly means different things to people all across the political spectrum, particularly among the more educated and aware groups. Yet the many understandings of the term notwithstanding, when an inquirer asks Americans to describe how affirmative action works in practice, he or she frequently receives two broad kinds of answers. Those who dislike it tend to argue that it violates the fundamental principle that employers ought always to hire the most qualified person, irrespective of race, religion, or whatever. They may proceed at that point to mention a particular event in their own experience in which a member of a minority group received special consideration, although he or she was in truth less qualified than were various white applicants. On the other hand, those who favor affirmative action tend to avoid the matter of qualifications, arguing that it provides a meaningful equality of opportunity by creating a more level playing field for the disadvantaged. Hopefully, through enlightened social policy, the historical "scars of racism" or other forms of discrimination will be erased.

Despite the controversy and the opposition it generates, affirmative action has put its indelible stamp on American institutions to such an extent that it is now engrained in the daily operations of our organizational life. To be sure, until recently there has been little open resistance. And given the innumerable reports of persistent racism in American society, perhaps it is not so odd that the opponents of affirmative action have been incapable of mounting a more effective response to the march of preferential policies. Whatever the reason for its successes, few politicians and journalists, in fact, dared call for its outright abolition before the Republican Party captured the U.S. House of Representatives and Senate in the 1994 congressional elections and a California citizen's group began to collect signatures for a petition to put a proposed ban of affirmative action on the 1996 ballot in that state. Political courage thus followed the election returns, and a short time after the new year, affirmative action suddenly emerged as a major issue on the public agenda.

In Washington, everyone from President Bill Clinton and his top officials to the leaders of the Congressional Black Caucus now admit that affirmative action has its flaws, although they still argue that it will continue to have a valuable role to play. But the admission itself suggests a signal retreat on the part of its supporters. No longer do they so easily occupy the moral high ground, nor do they control the terms of the debate. For the first time in at least 15 years, one can debate the merits of affirmative action in the public arena without fear of becoming a social outcast.[1]

For many, however, affirmative action remains a litmus test of one's human decency. No less a critic than Nathan Glazer, one of our most eloquent critics of racial preferences, concedes that as policy it is flawed, although he cannot quite admit that it ought to be abandoned. "Affirmative action has done precious little to ameliorate these problems [of blacks], but I am concerned that African-Americans will see the abandonment of affirmative action for them as a terrible rejection by an indifferent and hostile society. . . . It would have consequences—for example, a sharp reduction in the number of blacks in selective colleges and professional schools—that we should not accept whatever the value of the principle that justifies them."[2] In other words, even if it is bad policy, it apparently serves some higher good. Glazer suggests that affirmative action ought to be employed to place blacks in elite institutions where they can become role models for younger minority members. Perhaps he believes that if we eliminate affirmative action, we will bring on racial conflict and turmoil in our major cities.

How, then, are we to explain the persistent support of a public policy that leads such scholars as Glazer to defend affirmative action despite its many contradictions? In part, it owes its staying power to good organization in that a number of civil rights and women's groups campaign strenuously for its implementation, whereas few organized groups have waged open warfare against it. It also relies on public inertia and ignorance in that it is widely believed that racial preferences benefit blacks but do little or no harm to other groups. Indeed, most whites are either uninformed or misinformed about the nature and effects of this particular policy. Many individuals are ambivalent as well. They may oppose racial preferences in principle, but they are inclined to believe that blacks benefit materially from them. Hence, they believe that even if other values must be temporarily suspended, in the long run the majority of blacks will be better off and social peace more likely secured. Finally, there is fear of social sanctions in that opposition to affirmative action may earn one the label of racist.[3]

The majority of intellectuals in academia, media, and government are convinced that affirmative action confers substantial psychological and material benefits on blacks in general. But does it? Despite more than 20 years of affirmative action, racial preferences have produced little in the way of constructive results for the mass of black Americans, although we shall see that they have visited a number of political, economic, and social costs upon the general population.

Indeed, the costs of affirmative action are hardly negligible. Although much systematic work about its total cost to the economy remains to be done, a recent preliminary estimate by Peter Brimelow and Leslie Spencer puts the price tag at 4 percent of GDP.[4] For this sacrifice, however, relatively few black Americans appear to have actually profited. It is this failure of one of the great experiments in social engineering in America in this century that needs exploring. Only a full accounting of its real, as opposed to imagined, consequences will liberate the country from its attachment to a policy that may have made race relations worse than otherwise. First, however, we must take a small terminological detour.

A BASIC DISTINCTION: NONDISCRIMINATION AND AFFIRMATIVE ACTION

Although they are sometimes seen as identical concepts, nondiscrimination in employment and affirmative action are different notions. Title 7 of the Civil Rights Act of 1964 outlawed discrimination. Henceforth, the United States would be a "color-blind" society, officially committed to a policy of nondiscrimination. Equality before the law would be guaranteed irrespective of race. Title 7, in effect, instructed employers to hire and promote according to racially neutral criteria of potential job performance (e.g., by the recommendations of previous employers, civil service examination scores, prior work records).

Affirmative action, we must stress, was *not* part of the Civil Rights Act; indeed, as it came to be interpreted by the courts and administrative agencies, it clearly violates the 1964 statute in spirit and letter alike. By supplanting the ideal of "equality of opportunity" with "equality of result," it has placed the rights of preferred groups over those of the individual. Rather than speaking of the individual's right to equal treatment under the law, what is now called affirmative action declares that ethnic groups ought to be proportionately represented in various occupations, university positions, public bureaucracies, and so on. Its goal is to produce that representation in the workforce as well as in the distribution of other coveted resources generally. To take a specific example, if 15 percent of all skilled manual workers in a specific geographical area are black, it tends to *assume* that approximately the same percentage of each employer's skilled workforce ought likewise be black. An employer whose skilled workforce is only 5 percent black is said to be underutilizing or underrepresenting blacks.[5] This assumption that groups should be equally distributed throughout an economy is highly questionable, for, as Thomas Sowell has incontrovertibly demonstrated, ethnic and racial groups are never proportionately distributed. Indeed, quite the reverse is the norm throughout the world: Groups tend to specialize in occupations and industries.[6]

In a word, Title 7 of the 1964 Civil Rights Act unequivocally defined discrimination as a deliberate and intentional act. And that act rejected the revolutionary idea that mere underrepresentation of a particular group in an employer's workforce constituted discrimination.[7] To understand how nondiscrimination was transformed into affirmative action, one must look at the roles played by two government entities—the EEOC and the Office of Federal Contract Compliance (OFCC).[8]

The OFCC, housed in the Department of Labor, has played an especially significant role in the growth of affirmative action. It is responsible for issuing the regulations and guidelines of affirmative action concerning the obligations of companies and universities that hold federal contracts. Which is to say that it writes many of the rules and has responsibility for enforcing them. Thus, in 1968, the OFCC called for a written affirmative action program that required the "identification and analysis" of problem areas in minority employment. When deficiencies in the number of minorities on the payrolls were found, employers were subsequently obliged to develop goals and timetables for the hiring of additional minority members.[9]

Not until December 1971, however, were employers given a specific *numerical* goal to reach in order to be in compliance with the law.[10] Previously, employers could set their own goals and timetables; but after 1971, the goals were set for them. And while companies were not always compelled to meet their specific goals, they were nevertheless expected to display a "good-faith effort" in trying to reach them. The penalties for failure to exhibit a good-faith effort were potentially severe in that fines, loss of contract, and even exclusion from future contracts were possible.

Goals and timetables, it is true, are not technically quotas, but it is hard to deny that employers often pass over better-qualified whites to increase the number of blacks on their payrolls. What we now have is a de facto quota system, or soft quotas, as a more or less subtle device to reduce competitive pressures on minorities from nonpreferred groups. When we discuss the rule of law below, we will explain precisely why specific goals and timetables inevitably lead to racial preferences and what we refer to as soft quotas.

According to sociologist Nathan Glazer, the introduction in 1971 of mandated goals and timetables effectively transformed civil rights policy from ensuring equality of opportunity through nondiscrimination to enforcing equality of result. In retrospect, the transformation of the 1964 Civil Rights Act into "affirmative discrimination" against whites was an inexorable process, as courts, the EEOC, the OFCC and civil rights groups increasingly came to accept racial preferences as legitimate instruments of policy, so long as the favored group could claim a certified victim status.[11] Let us now turn to some of the justifications for a regime of soft quotas.

THE PROMISE OF AFFIRMATIVE ACTION

To justify racial preferences, the advocates of affirmative action usually advance as a foundational premise the assertion that labor markets are heavily biased against the interests of blacks. Their call for preferences rests on the claim that many black Americans cannot obtain positions in line with their skills, training, and abilities. Therefore, to the extent that employers do not allow blacks sufficient opportunities to compete with whites in any meaningful sense, affirmative action provides a necessary counterweight to the discrimination built into the American system of personnel placement. In other words, according to its supporters, affirmative action is fighting fire with fire. Moreover, aside from the question of whether affirmative action is "fair" to whites, its consequences for blacks are thought to be so sufficiently favorable that they far outweigh the inequities, however unfortunate.

The promise of positive results for its intended beneficiaries depends in large part on the extent to which racial bias is excluding qualified blacks from obtaining appropriate positions. Most advocates of affirmative action suppose that blacks are underemployed in low-level positions because racial bias is a ubiquitous obstacle to fair treatment in the labor market. By neutralizing this obstacle, affirmative action is expected to have several benign consequences. At the very least, it should raise the average income of blacks as well as the average prestige level of their occupations. But also, as the contact hypothesis predicts, it should improve race relations by exposing whites to competent middle-class blacks, whose very competence will dispel stereotypes and prejudice. We turn first to the foundational premise that labor markets are biased against minority job seekers.

Labor Markets Are Biased

Two sweeping indictments of the labor market are typically raised: In the first place, personnel policies are supposedly biased against blacks; and second, given the importance of networks of acquaintances in employment recruiting, blacks are placed at a severe disadvantage. Both criticisms reject the idea that employers actively seek to identify the applicants whom they regard as most likely to contribute to the profitability of their firms.

The bias, it is claimed, takes two forms. It may be intentional (referred to in legal theory as "disparate treatment" discrimination) or institutional (referred to in legal theory as "disparate impact" discrimination). As its name implies, intentional discrimination occurs when whites purposely treat the races differently. In contrast, institutional or disparate impact discrimination requires no intention to discriminate, in that it is addressed to the *outcomes* of employer practices and routines that would otherwise be fair on their face.

Although at present they can find very few concrete victims of intentional discrimination, many critics still maintain that employers willfully discriminate against blacks. In her much-praised defense of affirmative action, Gertrude Ezorsky writes, "We need definite numerical goals because . . . hiring procedures . . . can be manipulated by prejudiced personnel officers."[12] Like other proponents of racial preferences, she offers no evidence to support her indictment of personnel officers and employers. But as we suggested previously, since there is little direct evidence of such discrimination, it is hardly surprising that she would come up short of data.

Besides, although they apparently believe that deliberate discrimination is a great obstacle to black advancement, most supporters of preferences do not usually rely on it as their chief argument. Some critics even concede that intentional discrimination on the part of whites is not widespread; certainly, it is insufficiently broad in scope to account for the magnitude of labor market problems encountered by blacks.[13] Therefore, since discrimination must be the basic obstacle to black achievement in the labor market, discrimination is more likely to be institutional than intentional in nature. This fallback argument postulates bias even in the absence of any intention to discriminate. As such, personnel policies are said to be fraught with discriminatory practices that cannot be linked to the specific acts of individuals. How one can make a reasonable determination of discrimination in the absence of concrete data and where one assumes that institutions somehow exhibit humanlike qualities is a mystery.[14]

In general, the fallback position may be utilized as a rhetorical device to ridicule efforts that would establish merit in personnel decisions. For instance, employment examinations are often dismissed as "culturally biased" and "unrelated to job performance." Indeed, virtually all documents and statements that seek to establish objective criteria in the determination of the applicant's potential ability or worth to an organization are denounced. References and recommendations from former employers and colleagues are dismissed as little more than "mere personal connections," as if details about one's work habits and prior record have no bearing on the issue of future prospects for success. From this perspective, employment decisions are based on emotional or irrational attachments between employers, who presumably place more trust in the subjective evaluations of one another than in reasonably objective criteria. That the vast majority of such connections are made in order to ascertain present qualifications and prior performance is hardly entertained as a possibility. Even work experiences or attendance records may be deemed irrelevant to a decision to employ.

Yet most supporters of racial preferences in employment do not reject *all* attempts to impose objective standards in employment selection. They give special weight to college diplomas and other types of formal credentials. But the concerns of the employer have little to do with their acceptance of credentials, for the manner in which they wish such credentials to be appraised is of questionable value to most firms. They tend to assume that degrees from all high schools and colleges are roughly of equal value to employers. What counts is the degree itself, not the nature of the institution that bestowed the degree in the first place.

The motive that lies behind this argument is relatively clear. If the public in general and employers in particular can be persuaded that all high schools, colleges, and universities turn out graduates with similar qualifications and skills, it becomes impossible to make qualitative distinctions among individuals and institutions. The degree of the student from an elite university can rank no higher than one from a marginal college. Race or some other victim-related criteria may then be brought more easily to the forefront of the decision to employ.

Stated differently, employers are told to believe that all applicants who possess a given credential (e.g., a college diploma) have roughly the same capacity to carry out the tasks for which they were hired. In a word, it cannot be admitted that diplomas are qualitatively different or that a graduate with a C+ average from a selective school that recruits the best high school students is in all probability superior to the graduate with a B+ average from a school with an open admissions policy. In this way, it becomes difficult to make meaningful distinctions; therefore, the legitimate role played by credentials in the hiring process is undermined.

Just as all diplomas are assumed to be of more or less equal weight in the marketplace, so all test scores above a minimum passing grade are judged to be equal. It is apparently assumed that above a certain (usually low) minimum of training or ability as established by a test all job seekers possess the same ability. There are no real distinctions to be drawn between, say, applicants with a civil service examination score of 95 and those with a low passing score of 70. Each applicant is deemed sufficiently "qualified." (Yet there are apparent limits to this egalitarian approach to examinations. In the Foreign Service, for example, the government sees fit to accept individuals with modest scores, provided they are from designated victim groups. The majority of applicants who are hired must be among the top scorers on the Foreign Service Examination.)

In sum, the advocates of racial preferences assume rather than prove the existence of discrimination. Even their theory of institutional discrimination is unsubstantiated. We now know, for instance, that cognitive ability tests predict job performance and that employers use such tests for legitimate reasons. Still, allegations of discrimination are commonplace, and the call for various racial preferences is as strong as ever.

Why do they cling so desperately to the idea that discrimination is rampant and affirmative action necessary? One reason appears to be that its defenders believe that in the absence of the soft quotas of affirmative action's goals and timetables blacks would have no chance to obtain the more desirable positions. But another, although less obvious, reason is that it is always less painful to blame the out-group for the poverty and low social standing of one's own group. A third is that the promise of affirmative action is diminished once discrimination no longer accounts for the fact that many blacks are in low-wage and low-skilled laboring and service positions. Why? The reason is this: If discrimination is only a minor problem, as we have shown it appears to be, then at this time blacks are probably entering jobs for which they are well suited. The implications of this are very unsettling to the black community, especially the implication that many beneficiaries of affirmative action will enter positions and schools for which they are ill prepared. If the latter is the case, we can expect many to fail, in which case affirmative action will deliver much less prosperity and prestige than its advocates promise. Thus, racial preferences will be associated with failure as much as success. In other words, when discrimination is the ailment, a policy like affirmative action, which is designed to neutralize discrimination, should be very effective in conferring benefits on the group. But when discrimination is not the fundamental problem, affirmative action could well be the wrong medicine, with a number of disruptive side effects.

Affirmative Action Increases Income and Prestige

Although many advocates of affirmative action acknowledge that it violates the basic American norms of equal treatment and fair play, they nevertheless believe that racial preferences are a necessary evil in that they presumably deliver substantial benefits to blacks. Two desirable results in particular are mentioned by most writers when making a case for affirmative action. The first is a presumed increase in the average wage level of blacks compared to whites, and the second is improvement in the occupational status or prestige of black workers. The desirabilty of the first goal is obvious, requiring little comment; but the appeal of the latter is more complex.

Public officials compute a poverty line, and the public and its politicians spend money and energy worrying about the number of citizens who fall below it. Indeed, the effectiveness of economic programs and elected officials is determined in part by how successful they are in achieving reductions in the number of people in poverty. The government does not compute a prestige line; but the civil rights establishment and their allies are highly attuned to the relative prestige levels of the occupations blacks enter.

We can only speculate about the sources of the intense desire to upgrade the occupational status of blacks. But surely the status anxiety of blacks accounts for much of it. And many appear to believe that higher occupational attainment can alleviate status anxiety, which is not unreasonable since social standing appears to depend on the type of work one does as much as it does the amount of money earned.

But there is another reason for the effort to place blacks in more prestigious occupations. We are referring to the widespread, yet unsubstantiated, belief that blacks in middle-and upper-middle-class occupations can serve as role models for discouraged and demoralized black youths. Some critics even view the presumed role model effect as a crucial element in the resolution of the American race dilemma. As they see it, blacks in prestigious occupations inspire hard work, perseverance, self-denial, and other virtues, as younger or less successful blacks, by taking heart from the examples set by successful and older black Americans, strive to reach similar levels of achievement. Affirmative action, it is confidently predicted, will engender a wave of emulation, thereby invigorating the black community.

Whether the role model effect actually exists is so far an open question in the social sciences. The proponents of affirmative action routinely proclaim its existence in their defense of racial preferences, and most people appear to believe it exists.[15] Oddly enough, we have no research demonstrating its occurence at all. The extant research we do have about why we choose a particular career suggests that occupational choices are not based on either the presence or absence of role models. Rather, role models in the field one chooses have almost no effect, whereas parents and teachers— individuals a young adult knows and trusts from long-term relationships— have the greatest influence. Thus, it is very unlikely that the inclination of a minority youth to choose a prestigious occupation is greatly augmented by the presence of co-ethnics in a particular field.[16]

Occupational choice, as are many other decisions, is mostly shaped by concrete social relationships in the home, school, and community, not by abstract relationships with hypothetical role models. No doubt, this is what basketball star Charles Barkley meant when he said in the course of the 1993 National Basketball Association championship series that he was not a role model. Yet this perfectly reasonable statement—apparently buttressed by social science research—was greeted with a firestorm of denunciation. He was roundly criticized as irresponsible, which illustrates how many people have apparently been taken in by the idea that black children "model" their behavior after people whom they have never met. As a corrective, we would propose the following "law" of role models: The greater the period of time a young person spends in the company of the model (e.g., a teacher, parent, aunt, neighborhood businessman, etc.), the more likely he or she is to be influenced. Perhaps the least important attribute of any role model is the prestige of his or her occupation.

Affirmative Action Improves Race Relations

Since most proponents of affirmative action subscribe to the hypothesis that white stereotypes are the major obstacle to black progress, they are eager to reform the attitudes of white Americans. As they see the problem, whites will benefit from seeing more blacks in higher-status positions. Taken at face value, statements such as the following can be viewed as quite plausible: "Individuals socialized in a world where blacks are assimilated throughout the hierarchy of employment will no longer readily assume that they belong at the bottom."[17] This statement is consistent, of course, with the contact hypothesis, which, as the reader may recall, maintains that contact with blacks of equal status undermines traditional stereotypes, thereby changing the attitudes of whites toward blacks for the better. On the other hand, it is most important that the contact be between equals who recognize and respect each other's capacities. An obvious question intrudes at this point: If affirmative action lowers the standards for prospective employment to such an extent that the average black employee is relatively less skilled than the average white, can we expect a positive change in attitude? It is in this connection that hopes may be dashed, for if racial preferences are required to increase the number of blacks in high-level positions, does this fact not strongly imply that there will be relatively fewer competent blacks filling these positions? So even though whites, as Ezorsky and others have hoped, will see blacks working in upper-level positions, they will not necessarily assume that blacks have earned them nor increase their respect for blacks in general. In this sense a position gained through a racial preference is a Pyrrhic victory.

Indeed, such policies could actually backfire to the extent that blacks occupy positions for which they are less qualified than their typical white counterparts. It is highly likely that in the course of time their white coworkers will notice the inevitable performance discrepancies, drawing invidious conclusions—the very thoughts people of goodwill wish to discourage. Not all blacks who benefit from lower standards, of course, will do poorly at work, but we can anticipate that a higher percentage of the recipients of racial preferences will have performance-related problems. We cannot predict how specific whites will react to these blacks who are favored by quota systems, but the history of the first 25 years of affirmative action does not auger well for improvements in white attitudes or race relations in general if this line of attack continues to be pressed.

In the final analysis, it is deep-seated fear of failure in the black community that galvanizes the demand for preferences. Affirmative action proponents, white and black alike, presently share the assumption that blacks cannot compete with whites in the absence of a leg up in the competition. "[P]reference is necessary," as Ezorsky bluntly puts it, "because the handicap of a racist past has robbed many blacks of the wherewithal to compete equally with whites."[18] Once again, we see the gnawing fear of failure that fuels the prevailing status insecurity. This unfortunate fear is due of course to their relatively poor schooling and resulting lack of marketable skills. But the implications of this lack are difficult to accept fully. None of us wishes to admit his or her deficiencies, especially in a culture based on achievement norms and individual competition. To admit that the long-sought-after equality of opportunity—at least in law—and the use of racial preferences for certified victim groups have nonetheless failed to produce the anticipated progress toward equality of result is profoundly demoralizing. Excuses must be found.

SOCIAL THEORY AND THE CASE AGAINST AFFIRMATIVE ACTION

In most studies of affirmative action, there is a tendency to accent only one of its unfortunate consequences for the social and political order. Thomas Sowell, for example, stresses the practical failure of preferences to enhance the cultural development of the favored group.[19] In a similar fashion, many authors emphasize affirmative action's moral shortcomings, noting that it effectively punishes whites who are not guilty of harming blacks in any way.[20] We agree with these criticisms, but our approach to preferences is rooted more broadly in social theory. Affirmative action is an expression of that flawed theory we labeled the Victim Vision, and since bad ideas are likely to produce bad policy, it will have predictably undesirable results. Its advocates, we believe, are destined to discover over the long run that it confers few benefits but numerous costs.

This failure is lost on those social scientists who in their efforts to increase their understanding of their own narrow disciplines are apt to neglect important findings in other areas. One of the more significant obstacles to our grasp of social phenomena resides obviously in its sheer complexity. In our age, scholars are so hived off from one another that they have an unfortunate propensity to talk past each other. This limitation is especially apparent whenever scholars address the controversial issues surrounding affirmative action and race. One must ceaselessly cope with the political and social contentiousness surrounding the subject. Be that as it may, a proper comprehension of this issue requires the application of theories and data drawn from various sources, including economics, political science, and social psychology, no less than sociology and the specialty area of race relations.

To that end, we now intend to show that affirmative action fails to confer benefits on the society in that it violates a basic principle of the rule of law as it has evolved in the West—that it distorts the allocative processes necessary for the free market to function properly, that it stunts social and cultural progress within the black community in its encouragement of a reactionary retreat into the "warmth of the small group," and that it ultimately intensifies racial discord and divisions. All of these baneful consequences may be derived from elements of social theory.

Needless to say, much of what we have said previously and will discuss in the remainder will offend many liberals who tend to sincerely believe that the benefits of affirmative action to blacks and other groups far outweigh the costs to society as a whole. We can only plead with them that they not ignore two classes of costs inevitably associated with racial preferences: namely, those imposed at the expense of the health of our political, legal, economic, and other institutions and those imposed on the presumed beneficiaries of their policies and programs.[21] By ignoring these costs, over the long run our fragile sense of social and political unity can only be further eroded.

We contend that a constitutional system based on limited government, the rule of law, and a free market economy not only is consistent with racial harmony and minority group advancement but is indispensable for their attainment. Indeed, further erosion of the rule of law can only undermine the worthy goals that affirmative action itself was designed to reach. It is, of course, possible for the optimistic moralist to conclude that we give affirmative action too much influence in our lives and that we exaggerate its deleterious effects on American society in general. Perhaps, but does anyone believe that race relations have actually improved or that blacks are significantly better off materially now than in 1970? Our position at the very least has the virtue of empirical and theoretical consistency.[22]

Affirmative Action Is Illogical on Its Face

The proponents of affirmative action appear surprised by the intensity of the public's opposition to racial preferences. They even read this visceral dislike as a manifestation of racism. Yet strong revulsion is inevitable, as affirmative action rests on a notion long rejected by the legal systems of free societies—namely, that children can be held responsible for the sins of their fathers. In an area where moralists abound, it is strange that so many intellectuals encourage a policy so plainly contemptuous of one of our most basic precepts—that it is the guilty who ought to be punished. Dedicated to the production of an equality of outcome, they willingly apply the most questionable means to that end. They forget that no matter how well intentioned the ends, the use of bad means itself can produce dangerous results—something we have surely learned in a century when millions have perished in the name of collectivist ideologies.

Actually, the basic flaw of affirmative action is easily grasped if we can set aside for a moment the noble ends and lofty ideals its defenders regularly call upon in its defense. Quite simply, in preferring one race over the other in the development of public policy, the government and the advocates of racial preferences negate the time-honored principle that in a free society all citizens ought to be treated equally before the law.

Basically, proponents of affirmative action make their case in the following manner. Since a particular group in the population (blacks) suffered unjustly in the past at the hands of another group (whites), it is both "just" and "fair" that the particular segment of the population that made them unequal in the past itself be placed at a disadvantage in order to create a more equitable distribution of rewards and burdens. Specifically, since equal treatment before the law was violated in the days of slavery and segregation when black Americans were subjected to state-imposed coercion by whites, the proper remedy for the redress of old wrongs is to employ government power against whites, albeit less aggressively and without malice.

Unfortunately, the perpetrators of slavery and segregation against the minority have long departed. Justice in any meaningful sense would require that those blacks who are to benefit be the victims of discrimination and that those whites who are to suffer detriments be perpetrators of discrimination. Thus, the authorities would have to demonstrate that the black Americans who were treated unjustly in time I are the *same* blacks who are to receive just compensation in time II (today). Or conversely, the whites who are being denied equal treatment in order to advantage today's blacks must be shown to be the *same* whites who inflicted harm on the intended beneficiaries of racial preferences. It is surely a misplaced logic, therefore, that contends that present whites (time II) who did not themselves discriminate against the particular blacks subjected to slavery and segregation must "pay the price," as a member of President Jimmy Carter's EEOC admitted, for injuries inflicted on blacks in the past. As presently expressed, at least implicitly if not explicitly, this legal interpretation asserts that it is necessary to treat people unequally in the present in order to gain (presumably) a contrived equality of result in the more or less distant future. As such, it fundamentally negates the meaning of equal treatment at law. Thus, those white adults and students, for instance, who are denied at present a job or admittance to a university in spite of their obvious qualifications are nonetheless receiving just treatment, comforted as they presumably are by a legal theory that they are compensating a group whom they have not personally injured but whose ancesters their forebears ostensibly did harm. It would be interesting if this notion that we are guilty for the sins of our fathers and grandfathers made its way into the laws of nations!

In reality, this argument that the white majority should be held responsible for the sins of its fathers has no limitations, since the historical record has been one of plunderers on horseback dominating cultivators of the soil (or more broadly, one of the "political" over the "economic").[23] The rise of liberalism, in the old-fashioned meaning of that much-misused term, has been an effort to combat the historical impulse to subjugate the weak through various forms of serfdom, including different laws for different status groups.[24] The affirmative action mentality, therefore, can be said to stand classic liberalism (and the rule of law) on its head by demanding that the victims themselves be allowed to use state power in order to oppress, however lightly or marginally. Affirmative action thus leads logically to reparations for historical wrongdoing. And although its moderate defenders recoil at such a suggestion, it can be said that reparations in the form of the soft quotas arising from affirmative action's goals and timetables already exist.

What is more, these reparations are conferred on those blacks who arguably are the least victimized. Ironically, empirical studies of affirmative action find it tends to benefit the more financially secure, better-educated black middle classes. As one important study summarized its statistical findings: "[E]nforcement of affirmative action guidelines was beneficial, but only to more qualified blacks."[25] This irony is compounded by the argument that describes blacks as "shackled runners," handicapped by their history of racism. As we shall see, it is mostly the advantaged rather than the shackled members of their race who are the chief beneficiaries.

Affirmative Action Violates the Rule of Law

If there is one institution that may be said to embody the Western idea of freedom, it is what we call the rule of law. A nation ruled by laws rather than kings, politicians, or temporary majorities is one in which the subject is protected by rules that must be obeyed by soveriegn and subject alike. Unfortunately, with the advent of collectivist ideologies and the powerful welfare state of this century and the expropriation of income by high taxes, the rule of law has been gradually compromised and eroded to such an extent that we now have a legal system in which command elements increasingly supplant rule elements in the laws of the society. This is a necessary component of the modern welfare state, which, if it is to endure, cannot be bound by general rules of justice. It necessarily requires state-sponsored administrative decrees and legislative commands, which extract resources from some citizens in order to support the claims of other citizens.[26]

In this regard, affirmative action is merely a logical extension of the unremitting march of legal commands at the expense of legal rules. How and why this is the case will become apparent once we distinguish rules from commands.

As we have previously suggested, in their need to accommodate to the demands of the modern welfare state and to ensure their own electoral success, democratically elected representatives have increasingly been led to draft legislation based on elements of command rather than rules. It could hardly be otherwise; commands by legislatures and administrative agencies are crafted to achieve specific purposes. As such, they are addressed to known persons who are required to perform concrete tasks. Better still, commands are not only created to accomplish known ends; they are limited as well in scope and are bound to particular times and places.

A rule contrasts sharply with a command. The essence of a rule is quickly grasped if one thinks, say, of a game of football or basketball. Players on each team compete with one another, and referees ensure that each competitor adheres to the rules of the game. These rules, it is to be noted, do not confer a specific reward or impose a specific detriment. To the contrary, so long as the competitors obey the rules as previously laid down, they are free to compete in any way they see fit. In other words, they determine their own actions and pursue their own self-chosen ends.

It is most important that the reader grasp the clear distinction between rules and commands. A good rule, unlike a command, seeks no particular end. Put another way, it is "means dependent," not "ends dependent." As long as we observe the procedural requirements (the means) as laid down in advance, we are otherwise left free to pursue our own self-chosen ends. Thus, a rule is known in advance, is noninstrumental, and imposes obligations to subscribe to what the political philosopher Michael Oakeshott calls "adverbial conditions" in the performance of personal actions.[27] More generally, a legal system informed by the rule of law is fundamentally incompatible with the vast array of command-based administrative regulations and legislative laws that perforce draw distinctions between citizens.

Thus, the term *rule of law* merely expresses in a shorthanded fashion a legal order in which individuals, as long as they obey general rules announced beforehand, are to be treated in the same manner as other individuals. In short, provided they abstain from fraud, force, and theft, they are otherwise left free to pursue their own particular ends. It is a legal system in which the right of contract is enforced by courts.

Affirmative action, in contrast, is dependent on the imposition of legal and administrative commands. As such, it is incompatible with a rule-based order in which individuals contract freely with one another. Thus, under a set of race-conscious policies, the law of contracts is made subordinate to administrative decrees and statutory commands. In this regard, affirmative action mandates and orders merely follow historical trends that have been evident throughout this century. While technically it does not impose strict quota requirements, the real effect is to facilitate the establishment of soft quotas in the form of employment goals. Employers with government contracts, it will be recalled, are given numerical goals to reach and timetables for reaching them. These requirements demand a good-faith effort to increase the number of minorities on their payrolls. This system is the soft rather than the hard variety in that it does not compel employers to add a specific number of minorities to their payrolls, but it does insist on a display of good faith. In practice, this means that employers are expected to recruit additional blacks, even if they are less qualified than prospective white applicants. As a system oriented to legal coercion and administrative regulation, in effect it forces employers to discriminate against nonminority applicants.[28]

If the reader thinks that goals for minorities will not inevitably produce discrimination against whites, we ask him or her to imagine the likely behavior of the two major parties to affirmative action: namely, the employer and the government bureaucrat whose job it is to enforce the policy's goals and timetables. How can the bureaucrat know if a particular employer has made a good-faith effort? Conversely, how can the employer demonstrate his or her desire to meet the goal? In reality, there is only one answer to both questions: The employer must prefer blacks to whites.

The reader may object by noting that in the Civil Rights Act of 1991 "quotas" are specifically forbidden. Yet the same law expressly allows an aggrieved minority to bring suit in federal court by pointing to the underrepresentation of minorities in particular firms. This produces a dilemma for employers, the solution to which is to establish preferences for minorities but not an obvious quota. Thus, in the likely event that an employer wishes to avoid lawsuits, he or she may find it prudent to hire designated minorities, if at all possible. Whites will be relegated to a nonpreferred status and minority hiring artificially stimulated.

We appear to have in place a system that was disingenuously designed to conceal its true goal—mandatory racial preferences. In fact, one only grasps the true nature of affirmative action once one sees that numerical goals require quantifiable results. Under the current system insofar as there is a command to show a good-faith effort to increase minority representation, but no countervailing obligation to refrain from discriminating against whites, racial preferences are inevitable.

Many commentators dismiss objections that this policy is a blatant violation of the principle of equal treatment before the law by replying that it is only a minor price to pay for equality of result at some future time. Anyway, the preferred minorities have suffered in the past, so turnabout is fair play. But far more than a few jobs are at stake in this debate. The long-run damage done by affirmative action may therefore not be so much that it has bestowed special material and occupational benefits on preferred minorities at the expense of the majority but that its defenders have in effect contributed to a further erosion in the rule of law and the market economy that makes prosperity possible. Ironically, as we shall see, whereas it seems to harm the economy and social order, it appears to confer few benefits on the intended beneficiaries.

Affirmative Action Undermines the Market Economy

To the extent that affirmative action violates the principle of equal treatment under the law, it necessarily undermines the market economy and the efficient allocation of resources. As we have consistently insisted, not just any kind of legal order can coexist with just any kind of economic order. To the extent that economic liberty and private property cannot be guaranteed by the rule of law, the effectiveness of the market is likewise impaired. And since by guaranteeing the individual the freedom to utilize his (or her) knowledge and talents as he sees fit as long as he does not infringe on the rights of others, general rules of law provide a legal framework in which the freedom of entrepreneurs, capitalists, and workers may best meet the ever-changing demands of consumers. Thus, freedom of contract in buying and selling goods and services and exchanging titles to land, capital goods, and financial instruments is absolutely essential to the market economy. The absence of these rights can only lead to the misallocation of economic resources and to a wastage of capital, the effect of which is a general reduction in the living standards of the general population.[29]

The dedicated proponents of affirmative action, of course, are in the main American liberals who profess to believe in private property rights and free markets. Most definitely, they are not socialists who intend to nationalize the steel mills and other major means of production. On the other hand, they do tend to believe that government can easily regulate labor markets with few adverse effects on the economy as a whole. As they see it, affirmative action is a minor intrusion in employer-employee relationships, which can be handled with little or no cost to the public welfare.

Why do so many intellectuals assume that government intrusions in labor markets are virtually cost free? In the first place, they tend to make the Victim Vision assumption that many blacks are currently prevented by discriminatory practices from entering positions for which they are well qualified. So if it were not for discrimination, many would have already obtained jobs far better suited to their talents and education, or so the argument goes. Second, by compensating for this alleged discrimination in the marketplace, affirmative action measures presumably contribute to a more appropriate utilization of labor. In the absence of goals and timetables, employers would hire less-skilled whites rather than blacks and other preferred minorities with higher skills. Hence, affirmative action does not harm the market and may actually make it more efficient. The implication here is that employers prefer to make smaller profits by hiring "their own kind." Of course, in competitive labor markets in which government impediments to labor mobility are absent, such practices could hardly exist on any significant scale—the firm that refused to hire the more productive workers from the minority would soon find itself at a competitive disadvantage. Furthermore, as we demonstrated in Chapter 3, there is little sign of discrimination in the operation of the labor market.

In fact, this argument is seldom made explicitly by advocates of affirmative action in precisely this way, since these commentators would be forced to assert that the skills of blacks and whites are distributed in similar proportions between the races. However, this is certainly not the case at present, as these same critics implicitly admit when they demand that preferential practices such as "race norming" of tests be instituted or when they seek special subsidies for minority students and businesses. One is therefore left with the suspicion that defenders of affirmative action simply assume as an article of faith that the distribution of talents, interests, and work habits among various groups is similar. That ethnic groups may well differ in these important respects and that open markets tend to express those differences is summarily ruled out for serious consideration.

This refusal to accept inequality in any of its various manifestations probably accounts for the tendency both to exaggerate what affirmative action can actually accomplish for its intended beneficiaries and to underestimate its unfavorable consequences for the economy and social peace. In this respect, it must be seen primarily as an attempt to replace inequalities dictated in the marketplace with mandated equalities of outcome.

Yet inequality is part of the human condition. As we have previously argued in Chapter 3, it is differences in talents, knowledge, abilities, and interests that leads in the first place to the division of labor in society. So if some groups are on average less highly remunerated or hold less prestigious positions on average than do other groups, the difference in "success" need not be caused primarily by discrimination. Whatever disparities exist may be due mostly to a complex division of labor and impersonal free market allocations in which the distribution of income shares is dependent on the individual's contribution to the marginal product. On the other hand, if racism is seen as the primary obstacle to progress, one can easily conclude that government intervention designed to correct these outcomes is the most efficacious policy (through arbitrary assignment of blacks to more desirable positions). Such assumptions inform the unscientific notion so widely prevalent that "social justice" is most easily achieved by state intervention in the marketplace. Surely, the failure of eastern European communism and the present dysfunction of our "advanced" welfare state suggest otherwise.

But interfering with market processes has consequences. As a general rule, government intervention of any kind in the marketplace leads to the misallocation of resources; in the case of affirmative action, it is employees, of course, who are misallocated. And as is true in all markets, misallocation in the labor market lowers efficiency and prosperity. To the extent, therefore, that racial preferences result in the assignment of labor to inappropriate occupations and positions, we can expect to find signs of lower productivity, such as favored workers being more likely to experience problems performing their tasks. We will document the occurrence of negative outcomes from misallocation below.

It must not be supposed, however, that affirmative action is confined to labor markets alone. To appease minority activists, the Clinton administration is extending the quota revolution into the banking and insurance industries. Each has been accused of institutional racism, the former for providing mortgage loans to a lower percentage of their black than white loan applicants and the latter for charging higher rates to insure property in heavily black neighborhoods than in white neighborhoods.

The Clinton administration's intervention in the banking and insurance industries is potentially more threatening to the market economy than anything we have witnessed so far in the realm of employment. These recent efforts in the name of diversity to replace market allocations with state intervention constitute nothing less than a shifting of risk and responsibility from borrowers and property owners to banks, mortgage lenders, policy holders, and the general public. In various ways, lenders and insurers are being told to grant loans and policies to people who are bad risks.

This effort to limit the freedom of banks and insurance companies to set their own policies ignores the fact that the banks and insurance companies are refusing to grant loans and insurance for sound business reasons. Blacks and whites tend to differ in regard to a number of factors related to risk. Thus, the income levels, assets, credit ratings, and job histories of black Americans are on average less likely than those of white Americans to meet the traditional loan requirement standards of banks. And black neighborhoods are on average more subject to crime, fires, burglary, and vandalism than are white areas, which is the reason many blacks must pay more for insurance protection against fire, theft, and vandalism. All of this is a matter of public record. Nevertheless, regulators ignore the established differences in risk factors and assume that higher black rejection rates for loans and insurance mean that commercial banks, mortgage companies, and insurance firms discriminate on grounds of race and ethnicity.

The major evidence against banking has come from a Federal Reserve

Bank of Boston survey in 1992 of 6.6 million mortgage applications.[30] When black applications for loans were found to have been rejected more often than white ones, commercial banks and mortgage companies came under special scrutiny from federal agencies; but as various critics have pointed out, the government's own statistics do not show that discrimination actually exists. Indeed, a comparison of Federal Housing Administration insured loans made over a period of three years in the late 1980s found, in the words of one student, that the "average default rates for blacks were significantly higher than those for whites."[31] Yet, if marginally qualified whites were being preferred over marginally qualified blacks, the default rates would presumably be *higher* for whites than for blacks. But in truth they do not differ. Moreover, a subsequent study by the Federal Deposit Insurance Corporation (FDIC) questioned the initial Federal Reserve Bank conclusions.[32] Thus, when the data from the two banks that specialized in soliciting business from marginal black applicants were excluded, the initial conclusion that marginal whites were being accorded preferential treatment turned out to be groundless. As Jonathan R. Macey put it, "The government's willingness to proceed with litigation in the absence of evidence of discrimination may be good politics, but it is scandalous in a nation that purports to be governed by the rule of law."[33]

It is also questionable economics. Banks and insurance companies make profits by lending out money and issuing insurance policies. It is the marketplace, however, that ultimately determines interest rates and insurance premiums. Consequently, banking and insurance institutions have developed various means by which to assess the risk involved in lending or insuring. Banks, for example, take into account a person's ability to hold a job over time, his (or her) income level, the worth of his assets, his past record for repayment of debts, and other signs of creditworthiness. That the assets of the median black family are one tenth those of the median white family, that far fewer black households are composed of married couples, and that black income is on average lower than that of whites are hardly insignificant data to be regarded lightly by loan officers.[34] Race, per se, is unlikely to enter the equation, since banking institutions would hardly wish to pay the price for their racial prejudices by lending to risky whites rather than more trustworthy minority members. Obviously, those individuals in command of greater resources who have also demonstrated what bankers call "character" in their prior work habits and financial dealings are most likely to get loans. Llewellyn Rockwell, Jr., who has considered the ramifications of this problem, puts the matter bluntly: "Yes, there is discrimination in the market for loanable funds: people who pay their bills and otherwise act prudently are favored over those who don't. . . . The capital for loans comes from savings (present or future). If bankers are to make the two sides of the ledger balance over time, they must be able to predict the future behavior of borrowers."[35]

But the studies and logic that refute the allegations of discrimination have not deterred the activists who want "equality of result" in the loan market. In its endeavors to increase the number of loans to minority group members, the Clinton administration, in a reinterpretation of the Community Reinvestment Act, has introduced the notion of "performance-based standards"—in reality, numerical guidelines much like those of affirmative action in the labor market—as a method to assure that more minority loan applications will be acted on in a favorable manner. (Attorney General Janet Reno has justified the new regulations with the familiar argument of institutional racism.)

The government has other weapons in its arsenal to encourage more loans to minorities. Armed with unlimited funding to defray court costs, government regulators and the courts have already forced or pressured several banks to introduce sensitivity training to their personnel, to advertise on television or by radio as well as in newspapers aimed at the black community, and to initiate various projects directed specifically at black areas.

Even as the Clinton administration naively views numerical guidelines (i.e., quotas) as an unmixed blessing, it is certain that loan quotas will impose costs on society. According to a banking expert, one likely effect upon the industry of such regulations will be to encourage lenders to make bad loans based almost entirely on racial considerations, if they are to avoid government legal action and still greater regulation. Moreover, the amount of capital available to worthy borrowers will necessarily be reduced, for as bad loans are written off, mortgage rates will rise more than otherwise for the general public. Ultimately, all citizens will pay for the misallocation of capital to high-risk borrowers.[36]

As were the banks and mortgage companies, so the insurance industry will be compelled (if various members of Congress have their way) to make race a prime consideration in the conduct of its business. Data drawn from small census tracts, for instance, will be utilized to determine if they discriminate against black and Hispanic neighborhoods in order to benefit the white suburban areas. In general, they are accused of providing insufficient coverage to insufficient numbers of people at excessive prices. But given that inner-city neighborhoods are usually far more subject to violent crime, theft, vandalism, and fire, the premium assessments in such neighborhoods are in line with the costs of providing insurance to people in high-risk areas.[37] But choosing to disregard the evidence, Congress has moved to require insurance companies to supply information useful for a "community rating" system of small census districts in order to determine if racial differences in premium charges exist. When they find disparities, they will, of course, wax indignant. Yet this is what we should find in a healthy economy—the normal free market outcome of scarce resources being allocated to their more preferred uses by the pricing mechanism. Why should the insurance industry (and its customers) assume the burden of risk by insuring property in high-crime and low-crime neighborhoods at similar rates? Since they are private enterprises, after all, is it not their proper function to set premiums according to the probable risk they incur when they insure a property? And is this not desirable to the extent that it encourages property owners to reduce the risk (and the premium) by taking better care of their property?

Once again, we can anticipate a decrease in the public's overall level of well-being should this attempt to lower premiums in high-risk areas succeed. People living in high-crime areas will benefit at the expense of citizens in low-crime neighborhoods, who will have to pay higher premiums. Moreover, a community rate system in which companies are forbidden to "charge different premiums for different risks" will force many marginal firms to lay off employees, to reduce benefits, or to go out of business entirely. And there will be other costs associated with compelling insurers to lower premiums in high-risk neighborhoods. For instance, it will reduce the incentives for property owners in high-crime areas to turn to private means of security such as private guards and alarm systems.[38]

This recent extension of affirmative action fails to comprehend the role that savings and interest play in a market economy. As such, its potential for damage to the functioning of our economic system is more profound than that which has so far prevailed in the market for labor, since the pool of savings does not increase more or less automatically, immune to interest rate levels, political conditions, taxation, or even cultural influences. Savings, after all, represent a willingness by individuals to forego present consumption for future consumption. Interest paid on the loan market ultimately reflects this basic fact of life. Those who "wait" or "abstain" from consumption in the present must receive compensation—interest—in the more or less distant future. Otherwise, we would only spend and consume but seldom save, since we prefer present goods of the same kind and quantity to future goods of the same kind and quantity.[39]

As intermediaries between savers and borrowers, banks in particular play a crucial role in capital accumulation and economic growth. It is somewhat surprising in hindsight that it took the quota revolution so long to demand affirmative action in the allocation of credit. But now that affirmative action is spreading, we can expect it to invade other areas of American life. The next battlefield is likely to be pension funds, a massive pool of savings run primarily in the interests of future retirees. Already the Reverend Jesse Jackson has signaled a need to employ the savings in public sector investments for questionable (albeit job-generating) infrastructure rebuilding projects in the cities.

Affirmative Action Encourages Racial Antagonism

There is more at stake than our standard of living and our right to economic freedom, for affirmative action promotes racial discord. Conversely, economic freedom under the rule of law is conducive to the welfare of all groups over the long run. In the case of race relations specifically, it may be argued that market freedoms actually tend to reduce racial and ethnic tensions. This reduction is accomplished by a process whereby public relations are converted into private ones by impersonal exchanges between individuals. Let us therefore set aside for the moment the general benefits of economic liberty and assess the manner in which free exchanges under market conditions, unlike those under affirmative action, actually contribute to racial harmony.

Affirmative action understandably generates resentment, since it violates the basic rules of fair play in competitive circumstances. Good jobs are almost invariably in short supply; therefore, they elicit many more applications than the number of positions can accommodate. In our society, most applicants realize this and are willing to accept that they may not get the employment they seek. However, to maintain a willingness to accept loss in the competition, we must convince the losers that the decision to accept another candidate was appropriate. This can be done by predicating employment decisions on neutral criteria: lotteries, examinations, grades, prior experience, and so on. The one decision factor that is never acceptable is an open preference. That is, applicants can resign themselves to losing because of bad luck or some indicator of merit. They can even accept nepotism or the application of somewhat arbitrary standards. A flagrant preference, however, is intolerable.

But as if the inherent problem of resentment were not enough, affirmative action in practice is designed to maximize the number of people who feel victimized. Its flaws are well illustrated by the recent experience of the Louisville, Kentucky, police department when it hired new recruits by quotas. A total of 1,365 applicants took the examination for police officer. They were then ranked by score. Of those accepted into the police academy, the lowest-ranking white was 68th on the test with a score of 92. Conversely, the lowest-ranked black was 634th with a score of 73. In all, only a total of 35 black and white applicants were hired.[40] So more than 500 whites who had scores higher than 73 were not hired. Their resentment boiled over into a public controversy, as more than 500 whites felt cheated despite the logical impossibility of more than a handful of them being hired in the absence of an affirmative action program. In other words, to place a few more blacks on its police department, Louisville inevitably angered hundreds of whites. How can it be said that preferences are good for race relations?

But there is another weakness in affirmative action, which, it will be recalled, is based fundamentally on government commands. This reality is not lost on the contending social groups. In a word, what were previously private matters to be negotiated between employer and employee (buyer and seller of labor) are now transformed into a political contest over the distribution of the social pie. As all students of political conflicts will attest, the perennial political question concerns how scarce resources are to be extracted from some citizens in order to be distributed to others. That which stimulates collective efforts to obtain benefits tends to provoke public conflicts. Indeed, one of the outstanding students of such problems has argued that politics is essentially a struggle between those who wish to "socialize" conflict and those who desire to "privatize" it.[41] From this perspective, ideologies themselves are linked to political processes. Thus, nationalism and socialism, for instance, seek to encourage a socialization of the average conflict, whereas traditional liberals or conservatives would seek generally to keep arguments wedded to individual property rights and thereby keep arguments privatized and desocialized, outside the political arena, if at all possible.

An inherent weakness of affirmative action or almost any policy based on race or other ascriptive criteria is that the glare of publicity and contentious debate cannot be avoided, since its benefits cannot be bestowed by government officials equally upon all groups. Losers know they lose, and they invariably resent the winners. These kinds of struggles for political and material resources must activate a growing number of racial and/or ethnic groups in which differences are accentuated and ideological distinctions are magnified. Consequently, affirmative action expands the socialization of conflict as more and more groups, previously quiescent, feel compelled to join the public fray. It is a process we are currently witnessing as various ethnic, racial, or other groups seek to position themselves ideologically for similar rewards. Interpersonal relationships are therefore charged with political symbols and economic meaning or intent. We can expect many more groups to demand the preferences initially won by blacks and now granted to Hispanics, women, and the handicapped. An increasingly cynical majority will be politicized as others insist that their group be recognized. The list of candidates for victim status is almost limitless—immigrants, Catholics, gays, Appalachians, out-of-work mill hands, New England fishermen, and so on.

If one doubts that this process is typical of racial and ethnic political struggles when preferential policies are at stake, he or she need only consider what has taken place in other countries. In Malaysia, for instance, where diverse religious groups uneasily coexist and where legislative power is held by a dominant Malay majority, "laws" are fashioned to favor Malays at the expense of the ethnic Chinese. Malays are accorded special treatment in awarding scholarships and civil service positions and even in public funding for building places of worship. Similarly, the government earmarks taxpayer money disproportionately not only for mosques but for educating Malays abroad, although it is the Chinese who generally have superior academic records. Predictably, resentment in the Chinese community runs deep.[42]

Such practices of ethnic favoritism have existed in the past in America, although on a smaller and more local scale, particularly in the form of political patronage. The notable exception to smallness of scale, of course, was the Old South in which the legal system long sustained white rule. Nonetheless, although preferences in our day are blatantly written into law, we as a nation until now have never subscribed to the idea that racial preferences are quite legitimate. And whereas opinion elites in business, education, and law once either condemned altogether or at least did not justify racial preferences as legal instruments of policy, their counterparts today look upon racial preferences as evidence of progress and proceed to enshrine them as law as long as they can be justified by the principle of victimhood.

What is particularly distinctive about the United States is that a majority, through its laws and regulations, has actually agreed to discriminate against itself. Either through moral intimidation or indifference, a white majority has acquiesced to the idea that group quotas for the underdog are legitimate tools of policy and law as long as the victim obtains the spoils.

The supply of victims, needless to say, has risen to meet the demand, as new groups have bellied up to the bar. More predictable still, these status struggles have become increasingly clamorous and shrill, as the politics of victimization intensifies and the demands on the white majority escalate. At some point, however, the majority seems bound to resist openly the claims of minority groups for preferences. No doubt such a movement will be galvanized by those whites who have been pushed aside by soft quotas. That open opposition is an inevitable outcome may be found in the opinion polls (including a series of Gallup polls), which tell us that anywhere from 70 to 80 percent of whites are opposed to racial preferences. Moreover, increasing numbers of whites say they or a family member have been victimized by affirmative action.[43] Needless to say, the racial conflict fostered by this balkanization of American life is hardly a happy prospect; but it is unavoidable in an environment that encourages groups to assert their victimhood in order to obtain a share of what will be perceived as a dwindling number of positions. (Indeed, while it is an oversimplification to attribute the angry tone of "talk radio" to affirmative action, it is often the case that the listeners who call in mention it when voicing their complaints about the government and society.)

Much of our confusion over this issue arises because we have ignored one of the great benefits of the marketplace: its tendency to convert what would otherwise be political or social conflicts into impersonal market exchanges. In this regard, its capacity to foster impersonal, nonpoliticized social relations between individuals cannot be overestimated, whatever one might think about its other aspects. At heart, multicultural societies are therefore likely to achieve social peace only if the interactions between their various racial and ethnic components can be individualized and depoliticized through the marketplace. But by violating the rule of law upon which the market economy depends, the imposition of preferential policies literally invites the organization of political groups around issues of rank subsidization or spoils sharing. Whereas the pluralist politics of modern democracies are, as a rule, manageable when policies relate to concrete economic interests, the situation is likely to be far more volatile once the distribution of spoils concerns race and ethnicity.

Political stability ultimately requires an environment conducive to compromise and limited ends. Such is not the case with affirmative action. The inherent flaw in the policy is that it is impossible to favor one group without simultaneously offending others. For race, unlike impersonal standards that relate to general rules at law or to more limited yet impersonal standards for employment (such as test scores or previous experience), is seldom deemed a legitimate basis for reward. It can only generate resentment.

In contrast, the consequence of free exchange in the marketplace between individuals is to depoliticize potentially explosive group antagonisms through peaceful and mutually beneficial transactions. In the nineteenth century, Sir Henry Maine captured this distinction when he compared relations based on status with those based on "contract." According to his interpretation, societies prosper as they progress from legal orders characterized by ascriptive relations to those in which contractual ones are dominant.[44] It is the latter that have placed the highest value on individual rights, both economically and politically. In this respect, the right of individuals to enter freely into contracts with one another not only is dependent on the rule of law but also is an essential ingredient of the market economy. Personal rights, free markets, and rules are therefore intimately linked with the right to contract. Although the law of contract has been undermined by the advance of administrative and statutory law for more than a century now, it continues to play an important part in the modern democratic orders. A prosperous market economy in the absence of contract—in which the rights and duties of respective parties are clearly specified and penalties laid down for violation of their terms—is simply unthinkable in modern commerce.

Contractural relations (i.e., binding agreements into which individuals or groups enter for specific purposes for stipulated periods of time) offer immense psychological advantages, the foremost of which, perhaps, is the ability to trust members of an out-group. This consequence of the law of contract meshes neatly with our earlier argument about market relations generally. Just as market freedoms depoliticize relations between dissimilar individuals, so contract undermines status-linked relations based on ascriptive criteria. It performs this function by allowing people who differ in their customs, authority patterns, ideologies, religion, ethnicity, or race (and who may be objectionable to one another for many reasons) to set aside their differences for the moment by making mutually beneficial and binding agreements with one another as equals.

Since these agreements are limited in time and space, the status claims and distinctions of either one or both parties are less easily threatened. In fact, they are likely to be ignored, as through a contract a "part" of the "whole" person can be split off and offered to the other party. In that only a limited and specialized aspect of each party is at stake, the psychological burdens of social contact across status groups are reduced. In short, the ethnic, racial, religious, or other status attributes of the participants need not be invoked or, worse, affronted.

In short, affirmative action, unlike contractural relations in the market-place, is inherently linked to status considerations. Why? Because, from a legal standpoint, its purpose is not equality of treatment before the law but inequality of treatment according to ascriptive criteria. But even more profound status claims are present. In our era, when a right to preferential treatment is articulated, the claimant immediately assumes the victim role—with an implicit assertion of maltreatment of the victimized group by the majority. Under these conditions, it seems a group status is converted into a "resentment credit" used to define each party's rights and obligations.

AFFIRMATIVE ACTION IN PRACTICE

The nation has had numerical goals and timetables for over 20 years. In that time, relations between blacks and whites have deteriorated. And despite government enforcement of racial preferences, blacks as a group have made relatively little economic progress. This record of failure, need we say, is the antithesis of what the supporters of affirmative action had predicted. Nevertheless, it is entirely consistent with our discussion of social relations in contemporary society.

Before we can demonstrate that a widespread misallocation of black labor is taking place, we must distinguish the effects of Title 7 of the 1964 Civil Rights Act (a race-neutral policy of nondiscrimination) from those of affirmative action's soft quota system of race-conscious goals and timetables. Title 7, of course, called for color-blind hiring. In spirit, it was in line with the rational self-interest of employers, who would benefit from the opportunity to recruit from a larger pool of applicants. Thus, there is a fundamental difference between a policy demanding that employers apply the same standards to applicants across the board and one requiring them to show a good-faith effort in order to reach a government-imposed employment goal. The difference, in short, is that Title 7 was designed to foster equality of opportunity. Affirmative action was developed to impose a system of soft quotas in order to ensure equality of results.

While such a distinction would seem to be an obvious starting point for any assessment of the costs and consequences of affirmative action, many prefer to conflate race-neutral and preferential policies, by attributing all black gains over the past 30 years to the positive effects of affirmative action. This conflation is empirically unnecessary, since the enforcement of Title 7 precedes the enforcement of affirmative action's goals and timetables. It is therefore possible to compare the market effects of the initial civil rights legislation with the soft quotas of goals and timetables by examining those years when blacks made progress relative to whites.

The enforcement of the policy of nondiscrimination as defined by Title 7 began in 1965. In contrast, affirmative action as a system of government-imposed goals and timetables did not emerge until the 1970s. The OFCC, the agency responsible for enforcing affirmative action, did not require employers to create goals and timetables for eliminating the underutilization of minority employees until 1968, nor did it impose goals until December 1971, the year in which it may be argued that a system of soft quotas was begun in earnest. Moreover, these goals were not enforced effectively until the late 1970s, since the OFCC had a mere 34 positions budgeted in 1970 and by 1978 was still understaffed with a relatively scant 216 positions. It grew rapidly in 1979, and by 1982, it reached its current level of approximately 1,000 employees.[45]

In other words, affirmative action could hardly be enforced vigorously until approximately the mid-to late 1970s. Therefore, those advances in income that occurred *after* the early 1970s are attributable, in part at least, to affirmative action, but those that occurred in the 1960s and early 1970s have other causes—the most likely of which are an increase in black skills and education and Title 7 of the 1964 Civil Rights Act, which called for a color-blind policy of nondiscrimination.

The government statistics on black income relative to that of whites tell a surprising story. In 1965, the first year following the passage of Title 7, the median income of black males working full-time for all 12 months of the preceding year was 62.3 percent of the median for their white counterparts. By 1970, the median for blacks who worked full-time throughout the year advanced to 68.1 percent, a gain of almost 6 percent in just five years. At the end of the 1970s, however, the percentage was only slightly higher, at 70.4 percent. Thus, the decade of the 1970s, when affirmative action enforcement took root, witnessed little closing of the race divide in income. Similarly, the 1980s also saw scant progress, and by 1990, the median income of black males who worked throughout the year in full-time jobs was marginally higher at 71.4 percent to that of comparable whites.[46]

Clearly, most of the progress in reducing inequality of income was made in the late 1960s and appears to be attributable to a rising demand for black employees, encouraged to some degree, no doubt, by the 1964 Civil Rights Act. Why do we attribute the income advances of the late 1960s and early 1970s to market forces and/or Title 7 rather than to affirmative action? As we have already said, the OFCC lacked the manpower to conduct investigations; hence, it was unable to enforce affirmative action policies effectively until well into the 1970s. The 1964 Civil Rights Act, however, had a built-in enforcement mechanism in that individuals could file complaints with the EEOC or federal courts. Although the overall level of litigation was not great, firms now had reason to fear that they would henceforth incur burdensome costs from discrimination complaints and lawsuits. The corporate sector appears to have responded quickly to this legal threat by opening its doors to black applicants. As a result, the black-white earnings disparity closed significantly between 1965 and 1970, a period in which demand for labor was relatively high.[47]

Conversely, affirmative action appears to have added little or no increase in *average* black income. The small advances after the mid-1970s were probably due to improvements in black educational levels. We are left, then, with this intriguing question: If affirmative action does not close the income gap, and if it predictably intensifies black-white animosity by violating the accepted norm of color-blind treatment, why do black leaders so fervently campaign for it? Are they deluding themselves about its benefits? Perhaps, but since they are probably also aware of its general ineffectiveness at augmenting the income of the group as a whole, it seems reasonable to conclude that they seek it for other reasons—the most likely candidates being material advantages for specific sectors of the black population and a belief that an increase in occupational prestige for some blacks will redound to the benefit of African Americans in general.[48]

To be sure, there does appear to be a substantial payoff in prestige. Since 1970, blacks have entered white-collar occupations with growing regularity, narrowing, so to speak, the "prestige gap." Reynolds Farley, a sociologist and demographer from the University of Michigan, reports that in 1970 the percentage of white men and women who held white-collar jobs was 21 percentage points higherer than the percentage of nonwhite men and women in white-collar jobs. By 1982, however, the race difference had shrunk to only 14 percentage points. In 1992, it stood at 16 percent.[49]

What is the overall contribution of affirmative action to the economic conditions of black Americans? Although no one can be certain, it appears to be somewhere between small and nonexistent. By institutionalizing racial preferences, we have apparently produced a situation in which skilled, literate blacks enter slightly more prestigious positions, whereas blacks on the whole have benefited far less in a material sense. As a society, we may have simply moved skilled black workers from one sector of the economy to another (as if squeezing the end of a balloon) with little effect on the overall size of the black middle-income class or on the income disparity between the races.[50]

Although the recruitment of blacks into more esteemed occupations may be a positive development in itself, it does come with a possible price tag that it may somewhat delay the development of the black community. Let us consider the implications of the following facts. To begin, the majority of blacks have not so far entered the more prestigious occupations. In fact, only a relatively small, well-educated minority is suited for most of the positions that affirmative action can reasonably bestow. In general, these better-educated and more highly skilled individuals would obtain decent white-collar or blue-collar employment or self-employment in the absence of racial preferences. Thus, the effects of affirmative action on income are probably negligible overall. Black higher civil servants, professors, and corporate executives are neither plucked from unemployment lines nor are they sufficiently numerous to have much effect on overall income figures. Rather, they are a small, yet relatively highly skilled and motivated, group who may have been diverted from other, if somewhat less prestigious, middle-class occupations because of government-coerced affirmative action.

The diversion of blacks from some middle-class sectors to others is not without its detrimental aspects. One likely consequence is to discourage middle-class blacks from entering occupations more crucial to daily life in the black community. At present, black communities across the United States are in dire need of the services provided by people in lower-middle-class occupations. In black neighborhoods, there are, for example, shortages of black merchants, teachers, police officers, repair workers, small builders, and so on. The damage caused by this shortage is little noted by affirmative action proponents who tend to proceed as if occupations and communities are somehow separate from one another in terms of the consequences they have for one another. In reality, they are closely intertwined. We become aware of this interdependence once we begin to think of "local" grocery stores, schools, restaurants, gas stations, repair services, dry cleaners, hardware establishments, and drugstores. Merchants and other service providers must locate their enterprises so as to find and keep a steady stream of customers. Thus, the self-employed assume a vital place in the life of the community, including those who live elsewhere but form commercial relationships with local customers and clients.

These bonds can crisscross a neighborhood, contributing to stability and social control. One beneficial result is that the young males who are inclined to antisocial activities may confront a group of organized and relatively influential adults whose prestige and authority enable them to regulate and discipline the conduct of others on a daily basis. This form of community-centered regulation tends to be highly effective, since it is done through a combination of rewards (e.g., jobs and social relationships) and punishments (e.g., exclusion from desired locations and reports to parents).

To the extent that affirmative action "plunders" the lower middle class and skilled working class in order to stock the more prestigious upper middle class, its effects are socially destructive in the long run. It does not so much raise the marginal productivity of blacks as divert a portion of it crucial to the development of African-American communities. It encourages black professionals and administrators to abandon their less fortunate brethren in larger numbers than otherwise by moving away as quickly as possible from their old neighborhoods to the upscale housing of white suburbia.

We have here a perfect illustration of the law of unintended consequences. The use of racial preferences to create "role models for poor black youth" may have ironically had the perverse effect of reducing the likelihood that young blacks and lower-class adults would have daily contacts with successful middle-class blacks. Let us paraphrase our notion of role models. The more removed a particular role model is from daily interactions with young people, the less effect he or she will have on their behavior. It follows that a black high school teacher or neighborhood merchant is more likely to be an effective role model than a black university professor or corporate manager far removed from the neighborhood. Even if the former leave the old neighborhood to reside elsewhere, their place of business may well remain in the inner city. By contributing to the moral tone of their communities, they may then indeed serve as role models.[51]

This analysis is admittedly somewhat speculative, but it does accord with the much-documented decline in the percentages of black small businessmen and entrepreneurs. Robert Boyd, a student of minority involvement in small business, reports that between 1970 and 1980 the percentage of the black workforce that was self-employed in nonagricultural businesses declined by a staggering 18.5 percent. Meanwhile, the comparable decline for whites was only 4.7 percent.[52] This decrease occurred despite the best efforts of government to encourage the expansion of minority businesses with a variety of costly programs, including contract set-asides and low-interest loans for minority-owned firms. On the other hand, there was a simultaneous increase in the number of blacks with high school and college degrees, a development that one would expect to have stimulated a surge in self-employment, since small business owners tend to derive from the ranks of the somewhat better educated citizens. But as Boyd and others have observed, blacks deserted the private sector in droves to take employment in government, an institution with muscular affirmative action programs.

A shortage of black entrepreneurs has other damaging consequences for black neighborhoods. As business owners themselves, black employers would probably hire relatively more employees from their own race. Not only would more employment within the community be generated, but also highly useful skills would be taught, many of which are transferable to subsequent jobs. Such skills also seem to reinforce in an indirect manner the work of the schools. Indeed, it appears to be an empirical regularity that ethnic groups with large percentages of families in small business— Jews, Greeks, Armenians, Asians, et cetera—also perform disproportionately well in school, sending many of their members along the way into the more prestigious professions.

Historically, small business is thus an engine of upward ethnic mobility. One result of affirmative action, however, may be to encourage the deterioration in the social fabric of black community life, which actually retards group mobility. It is even possible that through its injurious effects on the quality of community life affirmative action contributes in the long run to lower aggregate income among blacks.[53]

That there is little or no increase in black income relative to that of whites suggests that misallocation of labor is occurring. But a number of other factors also suggest misallocation. Insofar as blacks are presently entering positions for which they are less prepared than whites, we may expect the recipients of preferences to experience more difficulty accomplishing their assigned tasks, especially in comparison with those employees, black and white, who meet the usual standards of employment. Unfortunately, there is no long-term study comparing the work performances and promotion histories of those who do gain racial preference with those in the same kinds of jobs who do not. (Such research would indeed violate the sensitivity imperative.) We do have a study, however, by Eugene Silverberg, an economist, that suggests that significant performance differences do occur. Silverberg assessed the results of affirmative action programs in the building trades. He found that black electricians had significantly lower high school grades than white electricians and significantly lower grades in the classroom portion of the apprenticeship program. Upon completion of their training, moreover, black electricians were far more likely to quit or to be terminated for a mistake during work. Silverberg obtained similar results for plumbers and pipefitters.[54]

Other such indications of differences in quality of work exist. It is known, for instance, that blacks employed by the post office, an employer with a vigorous affirmative action policy, are three times as likely as their white counterparts to be fired for cause.[55] For their part, industrial psychologists have established a powerful linkage between test scores and the quality of task performance.[56] Inasmuch as these tests predict an individual's work on the job, those blacks who are given a preference because of race (which often means they have lower test scores) will probably perform less well on the average than those blacks who are not recruited under the relaxed standards of affirmative action. We may presume, therefore, that those blacks with lower test scores will either quit or be discharged more often than those hired under the customary standards. And while definitive evidence does not yet exist on the performances of those who receive a preference compared with those who do not, the statistics on discrimination complaints filed with the EEOC suggest that blacks encounter more task-related problems at work.[57]

But perhaps the best evidence with regard to the specific case of affirmative action that a misallocation of labor is taking place comes from affirmative action experiments at our colleges and universities. In order to increase black and Hispanic enrollments, college officials have been forced to lower admissions standards substantially. As a result, minorities often have test scores on the verbal and quantitative sections of the SAT that are 100 to 150 points below the scores of white students.[58] At the University of California at Berkeley, for instance, the combined verbal and math scores of whites is 1232, whereas for blacks it is a much lower 952—a disparity of 280 points.[59]

A lower standard for admission to higher educational institutions is a dubious advantage at best, as it appears to set so many minority group members up for subsequent failure in school and elsewhere. It is known that students admitted under affirmative action programs frequently fail to graduate, and when they do obtain degrees, they are more likely to graduate in the less demanding and remunerative fields (primarily the social sciences, ethnic studies, and education), where markets are already more or less saturated. As far as the high dropout rates of students admitted under affirmative action are concerned, the statistics compiled at the University of California at Berkeley attest to the negative effects of preferential policies: Only 18 percent of blacks admitted under Berkeley's affirmative action program graduated within five years. In stark contrast, blacks admitted under the conventional standards in the regular admissions program graduated at a 42 percent rate. Hispanics admitted under the relaxed standards of affirmative action had similar problems; a mere 22 percent of those so admitted graduated in five years, compared with 55 percent for those Hispanics admitted under the more rigorous customary standards. Meanwhile, whites and Asians graduate at a rate of 65 to 75 percent. To make matters worse, those minorities who do ultimately graduate are disproportionately at the bottom of their class.[60]

Other evidence from across the country is similarly unequivocal. In the nation as a whole, 74 percent of the black students fail to win their diploma after five years, which gives black students only half the graduation rate of their white counterparts.[61] In other words, just as affirmative action has failed to close the income divide, it has failed likewise to boost black graduation rates.

In the case of education, preferences may leave even greater wreckage in their wake than in the workplace. In fact, catastrophic dropout rates demonstrate so well the limitations of programs guided more by wishful thinking tied to ideological egalitarianism than by realistic assessments of concrete realities. Thomas Sowell aptly observes in this regard that "the systematic mismatching of minority students with institutions [is] artificially fostering failure among students with the qualifications to succeed."[62] His point is a simple yet profound one. Many of the black students who fail at elite schools, where their qualifications rank well below the institutional average, would do very well at a college where they are as qualified as the average student.

Race-conscious policies therefore tend to promote failure for many minority members by placing them in situations for which they are not sufficiently prepared. Perhaps it is for this reason that the more prestigious occupations acquired through affirmative action programs result in minimal income gains for the average black over the long run.[63] It seems entirely possible that the number of recipients of preferences who subsequently fail or stagnate is great enough to counteract the income gains initially received. Obviously, we need much additional research to assess how well the beneficiaries of affirmative action cope with the demands of their occupations. Such research would help us to understand the true effects of this controversial policy, which quite possibly does much more harm than is generally supposed both to the recipients of preferential treatment and to the social order as a whole.

Our analysis is supported by another similarity between the campus and the corporation. Both are experiencing unprecedented levels of conflict and turmoil and are under constant pressure to promote diversity. Much of this concern with diversity can be understood as a "second stage of affirmative action" in that it is a response to problems caused by preferences. Thus, there is a growing effort to find ways to retain the beneficiaries of goals and timetables. In the schools, this second stage of affirmative action requires separate dorms, special tutoring systems, ethnic studies majors, and other efforts to ease the adjustment to university life, all designed to increase retention and graduation rates.

Within the corporations the second stage also entails an effort to retain and promote preferred groups. This stage has spawned a cottage industry of "diversity consultants" to help firms manage diversity by convincing them that "WASP culture," or more broadly, "white-male culture," somehow causes them to undervalue the performance of minorities.[64] The basic problem, say the diversity consultants, is the misguided attempt to emphasize such "ethnocentric" values as performance, efficiency, and mastery of skills.[65]

According to Heather MacDonald, hundreds of consulting firms have arisen in the past few years to help businesses "value differences." "The concept of valuing differences," she writes, "is the cornerstone of this managing diversity movement. It translates questions of competence into questions of culture."[66] What this is said to mean in practice is that workers recruited under affirmative action programs who fail to advance in the organization are not so much unqualified for promotion as "differently qualified." Diversity specialists unabashedly claim (without a scintilla of evidence) that each ethnic group has its own management style and that firms today must abandon their efforts to stress "white male management practices," the effects of which are allegedly to block the progress of minority employees. What are these ethnocentric personnel practices? MacDonald offers several examples: "treating people the same"; "reliance on traditional job qualifications"; and placing weight on such criteria as "math, science, and engineering credentials."[67] All of these personnel practices, even demanding literacy and writing ability, are condemned as institutional racism. MacDonald actually was informed by one diversity specialist that "[q]ualifications is a code word in the business world with very negative connotations."[68]

Diversity consultants are paid handsomely for conducting training sessions and workshops, the purpose of which is to engender compassion for and sensitivity to minority feelings. Arousal of guilt among the whites in the audience is attempted with skits, discussions of stereotypes, and videos displaying whites offending blacks in a variety of school and business settings. These skits and exercises dwell relentlessly on white transgressions. At a workshop attended by one of the authors, for instance, the diversity consultant led the members through a series of imaginary situations in which they were asked to discuss what it means to be a black man, a black woman, a white female, and a white male. The first three groups were depicted as the victims of the last.

With ever greater frequency, the efforts of these diversity workshops, sometimes called equity workshops, backfire. For example, the *New York Times* reported the fallout from a mandatory workshop given to the employees of the Washington State Ferry System. The ferry workers were told to refrain from posting pinups of unclad women in the locker room. Whereas this requirement seemed sensible enough, the workshop leaders also gave the ferry workers a new "politically correct" vocabulary. They were instructed not to call women "ladies" and to only refer to blacks as "people of color." Resentment inevitably emerged as sarcasm. One informant said they now refer to black trashbags as "bags of color."[69] At the workshop in which people were asked what it meant to be a white male in America, one participant whispered none too quietly, "It means always having to say you're sorry."

In practice, criticism of affirmative action and all remarks that threaten the self-esteem of its recipients are apparently slated for verbal extinction, however accurate they may be. It appears that we are witnessing the emergence of serious attempts to establish repressive speech codes. MacDonald reports that one New York law firm has taken the Sensitivity Imperative to its logical conclusion in censorship of ordinary speech, forbidding its partners to say a black associate was hired because of affirmative action or that persons of color are less qualified. Even asking a black where he or she attended law school is deemed a breach of etiquette with racial undertones.[70]

CONCLUSION

There is growing evidence that affirmative action is flawed in theory and practice. Its primary beneficiaries have been educated blacks, whose own backgrounds have been far from uncomfortable. Moreover, government-imposed affirmative action plans have often placed minorities in positions for which they are ill-equipped, setting them up for failure or frustration, not to mention the feeling that their own success was due less to their own abilities than to government pressure and white patronage. Inevitably, these doubts about their achievements contribute to resentment and hypersensitivity in interracial situations. Rather than improving race relations, affirmative action thus stimulates discord and division.

Most certainly, it fosters dishonesty and deceit among whites and blacks alike. As Lino Graglia, a professor of law, puts it, "[A]ffirmative action is a fungus that can survive only underground in the dark."[71] One must forever conceal its operation from scrutiny. To grasp the need for secrecy, just imagine introducing a new black coworker to some colleagues as an "affirmative action hire." We obviously cannot be so blunt, since describing someone as such implies that the new employee is, in reality, only the best of his or her race the organization could find.

Perhaps one of the most disagreeable aspects of affirmative action is that it traps minorities themselves in a tight web of self-doubt. At the very least, it is increasingly difficult to sustain the notion that racist white attitudes and discrimination are still a significant obstacle to black progress. Why, many inevitably wonder, is it necessary to have racial preferences and lower standards for blacks? Simultaneously, it implicitly resurrects in a new form the notion of "The White Man's Burden." Since blacks cannot succeed on their own, the white man must shepherd them along.

What, then, would an appropriate civil rights policy look like? Most certainly it would be color-blind and embrace ideas of equal treatment. That blacks will lose little from a policy of nondiscrimination is suggested in an article comparing minority employment in firms with affirmative action with firms practicing color-blind nondiscrimination. Contrary to their expectations, the researchers found no significant gains from affirmative action either in the overall number of black employees or in the number of management positions held by blacks. That is, nondiscrimination seems sufficient in itself as a means to ensure black employment. Thus, there appears to be no reason to fear a fall in either the aggregate employment of blacks or their numbers in managerial positions following the abolition of racial preferences.[72]

From a moral standpoint, much will be gained from an end to affirmative action. That racial quotas are inherently contrary to the rule of law is illustrated by the experience of journalist Jim Sleeper. After speaking to an audience in Paris, Sleeper observed that affirmative action does not travel very well. "[M]y French listeners," he noted, "serve to remind us how far American liberals and leftists have drifted from certain basic principles of social justice. Universalism . . . remains as important to the French as it once was to . . . many American liberals." Affirmative action, he concluded, "sandbags the universalism upon which racial justice ultimately depends."[73]

NOTES

1. See, for example, Terry Eastland, "Endgame for Affirmative Action," *Wall Street Journal*, March 28, 1996, A14.

2. Nathan Glazer, "Race Not Class," *Wall Street Journal*, April 5, 1995, A10.

3. There is good reason for fear of condemnation as a racist. Rhetorical excess can appear in the most unlikely forums. In a celebrated defense of affirmative action, literary critic Stanley Fish excoriates his opposition with the following: " 'Individualism,' 'fairness,' 'merit'—these three words are continually misappropriated by bigots who have learned that they need not put on a white hood or bar access to the ballot box to secure their ends." See Stanley Fish, "Reverse Racism: Or How the Pot Got to Call the Kettle Black," *Atlantic Monthly* 275 (November 1993): 136.

4. See Peter Brimelow and Leslie Spencer, "When Quotas Replace Merit, Everyone Suffers," *Forbes* 152 (February 15, 1993): 80–102. They conclude that the direct costs to regulate and enforce compliance in the private sector, schools, and colleges alone run between $16 billion and $19 billion yearly. This, however, is but the tip of a gigantic iceberg, for the indirect and opportunity costs associated with hiring the less able, which they can only measure roughly, may produce a total cost of $236 billion yearly.

5. Underutilization was defined as having fewer minorities or women in a particular job category than would reasonably be expected by their availability as determined by Census Bureau statistics on the workforce (e.g., the percentage of black workers who are unskilled laborers). So if 10 percent of the unskilled workers in a local area are black, 10 percent of each federal contractor's unskilled workers should likewise be black. Actually, the courts are willing to accept 80 percent of the goal, which in this example would be 8 percent. See Nathan Glazer, *Affirmative Discrimination* (Cambridge: Harvard University Press, 1987), esp. chap. 2.

6. For historical and cultural reasons, groups tend to specialize in various occupations and fields. Today, for instance, Koreans specialize in small grocery stores, Greeks in restaurants, subcontinent Indians in motels, and so on. (Blacks appear to specialize in civil service and other government jobs, as did the Irish at an earlier time.) In other words, underrepresentation is not prima facie evidence of discrimination. See Thomas Sowell, *Civil Rights: Rhetoric and Reality* (New York: Quill William Morrow, 1984), pp. 13–21.

7. Congress defined affirmative action as an intentional act and not one of mere underrepresentation. The actual wording of the law was: "703 (j) Nothing contained in this title shall be interpreted to require any employer . . . to grant preferential treatment to any individual or to any group because of the race, color, religion, sex, or national origin of such individual or group on account of an imbalance which may exist with respect to the total number or percentage of persons of any race, color, religion, sex, or national origin employed by any employer." From Glazer, *Affirmative Discrimination*, p. 44. Indeed, the intent of Congress was stated unequivocally in the *Congressional Record* by Senator Hubert H. Humphrey:

"The proponents of the bill have carefully stated on numerous occasions that Title 7 does not require an employer to achieve any sort of racial balance in his workforce by giving preferential treatment to any individual or group." Ibid., p. 45.

8. The term *affirmative action* appears in two places in American law—in the 1964 Civil Rights Act and in presidential Executive Order 11246. Just as Title 7 did not require proportional hiring of blacks and whites, the term did not refer initially to proportional hiring and other forms of preferential policy. When first used, it referred to the relief given to proven victims of discrimination. Ibid., p. 58.

9. Ironically, it was a Republican, not a Democratic, president who initiated specific goals and timetables. In 1969, an administrative decree was issued by Secretary of Labor George Schultz ordering contractors in the Philadelphia construction industry to impose a quota policy to increase the number of black apprentices in union jobs. Richard Nixon explained his support for quotas with the argument that "the Democrats are token-oriented—we are job-oriented." Richard Nixon is quoted in Seymour Martin Lipset, "Affirmative Action," *Washington Quarterly* (Winter 1992): 56.

10. On civil rights issues, administrative agencies (mostly the EEOC and OFCC) issue guidelines for employers, and the courts then rule on their constitutionality. Although many of the guidelines issued by the agencies were patently in conflict with the original intent of Congress, the courts generally accepted them, and Congress failed to challenge the agencies and courts, which it can do at any time.

11. See Glazer, *Affirmative Discrimination.*

12. Gertrude Ezorsky, *Racism and Justice: The Case for Affirmative Action* (Ithaca, N.Y.: Cornell University Press, 1991), p. 35. Victim Vision supporters tend to ignore recent social changes that have decreased discrimination. Personnel is now a field in which minorities have been heavily for some time. By 1980, for instance, blacks were 11.1 percent of all personnel and labor relations workers. How, one may ask, do white officials manage to impose racist employment practices when blacks are involved in the hiring process itself? Data on personnel may be found in U.S. Bureau of the Census, *Statistical Abstract of the United States: 1981*, 102nd ed., (Washington, D.C.: Government Printing Office, 1981), p. 394.

13. Perhaps the best example is to be found in William Julius Wilson, *The Truly Disadvantaged* (Chicago: University of Chicago Press, 1987).

14. See Joseph Agassi, "Institutional Individualism," *British Journal of Sociology* 26 (1975): 144–55.

15. For an example of this naive faith in role models, see Ezorsky, *Racism and Justice*, pp. 73–94.

16. The literature on occupational choice finds repeatedly that young people are influenced by parents, other relatives, friends, and teachers. For reviews of the literature, see John Saltiel, "Sex Differences in Occupational Significant Others and Their Role Relationships with Students," *Rural Sociology* 47 (1982): 129–46; and Michael Betz and Lenahan O'Connell, "The Role of Inside and Same-Sex Influencers in the Choice of Nontraditional Occupations," *Sociological Inquiry* 62 (1992): 98–106.

17. Ezorsky, *Racism and Justice.*, p. 73.

18. Ibid., p. 61. Unwittingly, Ezorsky reveals the status panic at the heart of the demand for preferential policies when she writes: "Today blacks still predominate

in those occupations that in a slave society would be reserved for slaves." Ibid., p. 74.

19. For an account of its worldwide failure to help people advance economically, see Thomas Sowell, *Preferential Policies: An International Perspective* (New York: William Morrow, 1990).

20. Nicholas Capaldi, a philosopher, argues that affirmative action, in theory and practice, violates ethical principles. See his *Out of Order: Affirmative Action and the Crisis of Doctrinaire Liberalism* (Buffalo, N.Y.: Prometheus Books, 1985).

21. For a detailed account of how the rule of law benefits the entire community, see the various works of Friedrich A. Hayek, especially his *Law, Legislation, and Liberty: Rules and Order*, vol. 1 (Chicago: University of Chicago Press, 1973).

22. We will discuss the absence of substantial benefit below.

23. For a discussion of this problem throughout history in general, see Alexander Rustow, *Freedom and Domination: A Historical Critique of Civilization*, trans. Salvator Attanasio (Princeton: Princeton University Press, 1980).

24. On laws defining status, see Randall Collins, *Weberian Sociological Theory* (Cambridge: Cambridge University Press, 1986).

25. See Soo Son, Suzanne W. Model, and Gene A. Fisher, "Polarization and Progress in the Black Community: Earnings and Status Gains for Young Black Males in the Era of Affirmative Action," *Sociological Forum* 4 (Summer 1989): 309–27.

26. On the rise of command elements, see Hayek, *Law, Legislation, and Liberty*; and Bruno Leoni, *Freedom and the Law* (Los Angeles: Nash, 1972).

27. See Michael Oakeshott, *On History, and Other Essays* (Oxford: Basil Blackwell, 1983).

28. For a discussion of how goals and timetables become "soft quotas," see Paul Craig Roberts and Lawrence M. Stratton Jr., "Color Code," *National Review*, March 20, 1995, pp. 36–51.

29. John Hunter, an industrial psychologist, estimates the current annual cost of not using cognitive ability tests to hire personnel at $150 billion, or 2.5 percent of gross national product (GNP). See Brimelow and Spencer, "When Quotas Replace Merit, Everyone Suffers."

30. Jonathan R. Macey, "Banking by Quota," *Wall Street Journal*, September 7, 1994, A14. Our italics. Also see Llewellyn Rockwell, Jr., "Welfarizing Credit, Ignoring Risk," *Washington Times*, May 24, 1994, p. E3.

31. See Jonathan R. Macey, "The Lowdown on Lending Discrimination," *Wall Street Journal*, August 9, 1995, p. A8. Macey points out that the average default rate for whites in 1987 was 4.3 percent. For blacks it was 9 percent. Also see Rockwell, "Welfarizing Credit, Ignoring Risk."

32. Llewellyn Rockwell, Jr., "Discreditable Reports," *National Review*, July 19, 1993, pp. 45–48.

33. See Macey, "Banking by Quota," p. A14. It may be "scandalous," but it must be remembered that the banking industry has long provided an inviting target for government agencies. Moreover, as closely regulated industries, they are extremely vulnerable to political pressures.

34. Rockwell, "Discreditable Reports," p. 46.

35. Ibid., p. 47.

36. Robert Stowe England, "Assault on the Mortgage Lenders," *National Review*, December 27, 1993, pp. 52–54.

37. Llewellyn Rockwell, Jr., "Insurance Industry Targeted," *Washington Times*, June 3, 1994, p. A17.

38. Ibid.

39. Ludwig von Mises, *Human Action: A Treatise on Economics*, 3rd rev. ed. (Chicago: Henry Regnery, 1966).

40. Gardner Harris, "White Applicants Say Police Test Biased," *Louisville Courier-Journal*, May 12, 1995, A1.

41. E. E. Schattschneider, *The Semisovereign People: A Realist's View of America* (New York: Holt, Rinehart and Winston, 1960), pp. 1–61.

42. For an account of affirmative action in Malaysia, see Thomas Sowell, *Preferential Policies*, pp. 41–89.

43. Polls show consistently strong white opposition to affirmative action. The Gallup organization has asked Americans on five occasions from 1977 to 1989 whether they prefer that minorities be given preference for jobs and places in education or that employment and educational decisions be based on ability as measured by test scores. On all five surveys, no more than 11 percent of the public ever endorsed preferential treatment for minorities. In all five, from 81 to 84 percent of those sampled thought that employment decisions should be based on tests. See Diane Colasanto, "Preferential Treatment for Women, Minorities," *Gallup Poll Monthly*, no. 291 (1989): 13–22. Opposition appears to be so strong that the public now wants laws against affirmative action. In fact, a recent nationwide poll conducted by the *Los Angeles Times* found that 73 percent of Americans favor a federal law that would make it unlawful for any employer to grant preferential treatment in hiring. See Steven A. Holmes, "Affirmative Action Backers Are Alarmed by Backlash," *New York Times*, February 7, 1995, p. C-18. For a report on white complaints about affirmative action, see David Johnston, "Study Finds Job Complaints Are Widespread at F.B.I.," *New York Times*, June 19, 1991, p. A-10.

44. See the classic work by Henry Sumner Maine, *Ancient Law* (New York: Henry Holt & Co., 1885), pp. 63–65.

45. James P. Smith, "Affirmative Action and Its Effects" (paper presented at a meeting of the American Sociological Association, Washington, D.C., 1990).

46. Two sets of employment statistics are relevant to the issue of black income advance: the median income of all black and white males 14 years of age and older (this includes the part-time and intermittently employed) and the median income of black and white males who work year-round. The income gains of all black males parallel those of full-time, year-round workers. In 1965 the income of the former was 52 percent of comparable whites'. It increased to 59.3 percent by 1970. By 1990, it had advanced only 1.3 percent to 60.6 percent of white income. Stagnation can also be found in the statistics for wages of black women relative to white women. By 1970 black women earned 91 percent of their white counterparts. During the 1970s they closed the gap slightly to 93 percent. But it widened during the 1980s and stood at 81 percent in 1990, as the wages of white women increased relative to all groups, including white males. Income statistics for 1970 and 1980 are from: U.S. Bureau of the Census, *Statistical Abstract of the United States: 1992*, 112th ed. (Washington, D.C.: Government Printing Office, 1992), p. 438. Income statistics for 1990 are from U.S. Bureau of the Census, *Statistical Abstract of the*

United States: 1993, 113th ed. (Washington, D.C.: Government Printing Office, 1993), p. 465. Income statistics for 1965 are from U.S. Bureau of the Census, *Statistical Abstract of the United States: 1967*, 88th ed. (Washington, D.C.: Government Printing Office, 1967), p. 337.

47. Smith, "Affirmative Action and Its Effects." In 1966, 3,254 individuals filed race discrimination complaints with the EEOC. That number increased to 11,806 by 1970. Each case filed with the EEOC is a potential federal lawsuit. By 1970, 344 Title 7 lawsuits had been filed in federal court. For an analysis of the benefits of Title 7 lawsuits, see Paul Burstein and Mark Evan Edwards, "Employment Discrimination Litigation and Racial Disparity in Earnings" (Paper presented at the annual meeting of the American Sociological Association, Pittsburg, Pa., August 1992).

48. Some statistical studies of affirmative action find a limited boost in the earnings of the young. For example, Jonathan Leonard, an economist, argues that the tight labor markets of the late 1970s conceal the positive effect of affirmative action, but he estimates only a 1 to 2 percent increase in average black male wages from affirmative action. See Jonathan S. Leonard, "The Impact of Affirmative Action Regulation and Equal Employment Law on Black Unemployment," *Journal of Economic Perspectives* 4 (Fall 1990): 47–63. And, of course, to say that most blacks do not gain an increase in income is not to say that some African Americans in specific occupations do not do so. A study of the pay of college professors found that blacks with Ph.D.s earn 10 percent more in income than their white counterparts, once research productivity was taken into account. See Debra A. Barbezat, "Affirmative Action in Higher Education," *Research in Labor Economics* 10 (1989): 107–56.

49. See Reynolds Farley, *Blacks and Whites: Narrowing the Gap?* (Cambridge: Harvard University Press, 1984). Similarly, Farley reports that the index of occupational dissimilarity (an index that shows the minimum number of either whites or nonwhites who would have to switch from one job category to another one to eliminate occupational differences) shows that occupational segregation by race declined during the 1970s, the index value shrinking from 30 to 23. In addition to its effect on average occupational prestige, affirmative action changed the structure of black employment with blacks (especially college-educated managers) moving into firms holding federal contracts. See Smith, "Affirmative Action and Its Effects." But most shifts to firms with federal contracts occurred prior to 1970 and probably represented a response to EEO laws, not to affirmative action pressures.

50. In a recent study of a large representative sample of young Americans below the age of 34, Charles Murray and Richard Herrnstein found evidence of widespread misallocation. Blacks, once cognitive ability is taken into account, are overrepresented in the professions and other higher-level occupations. The authors conclude that this overrepresentation is due to affirmative action. Among whites, the average IQ was 114 for professionals, 113 for technicians, and 108 for managers. Blacks had IQ scores that were more than one standard deviation lower than their white counterparts in each occupational category. (Some of this is probably due to the wide range of occupations in each category and the crowding of blacks into the lower-skill occupations. For example physicians, lawyers, and social workers are in the professional category; blacks are still rare in the first two occupations but overrepresented in the last). See Richard Herrnstein and Charles Murray, *The*

Bell Curve: Intelligence and Class Structure in American Life (New York: Free Press, 1994), p. 488.

51. Besides misallocation of labor, there are other possible reasons for affirmative action's failure. As noted in Chapter 3, there is some reason to believe that employers have moved some plants and facilities to rural areas where few blacks live. It is also possible, as Farrell Bloch speculates, that EEO law encourages small employers to avoid hiring blacks for fear of discrimination complaints. See Farrell Bloch, "Affirmative Action Hasn't Helped Blacks," *Wall Street Journal*, March 1, 1995, p. A14. This, however, seems unlikely as employers win the vast majority of such complaints, and many blacks work in the service sector, where the average business is small. In addition, one of the best defenses against a complaint of discrimination is to have some black employees on the payroll. So it is always in the interests of employers to hire some black applicants. Taking all of the above into consideration, it appears that the failure of affirmative action is due to the relatively small number of blacks with employable skills.

52. Robert L. Boyd, "A Contextual Analysis of Black Self-Employment in Large Metropolitan Areas, 1970–1980," *Social Forces* 70 (December 1991): 409–29; and idem, "Black and Asian Self-Employment in Large Metropolitan Areas: A Comparative Analysis," *Social Problems* 37 (May 1990): 258–74.

53. The relative decline in the number of black merchants in the cities may even aggravate race relations. Koreans, Palestinians, and people from other ethnic groups often fill the vacuum created by affirmative action by owning and operating retail enterprises like grocery and convenience stores, which provide basic services to the black community. For reasons not fully understood, these ethnic businessmen and -women are often disliked by the people they serve, a fact that appears to generate black-white and black-Asian conflict. Certainly, hostility toward Asian businessmen was evident in the Los Angeles riot in 1992, as Asians were attacked and their stores destroyed.

54. See Eugene Silverberg, "Race, Recent Entry and Labor Market Participation," *American Economic Review* 75 (December 1985): 1168–77.

55. Craig Zwerling and Hilary Silver, "Race and Job Dismissals in a Federal Bureaucracy," *American Sociological Review* 55 (October 1990):651–60.

56. For articles documenting the connection between tests of cognitive ability and job performance, see note 35 in Chapter 3. Also see Herrnstein and Murray, *The Bell Curve*, pp. 63–89.

57. See Lenahan O'Connell, "Investigators at Work: How Bureaucratic and Legal Constraints Influence the Enforcement of Discrimination Law," *Public Administration Review* 51 (March 1991): 123–30. For instance, blacks are far more likely than women and other minorities to file discrimination complaints. Moreover, over 50 percent of their complaints concern a discharge for cause (e.g., poor performance, rudeness, absenteeism). O'Connell also found that blacks were far more likely to have made a mistake of some kind at work.

58. See Herrnstein and Murray, *The Bell Curve*.

59. See Thomas Sowell, *Inside American Education: the Decline, the Deception, the Dogmas.* (New York: The Free Press, 1993), p. 144.

60. See Dinesh D'Souza, *Illiberal Education: The Politics of Race and Sex on Campus* (New York: Free Press, 1991), p. 39.

61. Sowell, *American Education*, p. 146.

62. Ibid., p. 136.

63. Another way to make this point is the following: If goals and timetables merely leveled the playing field so that the beneficiaries were as qualified as their white coworkers, affirmative action probably would significantly increase average black income. But once the market backed up by EEO law had effectively leveled the playing field, affirmative action had the perverse effect of setting blacks up in many cases for failure in the competition after hire with whites and Asians for pay raises and promotions.

64. For an interesting account of this "second wave" of affirmative action, see Heather MacDonald, "The Diversity Industry," *New Republic* 209 (July 5, 1993): 22–25.

65. Ibid., p. 23.

66. Ibid.

67. Ibid., p. 24.

68. Ibid.

69. Timothy Egan, "Teaching Tolerance in Workplaces: A Seattle Program Illustrates Limits," *New York Times*, October 8, 1993, p. A12.

70. Ibid.

71. See Lino Graglia, "Affirmative Discrimination," *National Review*, July 5, 1993, p. 29. Deceit seems to be inseparable from affirmative action in all its manifestations. For a discussion of the misleading tactics used to justify contract setasides in Atlanta, see Terry Eastland, "The Other Side of Atlanta's Affirmative Action Story," *Wall Street Journal*, July 24, 1996, p. A21.

72. See Alison Konrad and Frank Linnehan, "Formalized HRM Structures: Coordinating Equal Employment Opportunity or Concealing Organizational Practices," *Academy of Management Journal* 38 (Summer 1995): 787–820.

73. Jim Sleeper, "Back to Universals," *American Prospect* 10 (October 1992): 92.

6

Conclusion: Race, Status, and the Limits of Public Policy

In the conclusions of their books, students of public policy issues may offer their readers a series of specific proposals for social or political reform. Obviously, there has been no shortage of suggestions from race relations experts, but most of these "solutions" have not been notably successful. In general, they have aimed at reducing poverty and unemployment with transfer payments and abolishing discrimination with affirmative action policies. Unfortunately, affirmative action has failed to help the average black American, and a growth in welfare support has largely coincided with family breakdown, illegitimacy, inadequate educational attainment, persistent unemployment, and a drug culture in the great cities and elsewhere.

It is taken for granted by many scholars and public officials that white racism and discrimination remain the primary obstacles to black advancement. Since public authorities can justify the success of their programs only by referring to concrete results, it ought to have been plain to reformers from the outset that quotas and timetables, not "equal opportunity," would be what mattered once affirmative action was entrenched in law and administrative regulation.

Many Americans have predictably become disturbed by the heavy-handedness of administrative agencies and judicial bodies whose essential purpose is to intervene in hiring practices and other areas of individual, interpersonal decision making. When they discover that they, their friends, or their acquaintances are denied positions because of race or gender, they call it "unfair." At least intuitively, many have come to believe that affirmative action strikes at a fundamental principle of Western civilization, namely, that it offends the rule of law upon which our liberties and economic prosperity ultimately depend. Ironically, in their drive to demonstrate concrete results with statistics of African-American representation in various occupational categories, the political and intellectual classes, wittingly or unwittingly, have lent support to a system of "laws" whose chief beneficiaries turn out to be mostly middle-class blacks and well-educated women, not poorer, less advantaged African Americans. The consequence has been a growing public disillusionment and resistance at the ballot box against what they believe to be unfair treatment.

BESIEGEMENT AMID PROGRESS

It is hard to avoid the conclusion that a sense of being besieged has gripped the black community for some years now, a diffuse fear that the gains since 1964 are somehow ephemeral; that what whites have granted they might just as easily withdraw. To the disinterested observer of American events over the past 30 years, these fears may seem groundless, but to many blacks in all socioeconomic groups, it is not at all clear that whites are trustworthy. Thus, the most extreme or bizarre conspiracy theories have been routinely taken with the utmost seriousness, not just by the black masses but by their opinion leaders as well. The Tawana Brawley episode in which prominent black Americans were quite willing to believe the preposterous tale of a disturbed teenager and the theory that crack and AIDS were deliberately introduced into the inner cities in order to eliminate an entire race are among the most extreme examples. That the arguments of Minister Louis Farrakhan can be taken seriously by so many blacks from different educational backgrounds suggests the depth of these fears.

Simultaneously, blacks are confronted with a most disturbing reality within the heart of their own community—namely, the crime, unemployment, illegitimacy, weak educational attainments, and low incomes of the inner cities. It is impossible to lay the cause of all these social ills to white racism and discrimination, although some black spokesmen have made a valiant effort to do so. As whites have become acutely aware of black crime in our major urban areas, as social commentary spreads about the decline of the black family, and as the relatively poor performance of many blacks in integrated educational settings draws public attention, it becomes ever more urgent that this relative "backwardness" be explained. After all, have not fundamental rights been assured for some time? Are not the schools formally integrated? Then why, many inquire, is progress on a number of fronts so slow? To many of America's black citizens this is a question that cries for a reassuring answer.

Perhaps this sense of besiegement is not so strange as it may seem. Victimology is today a highly respected academic and political position. And who has been more victimized in this country than black Americans? Indeed, if whites in the eighteenth and nineteenth centuries embraced slavery, some reason, how can they ever be trusted again, even at the end of the twentieth century? Are black Americans not repeatedly informed by respectable political and educational leaders of all races that their present problems are due to white racism? Must it not be true if so many important people of all races agree? It is a vicious circle in which a victimist ideology, status frustrations, and concrete material interests mutually reinforce one another.

Much of this pessimism, we submit, arises from a reluctance to give sufficient attention to a black middle class caught in the throes of rapid social and political change. A long history of legal and political subordination to whites was rather suddenly dismantled in the 1960s. With the acquisition of full citizenship came inflated expectations for a quick entry into "mainstream" life. Disappointment with the pace of progress was inevitable. It was only a matter of time until tensions would erupt into open conflict. Disillusionment with the pace of progress since has fed on all the old fears of white repression and racism.

As the social balance of power between blacks and whites becomes progressively more equal, whatever barriers to parity that remain are fiercely resented. The consequence is an enhanced level of sensitivity to any perceived threats to dignity and respect, no matter how innocuous or unintended the particular affront. Disrespect or ignorance under the new circumstances, however mild, may be less bearable than ever for the minority individual.

When the roadblocks put in the way of social and political mobility are mostly eliminated, and when members of the established group profess their good intentions and willingly confess their own wrongs, it is increasingly difficult to attach consistent blame for one's misfortunes to any one particular individual or institution. At least it is difficult to affix cause and effect. Blame, therefore, tends to be framed in more abstract terms by the aggrieved party. Failures must be explained in a different way than formerly, made plausible not only to oneself but to the white majority as well. The changing definitions of what constitutes "racism" is a good case in point.

In the ensuing status struggle with the white majority, the black latecomer lays claim to the moral superiority of his or her own group. Under these conditions, whites on the whole agree that their race has much for which to answer. Faced with new circumstances and feeling some degree of guilt or responsibility for the wrongs of their ancestors, they acquiesce to pressures for reform. Their defenses crumble in the wake of the political and moral challenge. Their leaders admit their own errors and shortcomings, even going so far as to establish special days and months in honor of black heroes and events. In numerous cases, they agree to remove such despised symbols as the Confederate flag. Many white political elites and intellectuals even go so far as to support what has come to be called "reverse discrimination." In general, most whites are now agreed that race relations were in need of profound repair, although in the opinion of many blacks, the pace of progress has proved woefully inadequate to the times.

Is it not apparent that the psychological costs of potential failure are likely to be most severe in a society in which the individual member of a race historically oppressed and ridiculed is suddenly informed he (or she) can be anything he wishes, even as his own education and skills often leave much to be desired? The psychological stakes, however, are simply too great to admit failure; shortcomings need explanation. The idea naturally grows that racism is more entrenched than ever. Hence, we see a close connection between a strident victimist ideology and affirmative action in that the former requires the latter if it is to establish its legitimacy and eliminate other considerations. Those who gain from affirmative action cannot bring themselves to admit that their present good fortune may have been due in many instances to preferential treatment. To oppose affirmative action, to admit its inadequacies, would be an implicit acknowledgment that one's own achievements are somehow tainted. A result is the perpetuation of a flawed policy whose benefits accrue mostly to a minority of privileged black Americans.

Given the political will, affirmative action could be dismantled, but with the best of intentions, meaningful progress in other areas such as the family and education will be painfully slow in coming. It must be stressed that the balance of social power between the participants in the debate does not augur well for a significant resolution of these issues for some time. As we have argued in this work, one must not neglect the dynamics of group competition, that uneasy sociopolitical equilibrium presently composed, roughly speaking, of a white majority, a black middle class, and a black underclass. These three groups, broadly defined, are highly unequal in the power resources they respectively command, although even the weakest of the three is not bereft of influence. Put another way, they are functionally dependent on one another. The actions of one group can therefore affect, either positively or negatively, the "power chances" of the others. To employ the terminology of one sociologist, they may be said to form a network of "interdependent human beings, with shifting asymmetrical power balances."[1] Let us briefly consider what this balance of social forces portends for race relations and public policy initiatives in the near term.

RACE AND THE BALANCE OF SOCIAL POWER

Given its political, social, and economic power, the white majority can grant or limit access to an array of services and benefits upon which blacks directly depend for their welfare, everything from jobs in the public and private sectors for more advantaged blacks to welfare entitlements for disadvantaged ones. Of special concern to the black middle class are the numerous *symbolic* benefits that may be either proffered or withheld. It is hardly an exaggeration to say that the extent to which white "acceptances" coincide with black "announcements" profoundly affects the development of black individuals' identity, confidence, and self-esteem.

The black middle class has the power to affect the tone of the interracial dialogue. Because it possesses vital communication skills, its members are normally assumed by others to speak for the black community as a whole. In this role the attitudes and opinions of the middle class cannot help but influence both the manner in which the races will perceive the aims and actions of one another and the level of satisfaction or dissatisfaction within the black community. To what extent the African-American middle class exerts any direct influence over the overt behavior of the underclass is problematical, although its dissatisfaction with the present state of race relations must surely influence opinion among the black masses.

Even the underclass has various resources at its disposal to affect the balance of group power. Some social scientists have even concluded that the magnitude of "poor relief" is roughly proportionate to establishment fears of violence from below.[2] It goes without saying that the underclass potentially has ample power to disturb the peace. Its social pathologies also arouse resentment. As such, its behavior and attitudes partly determine how other races will respond to blacks *as a group*. Thus, what many middle-class individuals regard as "inappropriate" behavior by lower-class blacks on the streets, in the stores, or at the fast-food chains may be easily tucked away in memory for future reference.

Precisely because black poverty and social pathology are important factors in the formation of white attitudes, certain strategic choices press themselves upon the black middle class. At a minimum, the underclass potential for violence to person and property must obviously be taken into account. The manner in which the black middle class responds to these white fears, however, has consequences for its own interests.

If the black middle class distances itself too far ideologically and politically from the poor and the underclass, it endangers its leadership role within the black community as a whole. More directly, its access to affirmative action entitlements is put at risk. It is, after all, difficult to justify to both black *and* white opinion a policy that benefits a relatively small but hardly disadvantaged segment of black America. Once the public begins to sense just who benefits from affirmative action, the policy will probably lose whatever legitimacy it still commands. Consequently, there is every reason to anticipate that those who wish to maintain the status quo will continue making every effort to define the interracial political debate as one of white discrimination against *all* blacks, irrespective of income or social condition.

Let us suppose, however, that in the opinion of whites the black middle class does not appear to distance itself sufficiently from the lower class and the underclass. That is to say, black spokesmen seem to tolerate and excuse, if not actually support, standards of behavior that offend what generally passes for middle-class opinion. In this instance, the black middle class signals by various means its steadfast support for all members of its own race, whatever their behavior and values. The imperatives of race, in a word, take priority over the enforcement of agreed-upon norms of individual behavior. In order to make its position known, black opinion leaders with access to the media persist in laying the blame on "white society" for the high rate of crime, illegitimacy, inadequate skills, and poor schooling within the black community. Along the way, they lend their steadfast moral and ideological allegiance to policy positions that appear to be targeted overwhelmingly at the "welfare class." When this majority impression is joined with the reluctance of upwardly mobile blacks to adopt more or less wholeheartedly the behavioral norms of the dominant white majority, the distinct probability arises for mutual misunderstanding between the races. Under these conditions, one may be sure that the status struggle will persist.

THE STATUS STRUGGLE AND THE INFORMALIZATION OF BEHAVIOR

In the jockeying for positions of status among social groups, the issues in dispute can vary. The demand for affirmative action and its benefits is the most salient one at stake in the ongoing status struggle between blacks and whites. As we have seen, however, the struggle for social standing is linked more broadly to questions of self-esteem and victim status. In our age, these disputes are undoubtedly propelled by what the late Norbert Elias perceived as a major force in the development of Western societies in the twentieth century, namely, a growing "informalization" in general standards of behavior.[3]

Whatever one may say about these disputes, they are a permanent feature of sociopolitical life. One result has been to shift the balance of power much more favorably in the direction of outsider interests. Political and social power are now much more fluid, subject to shifting currents and unstable party alliances than at the beginning of this century when the nobility and a small elite within the middle class dominated the primary positions of leadership. People of modest backgrounds and circumstances have today entered party, military, and bureaucratic positions once dominated by narrow class interests. With social mobility, mass consumption, and a rise in productivity has come a marked growth in democratic attitudes and a general process of informalization of behavior.

Forms of behavior and standards of etiquette in existence in 1900, for example, were heavily laden with class meaning in which ritualized forms of language and behavior functioned as a means for social exclusion and distinction. Many of these rituals and standards, which encouraged social distance between social superiors and inferiors, were nevertheless adopted by other classes farther down the social hierarchy. As the wealth and power of the masses increased and class positions became more tenuous and open to challenge, formalization gave way on an ever-increasing scale to informalization of standards of conduct. Indeed, as the enemy of social distance, informalization of behavior is a natural ally of democratization of thoughts and feelings; hence, it is often the enemy of high culture. After all, to the extent that culture is employed as a means to create distance and distinctions in taste, it has the potential, directly or indirectly, of being translated into social and/or political power.[4]

In the United States, the ratio of formalization to informalization has shifted decisively in the direction of the latter. Evidence of the relentless increase in informalization is all around us, affecting in profound ways the relations between old and young, male and female, and higher-and lower-status and-class groups. In part because Americans have long been more accustomed to social change and are less class conscious and less inclined to deferential modes of behavior than are the peoples of Europe, they have likewise been more receptive to the informalization process. As a result, our bastions of social and political power are far less resistant to mobile outsiders than was true of previous generations. The power chances of outsiders have been enhanced as never before.

More traditional cultural, social, and political elites, of course, may be expected to resist to varying degrees the informalization of manners and behavior, to insist on conformity to the practices of the established group. This pressure to conform, however, is resented by outsiders, especially as their own social and political power more nearly approaches that of the established group. In this respect, the strength of white Americans in terms of numbers and resources is overwhelming on paper, but black moral and ideological leverage are far from negligible. Barriers traditionally put in the way of minority advancement have therefore either been severely compromised or eliminated entirely over the past three decades. Just as the informalization process has helped to erode the power of men over women, it has likewise reduced barriers between the races, easing the way for black advancement and white acceptance.

Nevertheless, the informalization of behavior and a general tolerance for behavior thought unacceptable by much "respectable" opinion only a short time ago does not mean that resistance from established groups has completely disappeared. It is plain that informalization has its limits. An insistence on "showing my color" or steadfast opposition to "acting white" may be emotionally satisfying for those confronted with pressure to conform to "white" norms and values. Similarly, rebellion against contemporary standards of behavior may also play well with younger, more self-conscious individuals in search of secure identities and resentful of particular restraints meant to enforce conformity to what they regard as white culture. But a refusal to comply with majority standards may have a detrimental impact on the fortunes of minority members who will not or cannot comply.

Many blacks, to be sure, regard formalized behavior as a threat to black culture. In an assessment of Clarence Page's *Showing My Color*, David Horowitz aptly remarks that when the African American is warned by another member of his race against "showing your color" to whites, the real message is that he ought not display his "culture."[5] Otherwise, he may not only embarrass himself but, in addition, encourage disrespect for his race. If this saying refers to overt behavior alone, it may be little more than an attempt to bring the erring individual around to more acceptable forms of behavior. Much depends on whether it is intended to apply mainly to the particular individual or to the group in general. In either case, an element of self-hatred is apparent.

The conflict over standards of behavior probably explains much of our interracial tension. If color and culture are regarded by many black Americans as essentially interchangeable concepts—if they are synonymous—the implications for race relations are alarming, to put it mildly. One's personal style or "culture" can presumably be altered, but color is another matter altogether. Color must therefore be somehow prior to culture. But if that is the way many black Americans think and believe, the status struggle will not soon subside, least of all in the professions, management (middle and upper-level), finance, sales, and other occupational areas in which appearance, personality, and language skills heavily influence recruitment and success.

To the extent that it is possible for the mind to reduce culture to color—that is, to race—there arises the temptation to resist steadfastly the effort to impose standards of behavior and values at odds with black standards, styles, and traditions. The black individual, it would seem, is thus under more or less constant pressure in school, the workplace, and elsewhere to choose between the demands of the racial group and the necessity to adapt his (or her) own behavior to majority customs and habits, including the standards of his white employers, peers, and clients. Because getting promotions, winning contracts, or making sales is so dependent on "making a good impression" and other more or less subjective criteria, it is easier to convince oneself in the face of rejection that racism must be the cause of failure. Without a serious effort to adjust to white behavioral standards, tastes, and expectations, however, many in the rising black middle classes may fall along the way, while others will regard themselves as permanent outsiders denied the fruits of their labors by a racist society.

The militant defense of affirmative action at all costs by black spokesmen exposes these many contradictions at war within the black middle-class soul. By creating an impression among many whites that blacks as a whole, irrespective of their particular status or class, disparage values that reward ability, skill, and hard work, they reveal less the principled stance of a deprived race than the pecuniary demands of the narrow interest group. The demand for racial preferences implies that in their quest for quotas, timetables, and diversity, black Americans more or less uniformly support hiring by race, whatever the cost to employers, employees, or the economy. This impression, once it is firmly linked in white minds with the objective conditions of black crime, relatively low educational achievement, illegitimacy, and welfare, provides fertile soil for the growth of the negative stereotypes that affirmative action and the role models it supposedly develops are expected instead to undermine. By appearing to excuse the social pathology within the black community and by linking itself to a vision of blacks as a besieged group united against a hostile majority, the black middle class inadvertently encourages the stereotypical behavior it so rightly detests.

In sum, the black middle class is caught in a double bind between a white majority, whose respect and deference it craves and whose support it requires, and a population of poorer, less advantaged blacks whose lower-class patterns of behavior are an embarrassment in its status struggle with whites but whose own yearning for social recognition and respect grows ever stronger. By championing the interests of the black lower class in general and the underclass in particular, by seeming to make their aspirations its own, the middle class at present seems to opt simultaneously for moral leadership within the black community *and* the emotional sustenance of the group, representing to nonblack opinion what passes for *the* African-American position on an array of political and social issues.

PROGRESS, BLACK COHESION, AND THE LIMITS OF PUBLIC POLICY

Because growing numbers of black Americans are finally entering the mainstream of American life, but because they also carry painful historical memories from their long trip, their road will continue to be a bumpy one for some time. If the theory of status insecurity articulated in this work is applicable to upwardly mobile outsiders in general, why should it not apply with special force to this particular generation of black Americans? This kind of analysis raises few eyebrows where other American ethnic groups or peoples in other nations are concerned, but social scientists in this country seem reluctant to study black Americans in quite the same manner as other ethnic groups here and abroad. Perhaps if more American specialists in race relations reasoned in comparative terms, their pessimism about American institutions and even majority behavior and attitudes might be open to some revision.

Although status anxiety and the search for self-esteem within the black middle class are to be with us for some time, the long-term prospects are more positive. As the paradox of progress implies, many of our current problems are those "natural" growing pains that generally accompany the social advancement of latecomer groups. History tells us that sooner or later they enter the mainstream in the full sense of the term. In fact, there are clear signs of progress already evident. Increased skills, rising family incomes, educational achievements, and entry into the more prestigious occupations suggest improvement.[6]

If we assume a more or less steady increase in economic growth, we may be confident that the expansion of opportunities in the marketplace will continue to raise aggregate black income and employment. In this respect, the reduction or elimination of affirmative action would divert relatively more black labor away from government and the huge private bureaucracies into the private sector, particularly into small business and those occupations within the black communities in which viable role models would be readily available for young people. One consequence would presumably be a change in the socioeconomic and ideological composition of the black bourgeoisie, which until now has been heavily dependent on public sector and corporate employment.

Needless to say, we have been discussing long-run trends. Public policy and politics, however, take place in the short run. If, as we have argued, much of the existing tension between the races is due to status frustration and competition, it is hard to see how government programs can alleviate this particular problem in any significant manner. How does one craft legislative or administrative rules that ultimately relate to the psyche? It is clear that to the extent anxiety breeds resentment, alienation, and a sense of victimization among members of a group who are not typically disadvantaged in any material or educational sense, public policy is a hapless tool. After all, a principal purpose of race policy today is not so much an attempt to create situations favorable to the rights of the individual and a true equality before the law—witness affirmative action—as an effort to draw distinctions between special categories of citizens, the usual effect of which has been to reinforce existing racial divisions. Particularly in the case of the black middle classes, no amount of government support in the *short run* will satisfy those needs that at bottom are status related rather than merely economic in nature.

At the same time, it is undeniable that, over and above status competition, an economic component reinforces the sense of racial besiegement and alienation within the black community. To retain its legitimacy, affirmative action must be justified as beneficial to the entire black community and not merely to its middle-class component. That so many blacks, relatively speaking, work in the public sector or are dependent on public welfare for their sustenance deserves emphasizing. In such areas as welfare and education policy, therefore, important changes in the status quo will be fiercely resisted. If this is true, the course of the interracial dialogue will depend less on any specific political and economic reforms or white attitudes than on the ideological and structural development of the black middle class. Not only does the black middle class have little incentive to abdicate its role as spokesman for the underclass and the poor, but the majority of African Americans are likely to follow its lead in the same direction.[7]

If racial cohesion remains a symbolic or economic imperative for so many black Americans, it is not difficult to grasp the larger implications in the near term, not only for the majority of African Americans but for American society as a whole. For one thing, it makes blacks perpetually dependent on a single political organization, namely, the Democratic Party and the public policies that sustain the social security state. The implication is obvious: Blacks' interests are to be defined in terms of the liberal wing of the national Democratic Party. As such, they are automatically deprived of a pivotal role between the two major political parties. Taken mostly for granted by the Democrats, their group concerns are largely ignored by the Republicans.

Thus, despite the great changes since 1964, the segmentation of the African-American community continues to exist. This separation is expressed in a sense of besiegement and victimization, both of which are reinforced by the economic and political conditions in which many blacks find themselves. Thus, as compared with other middle classes, blacks are more likely to be employed in the public sector, which in turn makes them as a group especially receptive to the Democratic party and public policies based upon redistribution and state intervention in economic life. The combined effect of these various forces is the creation of a certain uniformity of outlook in which deviation from the accepted path is not easily tolerated.

Specifically, the individual's daily experiences bring him (or her) into repeated contact with others whose own basic ideas and opinions continually reinforce his own inclinations. Family, peers, neighbors, coworkers, political affiliations, and the like, mutually support one another, in the process socially isolating him from contrary ideas. There is a cumulative effect in which the individual's opinions and prejudices are continually reinforced in different social environments. As a result, the individual will tend to be less tolerant of divergent views. Since they are unlikely to interact with those who might disagree with them on a broad range of topics, the positions and attitudes of others outside their orbit are unlikely to be considered as worthy of consideration. Lacking, in a word, are sufficient "cross pressures" on the individuals that normally take place in the course of their daily lives as they interact with others who have different attitudes from their own. According to social scientists, the individuals who belong to various groups are more likely to be characterized by tolerance of others and open-mindedness in general than are those who belong to few, if any, groups.[8]

It is true that members of the black middle class may interact frequently with whites in the course of their daily activities in the workplace or in public. On the other hand, it is doubtful that very many have close friendships with whites or other ethnic group members. It is not so much that interracial contacts are absent altogether as that they are often devoid of positive affect. More than one observer of college life, for example, has noted the absence of white and black student interaction when students sit at tables in cafeterias, converse outside classrooms, and mingle in dormitories. The desire to self-segregate may be seen in the rise of separate dorms and black cultural centers, hardly an encouraging omen, since these are the people who will enter the ranks of the black middle class. The factor of race seemingly cancels out many mutually satisfying experiences that one might ordinarily anticipate, so powerful are the pressures for racial conformity and racial cohesion. Our personal observation is that these youngsters are under continual pressure to repudiate their friendships with the other race.

Undoubtedly, the argument we have advanced in this book will be dismissed by some readers as a case of "blaming the victim." There are indeed black victims, but with the end of legal discrimination, it does not follow that government is equipped to end racism. As it is, public policy would be called upon to eliminate practices and attitudes that challenge one's preferred status or offend one's sense of dignity. In short, we enter the realm of good manners and everyday consideration for the feelings of others, especially on the part of whites. Realistically speaking, we face a problem of civility, not civil rights, in an era in which these virtues are sorely lacking.

The social system that supports the aged, the ill, the poor, and the unemployed has come under pressure from all sides. As we write these words, the United States, unlike the major European powers and Japan, is roughly at full employment, although our relatively lower level of productive growth has adversely affected family incomes for about a generation now. If the political authorities cannot or will not seek a "reasonable" balance between the saving and investment needs of the real economy and those of the welfare state and its clientele groups, there will surely arise even greater social tensions between whites and blacks over employment and affirmative action than presently exist.

NOTES

1. The statement is that of Van Benthem van den Bergh, as reported in Stephen Mennell, *Norbert Elias: An Introduction* (Oxford: Blackwell, 1992), pp. 251–52.

2. For example, Frances Fox Piven and Richard Cloward, *Regulating the Poor* (New York: Vintage), 1971.

3. Norbert Elias, *The Germans: Power Struggles and the Development of Habitus in the Nineteenth and Twentieth Centuries* (New York: Columbia University Press, 1996), pp. 25–63.

4. Pierre Bourdieu, *Distinction: A Social Critique of the Judgement of Taste* (Cambridge, Mass.: Harvard University Press, 1984).

5. David Horowitz, "Clarence Page's Race Problem, and Mine," *Heterodoxy* 4 (May-June 1996): 4.

6. For example, the National Assessment of Educational Progress, an annual study of the reading and other abilities of the nation's 17-year-olds, reports that blacks have significantly narrowed the gap in literacy over the past 15 years. This increase in such an important skill will undoubtedly be translated eventually into higher incomes and more rewarding lives for many more minority individuals in the years ahead. See Richard Herrnstein and Charles Murray, *The Bell Curve: Intelligence and Class Structure in American Life* (New York: Free Press, 1994), p. 291. Their data were drawn from the National Center for Education Statistics, *Trends in Academic Progress* (Washington, D.C.: National Center for Education Statistics, 1993).

7. In the debate of requiring English as the national language, the black middle class apparently has been more supportive of bilingualism than has the black majority. While this stance may be read as support for the civil rights of another minority group, it may also reflect the greater degree of black alienation from the dominant majority. For an excellent study, see Raymond Tatalovich, *Nativism Reborn?: The Official English Language Movement and the American States* (Lexington: University of Kentucky Press, 1995), pp. 240–43, 247–49.

8. The literature on the role of cross pressure and its role in degrees of tolerance, attitudes toward democracy, and even the role it plays in political stability is very large. See, in general, Seymour M. Lipset, *Political Man: The Social Bases of Politics* (Garden City, N.Y.: Doubleday, 1960); a particularly good treatment is Arend Lijphart, *The Politics of Accommodation: Pluralism and Democracy in the Netherlands* (Berkeley: University of California Press, 1968), pp. 7–15; and for a critique, see Sidney Verba, "Organizational Membership and Democratic Consensus," *Journal of Politics* 27 (August 1965): 467–97.

Selected Bibliography

BOOKS

Allport, Gordon. *The Nature of Prejudice*. New York: Addison-Wesley, 1954.

Barnett, Randy E., and John Hagel, eds. *Assessing the Criminal: Restitution, Retribution, and the Legal Process*. Cambridge: Ballinger, 1977.

Berger, Peter L., and Thomas Luckmann. *The Social Construction of Reality*. Garden City, N.Y.: Doubleday, 1967.

Bunzel, John. *Race Relations on Campus: Stanford Students Speak*. Stanford, Calif.: Stanford Alumni Association, 1992.

Coleman, James S., Thomas Hoffer, and Sally Kilgore. *High School Achievement: Public, Catholic, and Other Private Schools*. New York: Basic Books, 1982.

Cose, Ellis. *The Rage of a Privileged Class*. New York: HarperCollins, 1993.

Cuddihy, John Murray. *The Ordeal of Civility: Freud, Marx, Lévi-Strauss, and the Jewish Search for Modernity*. New York: Basic Books, 1974.

D'Souza, Dinesh. *Illiberal Education: The Politics of Race and Sex on Campus*. New York: Free Press, 1991.

Elias, Norbert., and J. L. Scotson. *The Established and the Outsiders: A Sociological Inquiry into Community Problems*. London: Frank Cass, 1965.

Ezorsky, Gertrude. *Racism and Justice: The Case for Affirmative Action*. Ithaca, N.Y.: Cornell University Press, 1991.

Gates, Henry Louis, Jr. *Colored People: A Memoir*. New York: Alfred A. Knopf, 1994.

Gehlen, Arnold. *Man in the Age of Technology*. New York: Columbia University Press, 1980.

Gerth, Hans, and C. Wright Mills. *Character and Social Structure*. New York: Harcourt, Brace & World, 1953.

Glazer, Nathan. *Affirmative Discrimination*. Cambridge: Harvard University Press, 1987.

Gutman, Herbert G. *The Black Family in Slavery and Freedom, 1750–1925*. New York: Vintage Books, 1977.

Hamilton, David, ed. *Cognitive Processes in Sterotyping and Intergroup Behavior*. Hillsdale, N.J.: Lawrence Erlbaum, 1981.

Hayek, Friedrich A. *Law, Legislation, and Liberty: Rules and Order*. Vol. 1. Chicago: University of Chicago Press, 1973.

Herrnstein, Richard, and Charles Murray. *The Bell Curve: Intelligence and Class Structure in American Life*. New York: Free Press, 1994.

Hutt, William H. *The Economics of the Colour Bar*. London: André Deutsch, 1964.

Jaynes, Gerald, and Robin Williams. *A Common Destiny: Blacks and American Society*. Washington: D.C.: National Academy Press, 1989.

Jencks, Christopher. *Rethinking Social Policy*. Cambridge, Mass.: Harvard University Press, 1992.

Katz, Phyllis, ed. *Towards the Elimination of Racism*. New York: Pergamon Press, 1976.

Kelso, William A. *Poverty and the Underclass: Changing Perceptions of the Poor in America*. New York: New York University Press, 1994.

Klapp, Orrin E. *The Collective Search for Identity*. New York: Holt, Rinehart and Winston, 1969.

Lachmann, Ludwig M. *The Legacy of Max Weber*. London: Heineman, 1970.

Lee, Yueh-Ting, Lee J. Jussim, and Clark R. McCauley, eds. *Stereotype Accuracy: Toward Appreciating Group Differences*. Washington, D.C.: American Psychological Association, 1995.

Levy, Marion J. *Modernization: Latecomers and Survivors*. New York: Basic Books, 1972.

Mead, George Herbert. *Mind, Self and Society: From the Standpoint of a Social Behaviorist*. Chicago: University of Chicago Press, 1934.

Mennell, Stephen. *Norbert Elias: Civilization and the Human Self-Image*. London: Basil Blackwell, 1989.

Mises, Ludwig von. *Human Action: A Treatise on Economics*. 3rd rev. ed. Chicago: Henry Regnery, 1966.

Murray, Charles. *Losing Ground: American Social Policy 1950–1980*. New York: Basic Books, 1984.

Oakes, P. J., S. A. Haslam, and J. C. Turner. *Stereotyping and Social Reality*. Oxford: Basil Blackwell, 1994.

Oakeshott, Michael. *On History, and Other Essays*. Oxford: Basil Blackwell, 1983.

Page, Clarence. *Showing My Color: Impolite Essays on Race and Identity*. New York: HarperCollins, 1996.

Rabushka, Alvin. *A Theory of Racial Harmony*. Columbia: University of South Carolina Press, 1974.

Roepke, Wilhelm. *A Humane Economy: The Social Framework of the Free Market*. Chicago: Henry Regnery, 1960.

Rokeach, Milton. *Beliefs, Attitudes, and Values*. San Francisco: Jossey-Bass, 1968.

Rose, Arnold M., ed. *Human Behavior and Social Processes*. Boston: Houghton Mifflin, 1962.

Rothbard, Murray N. *Freedom, Inequality, Primitivism, and the Division of Labor.* Auburn, Ala.: The Ludwig von Mises Institute, 1991.

Schattschneider, E. E. *The Semisovereign People: A Realist's View of America.* New York: Holt, Rinehart and Winston, 1960.

Schumann, Howard, Charlotte Steeh, and Lawrence Bobo. *Racial Attitudes in America.* Cambridge: Harvard University Press, 1985.

Schutz, Alfred. *Collected Papers II: Studies in Social Theory.* Edited by Arvid Brodersen. The Hague: Martinus Nijhoff, 1971.

———. *On Phenomenology and Social Relations.* Edited by Helmut R. Wagner. Chicago: University of Chicago Press, 1970.

Sowell, Thomas, ed. *Essays and Data on American Ethnic Groups.* Washington, D.C.: The Urban Institute, 1978.

———. *Preferential Policies: An International Perspective.* New York: William Morrow, 1990.

Steele, Shelby. *The Content of Our Character: A New Vision of Race in America.* New York: St. Martin's Press, 1990.

Wilson, Julius. *The Truly Disadvantaged.* Chicago: University of Chicago Press, 1987.

Zijderveld, Anton C. *The Abstract Society: A Cultural Analysis of Our Time.* Garden City, N.Y.: Doubleday, 1970.

ARTICLES

Agassi, Joseph. "Institutional Individualism." *British Journal of Sociology* 26 (1975): 144–55.

Amir, Yehuda. "Contact Hypothesis in Ethnic Relations." *Psychological Bulletin* 71 (May 1969): 319–42.

Beer, William R. "Sociology and the Effects of Affirmative Action: A Case of Neglect." *American Sociologist* 19 (Fall 1988): 218–31.

Brigham, John C. "Ethnic Stereotypes and Attitudes: A Different Mode of Analysis." *Journal of Personality* 41 (1973): 206–33.

Brimelow, Peter, and Leslie Spencer. "When Quotas Replace Merit, Everyone Suffers." *Forbes* 152 (February 15, 1993): 80–102.

Cohen, Elizabeth. "Expectation States and Interracial Interaction in School Settings." *Annual Review of Sociology* 8 (1982): 209–35.

Cohen, Elizabeth, and Susan Roper. "Modification of Interracial Interaction Disability: An Application of Status Characteristic Theory." *American Sociological Review* 37 (December 1972): 643–57.

Dauenhauer, Bernard P. "Making Plans and Lived Time." *Southern Journal of Philosophy* 7 (1969): 83–90.

Fordham, Signithia, and John U. Ogbu. "Black Students' School Success: Coping with the Burden of 'Acting White.' " *Urban Review* 18 (3) (1986): 176–205.

Jones, Edward W. "What It's Like to Be a Black Manager." *Harvard Business Review* (May-June 1986): 84–93.

Lewis, Oscar. "The Culture of Poverty." *Scientific American* 15 (1966): 19–25.

Macey, Jonathan R. "The Lowdown on Lending Discrimination." *Wall Street Journal*, August 9, 1995, p. A8.

Mackenzie, B. K. "The Importance of Contact in Determining Attitudes towards Negroes." *Journal of Abnormal and Social Psychology* 43 (1948): 417–41.

McCauley, Clark, and Christopher Stitt. "An Individual and Quantitative Measure of Stereotypes." *Journal of Personality and Social Psychology* 36 (September 1978): 929–40.

O'Neill, June. "The Role of Human Capital in Earnings Differences between Black and White Men." *Journal of Economic Perpectives* 4 (Fall 1990): 25–45.

Rockwell, Llewellyn, Jr. "Welfarizing Credit, Ignoring Risk." *Washington Times*, May 24, 1994, p. E3.

Rokeach, Milton, and Louis Mezei. "Race and Shared Belief as Factors in Social Distance." *Science* 151 (January 1966): 167–72.

Schmidt, Frank L., and John E. Hunter. "Employment Testing: Old Theories and New Research Findings." *American Psychologist* 36 (October 1981): 1128–37.

Smedley, Joseph, and James A. Bayton. "Evaluative Race-Class Stereotypes by Race and Perceived Class of Subjects." *Journal of Personality and Social Psychology* 36 (1978): 530–35.

Smith, T. Alexander. "A Phenomenology of the Policy Process." *International Journal of Comparative Sociology* 23 (March-June 1982): 1–16.

Steele, Claude M., and Joshua Aronson. "Stereotype Threat and the Intellectual Test Performance of African Americans." *Journal of Personality and Social Psychology* 69 (November 1995): 797–811.

Swidler, Ann. "Culture in Action: Symbols and Strategies." *American Sociological Review* 51 (April 1986): 273–86.

Wineburg, Samuel S. "The Self-Fulfillment of the Self-Fulfilling Prophecy." *Educational Researcher* 16 (December 1987): 28–37.

Index

achievement: and occupation, 34–35; and self-esteem, 35–37; and status, 34–37; and testing, 35–37

affirmative action: and black income, 146, 166–68; and black progress, 88–90; costs of, 141, 175 n.; and credentialism, 145–46; and cultural bias, 144–45; and discrimination, 141–42; and diversity, 172–73; and the economy, 155–60; and education, 171; enforcement of, 165–66; and general case against, 149–65; as goals and timetables, 142–44; illogical, 150–52; and income, 146, 166–68, 178 n.46; and labor markets, 143–46, 167–73; in other nations, 162; racial antagonism, 160–65, 178 n.43; racial harmony, 148–49; socioeconomic progress, 88–90; and status prestige, 146–48, 165–65, 167–68; as stimulus for politicization of private exchanges, 162–64; success of, 166–72; and testing, 145–46. *See also* black employment; black middle class; market economy; quota revolution; role models; rule of law; stereotypes; Victim Vision

Allport, Gordon, 67, 126

Aronson, Joshua, 124–25

balance of social power, 11–12, 185–88

Barkley, Charles, 148

Berger, Peter, 47 n.16

Bernal, Martin, 36

black alienation: and group pride, 38; middle class, 2–3, 9–11, 37; and "white institutions," 37–39

black employment: and affirmative action, 27–28; in corporations, 172–73; in general, 2, 168–70; in public sector, 26–27; in universities, 167–68

black middle class: and black lower class, 11–12; and black underclass, 32–34; depictions of, 13 nn.4, 5; and entrepreneurship, 169–71; and inner cities, 168–69; and racial unity, 34; and whites, 3, 4, 11. *See*

Steele, Claude, 124–25
Steinberg, Joel, 58, 64
stereotypes: accuracy of, 5, 113–14,
117–18, 120–25; definitions of,
67–68, 102, 106; employers and,
67; eradication of, 129–32; and expectations, 110, 114; flexibility of,
108, 125–29; in general, 67–68,
102–3; of groups, 113–16; and
prejudice, 67; of teachers, 77–80;
and typicality, 5, 6, 111–16; of
whites, 5–6, 109. *See also* Victim
Vision
Stitt, Christopher, 121
Stone, Gregory P., 21
Sykes, Charles J., 39, 50 n.51

Victim Vision: and affirmative action,
88–90; and class interpretations, 80–
83; definition of, 57–58; and
discrimination, 67–75; negative stereotypes, 75–80; and skill differer-
ences, 83–88, 96–99; and
unemployment, 71–72. *See also* affirmative action; stereotypes

Walton, Anthony, 1–2
West, Cornel, 28, 33
white exploitation, of economy, 58–
66. *See also* racism; Victim Vision
white racism: in general, 4–5, 25, 29–
44, 184–85; and violence, 72–73
Willie, Charles, 58

About the Authors

T. ALEXANDER SMITH is Professor of Political Science at the University of Tennessee-Knoxville. His major areas of interest are comparative political institutions and political economy.

LENAHAN O'CONNELL is Professor with the Center for Rural Economic Development at the University of Kentucky. He has written extensively on American race relations.

ISBN 0-275-96054-4

HARDCOVER BAR CODE